MW00427217

Gila Monsters and Red-Eyed Rattlesnakes

Gila Monsters and Red-Eyed Rattlesnakes

Don Maguire's Arizona Trading Expeditions, 1876–1879

Edited by Gary Topping

University of Utah Press
Salt Lake City

Printed on acid-free paper

Library of Congress Cataloging-in-Publication Data

Maguire, Don, 1852–1933.
Gila monsters and red-eyed rattlesnakes : Don Maguire's Arizona trading expeditions, 1876–1879 / edited by Gary Topping.
p. cm.
Includes bibliographical references (p.) and index.
ISBN 0-87480-537-6 (alk. paper)
1. Arizona—Description and travel. 2. Maguire, Don, 1852–1933—Journeys—Arizona. 3. Peddlers and peddling—Arizona—History—19th century. I. Topping, Gary, 1941– . II. Title.
F811.M25 1997
917.9104'4—dc21 96-49852

Frontispiece photograph of Don Maguire from J. Cecil Alter, *Utah: The Storied Domain* (1932); photographer unknown.

Book design by Richard Firmage.

Contents

Introduction

DON MAGUIRE'S NARRATIVES of his three remarkable trading expeditions through Utah, Nevada, California, Arizona, and Mexico during the years 1876 to 1879 are original and colorful contributions to the literature of the American West. For one thing, they open a large window onto the experiences of an itinerant peddler. While we know a good deal about other types of Western traders—those working for the great fur companies or the settled Indian traders, for example—the life of a wandering peddler among the mining camps and Indian tribes of the Southwest is largely a historiographical blank. Another asset is Maguire's elaborate (though sometimes faulty) descriptions of the communities he visited, some of which—Phoenix, Arizona, for example—have changed completely into modern metropolises, while others have vanished almost completely into sketchily documented ghost towns. Finally, his narratives acquaint us with the inimitable Don Maguire himself, a genuine Western character whose courage, curiosity, resourcefulness, and offbeat sense of humor stand out even in a region famous for people with such qualities.

All of the major biographical sources for Don Maguire originate with Maguire himself—no small problem, for there are reasonable suspicions that he was inclined to overstate the truth.[1] He was born at St. Johnsbury, Vermont, on 13 June 1852 to Irish immigrants John and Sarah Conwell Maguire. Politics was in the family blood, for Sarah claimed to be related to James G. Blaine and John was an Irish separatist with a price on his head. John Maguire made a significant fortune in livestock and land speculation in Iowa during the 1850s. Sometime in the early 1870s he followed the transcontinental railroad to Ogden, Utah, an effective supply depot from which he and his five sons could engage in various mercantile ventures in the developing West.

Don Maguire (his given name was Dominick, but he never used it) was the youngest of the children and a true Maguire in his devout Catholicism,[2] his business sagacity, his wanderlust, and his political radicalism. The last two qualities led him to participation, or so he claimed, in the planning of abortive ventures to overthrow both the Emperor Maximilian of Mexico and British rule in Canada. Although both of those quixotic expeditions failed to come to pass, Maguire spent most of his youth on the move. He worked as a livestock buyer for an army quartermaster in the Midwest, a packer for a U.S. Geological Survey party, and a miner. With money from those occupations, he put himself through a Franciscan college in Santa Barbara, California, where he studied engineering, mathematics, and the French, Spanish, and Arabic languages—all of which became useful in his trading and mining ventures.

During and after college, he traveled throughout the mining districts of California, Nevada, and Utah, as well as into Central America. His first narrative gives details of a North African trading expedition that ended in frustration, sparking inquiries that eventually produced his three great Arizona trips and a similar one to Idaho and Montana. His life continued his mining speculations and other business ventures, as well as significant prehistoric excavations, particularly at Willard, Paragonah, and Grand Gulch, Utah.[3] As an avocation, Maguire wrote voluminously, producing a novel, poems, short stories, biographies, and the narratives included here.

The historian Charles Kelly, who knew Maguire in his later years, reported that his Ogden home (a Victorian duplex now on the National Register of Historic Places) was packed with manuscripts and an immense library; and, in an extensive correspondence, the younger man often drew upon Maguire's erudition about Utah mineralogy and history.[4] But those years were punctuated with tragedy. In 1927 his wife of forty-six years, Agatha Wells Maguire, died. Then in 1929 a fire in his home burned virtually all of his library and manuscripts. His death, too, was tragic, for he was struck by an automobile on the night of 7 January 1933 while crossing a street near his home.[5]

The Don Maguire Papers at the Utah State Historical Society, which include the narratives presented here, were donated after Maguire's death by Charles Kelly. They are not very extensive. Besides the Arizona narratives, they include a few short stories, a badly charred diary of the Arizona trips obviously barely rescued from the 1929 fire, correspondence files kept by Kelly himself, and a few odd volumes from Maguire's library. Out of a long, varied, productive, and adventurous life, only the brief period of his Arizona expeditions is adequately documented.

Although the manuscripts indicate that Maguire wrote these narratives in San Francisco in 1883, they probably remained in handwritten drafts until 1931, less than two years before his death, when he hired a secretary and began putting them into typescript in preparation for publication.[6] It appears that the secretary's role was to record Maguire's dictation of the narrative, which convincingly accounts for its repetitiveness and verbosity, as well as for some phonetic misspellings which Maguire would not have made (for example, Remi Nadeau, the freighter, mentioned in the first expedition, appears in the typescript as "Nado," even though Maguire tells us that he had been reading *Telemachus* in French and thus would have known the correct spelling).

Although the typescripts were completed at the time of Maguire's death, there is no evidence that he offered them to a publisher. The postulated handwritten drafts have not survived. The only other primary sources for the Arizona trips are the diary and a series of articles Maguire mailed to the *San Francisco Chronicle* from various points along his itinerary. Because of their lack of detail, neither of those sources is of much value in supplementing and corroborating the narratives. Although I have augmented and revised the first narrative in minor ways through use of the diary, it is of little help on the other expeditions, and the newspaper articles are nothing more than general descriptions of the country, much less detailed than the narratives.[7]

Realizing that the extant typescript never had the benefit of revision by Maguire or any other editor, I have not thought it improper to exercise the same free hand with it that any editor would with a rough draft. The text presented here thus is vastly reduced from Maguire's typescript. In the first place, I have clipped the wings of Maguire's prolix prose not only to make it more palatable to readers of the late twentieth century but also to mitigate the tediousness of his repeated descriptions—for example, of the nightly routine of feeding the animals, erecting the tents, building the fire, and cooking the food. I have left enough of that to give the reader an idea of the camp routine, but there is a sameness to it that the reader can presume to have existed on other nights unless something unusual occurred, which I of course in those cases have left in. I have not completely docked his verbosity, for one of my primary editorial goals has been to reveal Maguire's engaging personality. Many more editorial cuts could have been made, but I have thought it dishonest to try to change Maguire's florid nineteenth-century prose into something else.

Also, I have omitted many lengthy passages of only tangential relation to Maguire's own story. Maguire included several lengthy narratives of adventures of people he met along the way as well as a long, hostile history of the Mormons, for example, that seriously interrupt the account of his own journey, which it seems to me ought to be the continuous focal point. One generic exception to this policy is Maguire's anthropological descriptions of the various Indian tribes he encountered. While some of these are not free from inaccuracies, they do reflect his serious scientific interest in the American Indian, both historic and prehistoric, and, as I mention in some of the footnotes, there is reason to believe that they represent his own observations and fact-gathering rather than data imported from some other source to pad his narrative. To repeat, my interest centers on Maguire's own experiences and observations. Readers interested in Maguire as folklorist or raconteur are invited to consult the unabridged manuscripts at the Utah State Historical Society.

This attempt to focus on Maguire's own experiences has also governed my efforts to identify and corroborate the multitude of people and places he mentions. In addition to relying heavily upon the work of local historians, I have searched the federal census schedules of 1870 and 1880 for the communities through which Maguire passed. While I have given what I regard as every reasonable effort to corroborate people and places in the narrative, many have yet eluded my net, either because they appear in no other extant records or because they are phantoms of Maguire's hazy memory. The well-known transience of much of Western society, which was heightened in the mining camps where Maguire found most of his business, enabled many of his acquaintances to elude mention in any written record that I have been able to locate.

The most useful aspect of these narratives is their documentation of the life of an itinerant trader, with their data on prices, profits, supply and trading techniques, and other business practices. Maguire's memory is likely most trustworthy on those matters, and they fortunately fill a large historiographical gap. Maguire emerges here as a shrewd businessman who seized a brief, unique opportunity and made the most of it.

Lack of transportation and formidable Indian hostility inhibited development of Arizona mining until after the Civil War. Although the Colorado River provided a valuable link to the outside world for western Arizona and permitted the importation of light mining equipment that could be broken down and freighted by wagon into the interior mining districts, it was not until the railroads began reaching the territory in 1879 that truly industrialized mining became a possibility. Getting food, clothing, and other supplies to the mining camps was equally arduous. Until the 1870s, Indian resistance to white incursion also was a formidable barrier. While the Navajos had been in large part subdued by army troops under Kit Carson in the 1860s, the Apaches kept up a vigorous resistance until put down by General George S. Crook in the early 1870s. Some resisted even into the 1880s in some places. Other tribes like the Mojaves and the Hualapais offered less, but still significant, resistance.[8]

It was Maguire's genius to perceive this situation as a whole. He saw that Arizona's mining districts—and those of a good part of Nevada and eastern California—were often well populated yet poorly supplied. And he saw that the Indian barrier, while still significant, had lowered enough to admit with reasonable risk a cautious and well-armed party of traders. This opportunity would last only for a few years, for the railroads also perceived the economic potential of the region and were moving into it; in fact, Maguire used the expanding railroad network himself to reach resupply points.

Although Maguire had previously investigated much of the region in which he proposed to trade, his first expedition was experimental. Because there were large parts of his proposed itinerary about which he was poorly informed, he used a pack train rather than wagons because of its greater mobility over rough terrain. On his later trips, after he had seen the country more thoroughly, he used wagons, which could carry large payloads without the nuisance and toil of repeated packing and unpacking. His first trip also gave him information on the types of goods demanded by his varied clientele of miners, ranchers, and Indians, as well as the locales where the highest prices could be charged. Furthermore, as a hedge against the inherent risks of his ventures, he arranged to supplement his income by acting as agent for mining speculators wishing to purchase promising properties and as a correspondent to the *San Francisco Chronicle*, submitting colorful descriptions of the wild country through which he was traveling.

Maguire's relationship to his employees was an interesting aspect of his expeditions. Since he apparently hired most of them on the spur of the moment, he admits in a couple of places that he was extraordinarily lucky in getting honest, hard-working, and agreeable men. It is apparent that he worked them hard, and his requirement that they remain separate and silent in the communities they entered, for fear of tipping off bandits with information on the amount of money they were carrying or their itinerary, cannot have been to their liking. On the other hand, Maguire compensated by carrying the best food he could obtain and hiring Chinese cooks to prepare it, and by allowing little vacations like a few days in Santa Barbara on the first expedition and side trips to interesting places such as the Petrified Forest and the Hopi villages. Still, even though Maguire stayed in touch with some of them in later years, none of his men ever repeated a trip with him. And forcing Sam Hing, his Chinese cook on the first trip, to remain in Mojave, California, and obtain employment to support himself while Maguire and his white employees lived it up in Santa Barbara can only strike a modern reader as egregiously unjust.

Like successful businessmen of all times and places, Maguire was a quick student of human nature, and he could become firm, generous, unscrupulous, or even duplicitous as circumstances warranted. After trading with the Hualapais at a remote rendezvous near the Colorado River, for example, during which he sold them a considerable number of guns, he saw the wisdom of quietly sneaking away over the sandy road at 2:00 a.m. before the Indians realized they now held.the upper hand and could overpower him and his men. During his stay at the Mormon colonies on the Little Colorado River, Maguire concealed his dislike of their autocratic leader, Lot Smith, and his outrage at the prices Smith charged to board his animals. Instead, he bided his time until Smith was ready to trade, then raised his own prices commensurately. And his parting gesture was to sell the remainder of his stock of guns, after Smith had bought what he wanted, to the very Navajos against whom Smith and his people wished to defend themselves. Finally, Maguire took his market where he found it, and near the end of his second expedition sold a large stock of guns "useful for revolutionary and other social purposes" to a Mexican gun-runner who then "might well return into his own country without giving the Mexican revenue officers any annoyance, and in that way make the smugglers' percentage."

If, as Howard R. Lamar claims, we have made the Western trader "myth's victim" through our facile condemnation of his immense markups and shrewd trading practices—features of frontier commerce well understood, accepted, and acted upon by white and Indian alike—then Maguire deserves the same tolerance we should be giving to other historic traders.[9] If Maguire sold his seventy-five-cent surplus muskets to Indians for ten dollars and exacted a markup of 200–300 percent on other goods, we should remember the labor and risks he undertook to bring those commodities to his customers and their lack of complaint, so far as we can tell, about his prices.

But Maguire was much more than just an entrepreneur with an eye for the main chance. Several times he refers to himself as a student, and while it is obvious that he enjoyed cutting profitable deals, he in large part used his trading as a way of paying for his archaeological and anthropological investigations. While waiting for the soldiers at Camp Verde, Arizona, to be paid during his last expedition, for example, he and his men disdained killing the time in Prescott saloons as one might expect and instead spent several days living in and exploring a magnificent prehistoric ruin.

The literary quality of the narratives is also significant. Maguire's colorful expressions, his unsentimental assessment of the people he encountered (though he lost his objectivity in the presence of personal heroes like John C. Frémont), the toils and dangers of the journey with its lurking bandits and "red-eyed rattlesnakes," and the joys of a warm campfire on a starry Arizona night all emerge memorably from Maguire's pen. His unwavering sense of humor, often revealed in spicy Western expressions, is a constant source of delight. The wine made by southern Utah Mormons, which he calls "villainous stuff, containing about as much of the juice of the yellowjacket and wasps as it does of the grape," was one butt of his humor. "So rascally is the nature of this drink," he reports, "that people of Arizona and Nevada claim that a man who drinks a quart of it will get up in the night and steal his own clothes." The stories told by an old Mexican War veteran with whom Maguire had dinner in Wickenburg, Arizona, "were bloody enough to put snakes into the boots of old Homer, the ancient poet." The lazy inhabitants of one run-down Arizona ranch were put to shame by the enterprise of "a smart-looking old sow industriously prospecting for bugs and worms or corn grains in a pool of water near the door. Around her played seven little snow white pigs with all the innocent looks of infant pork. O snap and vim, I respect thee in man or hog." The animal population of the Pima Indian reservation consisted, he says, of "about 1,800 head of sheep, about 1,000 head of goats, and from one to two thousand dogs, more or less." Dogs play a role, too, in one final example of Maguire's mysterious expressions. After a long, forced drive in northern Arizona during which he and his men had had no time to stop for lunch, they arrived at an isolated ranch as hungry, he says, "as yellow dogs of Constantinople."

Historians are cautioned not to yield too easily to the temptation to take at face value Maguire's descriptions of people and places even though he claims in his preface, "It was while the impressions were still fresh in my mind that I produced these records from my diaries, notebooks, and memory." The surviving diary contains sketchy entries from all of his Arizona expeditions, so one may safely assume, despite the plural, that it was the only written diary. The notebooks, which he implies were separate from the diary, have not survived. They must have contained his business accounts, which are given with great precision in the narratives, and the details of people and places, though some of the latter came only from his memory. Those latter details were not as "fresh in mind" as he thought, for demonstrable errors in them are common. The historian must therefore use those parts of the narratives with care and as much corroboration as possible. The greatest possible mistake would be to neglect their use because of those known inaccuracies, however. Instead, the reader is encouraged to utilize Maguire much as he would utilize Herodotus, for example, in spite of his credulous reporting of absurdities, or Livy, in spite of his transparent mythmaking. The shortcomings of those ancient historians, like those of Maguire, do not invite rejection, but rather challenge our own intelligence and creativity.

Acknowledgments

WHILE EDITING THE NARRATIVE of a man who ranged widely over four western states and territories—Utah, Nevada, California, and Arizona—in addition to one trip into northern Mexico, I have naturally incurred many debts to local historians and records repositories in those areas. My notes are my most eloquent acknowledgment of those obligations, and there would be no point in trying to duplicate them here. Nevertheless, I believe several specific acknowledgments are in order at this point.

The Utah State Historical Society was particularly helpful, not only in providing access to the original manuscript but also through its magnificent library of local histories with which I began my research. Many other local historical sources were available in the American history library at the University of Wisconsin, where I spent two very productive weeks in the summer of 1994. For the California leg of Maguire's first expedition, I found useful material in the California Historical Society archives and the San Francisco Public Library. Sue Abbey, of the Sharlot Hall Museum in Prescott, Arizona, went far out of her way to provide answers to most of my questions on obscure aspects of the history of that city and other Arizona matters. Stan Jones, former publicist for Colossal Cave, helped me with some of my speculations regarding Maguire's itinerary in southern Arizona, and Dr. Francis J. Serpa, my colleague in Latin American history, helped my interpretation of Maguire's journey into Mexico.

During the last stages of preparation of this manuscript, I benefited greatly from participation in the National Historical Publications and Records Commission's annual seminar in historical editing, affectionately nicknamed "Camp Edit," at the University of Wisconsin. In that congenial and intellectually stimulating setting I received a great deal of helpful advice and encouragement from both faculty and fellows. I should particularly like to thank Beth Luey, my personal advisor there, for encouraging me to believe that I was proceeding in a basically sound direction; and it is my hope that the final product satisfies at least some of her exacting standards.

Among the aforementioned local historical literature I have found so helpful, I should like to isolate for a particular expression of gratitude the authors of several books on western ghost towns. Without their tenacious spadework, my research could easily have taken a lifetime to achieve its present level of documentation. I refer to the work of Dr. Stephen L. Carr on Utah, Stanley N. Paher on Nevada, Philip Varney on southern California, and James E. and Barbara H. Sherman on Arizona.

My last expressions of gratitude go to the two anonymous readers provided by the University of Utah Press, whose enthusiastic reviews led to acceptance of my manuscript for publication and whose criticisms improved it significantly. Thanks as well to my editor at the press, Mick Gusinde-Duffy, whose interest and support never flagged during the publication process.

Preface

MORE THAN FIFTY YEARS have passed since the days and nights when I penned the records of my three commercial and exploration expeditions into the wonderful land of Arizona. It was while the impressions were still fresh in my mind that I produced these records from my diaries, notebooks, and memory.

Army men, miners, ranchers, adventurers from across the country and the seven seas looked upon Arizona as the land of dreams, inviting them to come and possess her wealth, drink of her mountain streams, and rest in her forest shades. It was a region of romance; but danger and death also lurked in a hundred places where the Apaches made blood-stained trails, where lone deserts and black lava plains, waterless wastes, and long forbidding reaches of desolation discouraged man's coming.

But for one who would brave the dangers, there was much to secure in a land where life was yet primitive and civilization was yet in the making. It was the officers and men of the United States Army who were given the work of bringing peace and civilization to the region. It was while that work of transformation from barbarism to civilization was in process that the author of these pages took part in the life of that romantic country.

The fifty-five years since the events recorded here took place have seen vast changes in western America. Arizona then was an unsettled territory with no railroads and only a few unimportant villages whose white inhabitants, with a few thousand ranchmen, miners, and freighters, enjoyed a precarious protection by the army from robbery, outrage, and death by Indians. The army posts were so many places of refuge where food supplies and protection could be obtained.

While Arizona was terrorized by ruthless Indians, other western territories were little better. Eastern Idaho was yet an unsettled wilderness, and southern Nevada and southeastern California were less civilized and fully as desolate as the Sahara. Social conditions in Utah placed that territory outside the accepted form of American civilization.

Since then, the work of the American pioneer has gone on until Arizona's many valleys are now watered by a hundred irrigation canals, so its rich soil and semitropical climate produce vegetables to rival the Mississippi Valley, citrus fruits to rival Mexico and Old Spain, and grapes to rival France and Italy. Where once stood the straggly adobe villages, we now find modern cities with paved streets, modern architecture, schools, a state university, and railway lines.

But, oh, the men of those old days! There were amongst them many of heroic mold. They have passed away, and I, one who was with them in that land of romance, have prepared this narrative of times and scenes that are gone forever.

D. M.
February 17, 1932

Gila Monsters and Red-Eyed Rattlesnakes

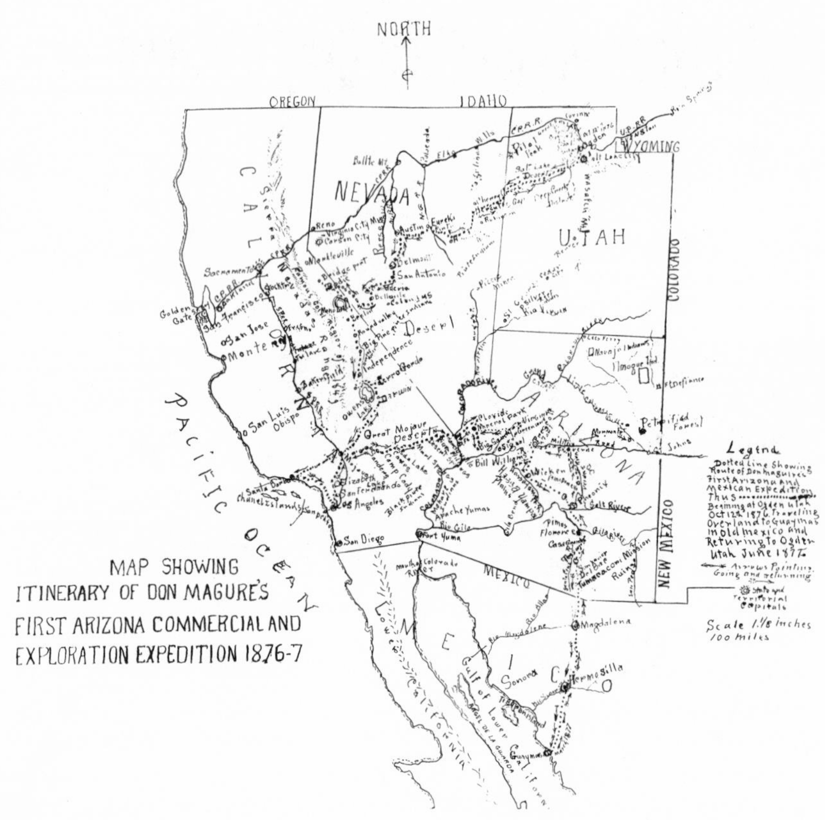

Map of Don Maguire's first expedition, found with manuscript and believed to have been drawn by Maguire. USHS

1.

First Arizona Expedition

IT WAS IN THE LATTER PART of the year 1876 and in the twenty-fifth year of my age. I had just returned to the United States after having made a protracted period of travel over several nations of Europe, as well as Egypt, Algeria, and Morocco in Africa. Upon returning to New York City, I planned an expedition for trade and exploration into the then wild territory of Arizona and the regions of Chihuahua and Sonora in Old Mexico.

My work in Europe was that of a student. I was accompanied into Africa by a young man from Toledo, Ohio, named James W. Garner.[1] Our travels into Egypt and Algeria would be as students, but into Morocco we would go as traders in merchandise that we had purchased in Marseilles and shipped in bond to Gibraltar, intending to ship the same to Tangiers in Morocco. We expected to exchange these goods for such things as attar of roses, ivory, sandalwood, gum copal, morocco leather, ostrich plumes, gold dust, and Moorish brass work. We soon found, though, that knavish Arabs, Berbers, Moors, and Negro chiefs of northeast Africa were such a rapacious lot that we were robbed first by officials for permits to trade at Fez, Mogador, and in the Arab villages along the north base of the Atlas Mountains. Along with the astoundingly high permit fees, we were compelled to pay a high export and import duty, which left the results of our African venture three thousand dollars in loss.

After the above venture, James Garner and I took an educational trip into southern Spain by way of Malaga, whence we went up into the Vega of Granada and spent almost two weeks in the famous old city of Granada itself, and Santa Fe on the Xenil, and along the Duaro River. After thus studying the remains of former Moorish glory in the south of Spain, we returned to Gibraltar, where we parted. I took a steamship for New York by way of London. In London and Manchester, I prepared a shipment of merchandise to be shipped to New York City. This merchandise was such as would afford a very wide margin of profit when gotten into Nevada, southeastern California, Arizona, and the states of northern Mexico.

Previous to my going into northern Africa, as I was somewhat in doubt about our success in the latter country, I had written letters to many of my scattered friends in Peru, Bolivia, California, Mexico, the Sandwich Islands, Idaho, Montana, and Arizona inquiring into the probable results of a trading expedition into any of those regions. Gold and silver mining in the above areas was yet in a fair state of prosperity.

After leaving Marseilles and reaching Gibraltar, in my mail at the American consulate I found several letters in reply. Some gave encouragement, reports of what might be done in gold and silver mining, but the most interesting was from an old friend, Alexander Hamilton of Fort Yuma, Arizona.

Some four years previous, Mr. Hamilton had gone to Peru in the service of Colonel Harry Meigs, who was building the first railroad in that country. Hamilton made good in Peru, married into a prominent Spanish family, and made his home at Lima. But he had made his home for the past six months in Arizona, where he had a brother, Charles Stewart Hamilton, who was engaged in mining and had been very fortunate in the outcome of a gold mine in the Vulture Mountains in south-central Arizona. Two years before, Hamilton had financed his brother on conditions that they were to stand fifty-fifty in any important discovery that might be made. Such a discovery having been made, Hamilton was induced to come back from Peru, and in reaching Arizona, he and his brother disposed of the gold discovery for thirty thousand dollars, which they shared equally.

Hamilton had his wife with him when he wrote me from Fort Yuma. He stated that were it not that he was then anchored in Peru, where he was to return in a few weeks, he would certainly begin life over again in Arizona. It was a land of opportunities in ranching, cattle raising, trading in most lines of merchandise, and mining and exploration. Gold, silver, lead, and copper were plentifully in evidence.

From fifteen military posts or forts, the government was sending out infantry and cavalry forces constantly in conquering the Apache Indians. As yet there were no railroad lines entering Arizona or New Mexico, nor were there any railway communications in the Mexican states of Chihuahua, Monterey, Sonora, Durango, or Zacatecas.[2] In Arizona prices were high for all sorts of merchandise because of the lack of railroads, and goods were being hauled into the country by mule- or ox trains across dry, inhospitable deserts from California. Freight charges were unmercifully high. Money was plentiful and opportunities of making money were good, but, on the other hand, Indian depredations were high. The Apaches were yet unconquered in most parts of the territory. In the mountains, on the deserts, and along the highways, both Americans and Mexicans were being murdered almost daily, and their bleaching bones might be seen yet unburied in almost any part of Arizona.

Notwithstanding Apache Indians and Mexican bandits, Hamilton said that he believed that if I came to Arizona with a stock of merchandise, I would make good, or if I gave my whole attention to gold and silver mining or to cattle raising, that all chances were in my favor. Knowing Alexander Hamilton very well, and relying on his judgment, I also had a premonition that of all countries, Arizona and northern Mexico were the best fields for my next venture.

Quite true, Arizona was then a region of difficult approach; the traveler was confronted by mountains and sandswept regions on its east, west, and north, and on its western border the approach from California was difficult. In its interior, Apache Indians were the most treacherous and inhuman of all the American tribes. But, all these features considered, had I not just come out of Morocco, one of the most barbarous and uncivilized of all countries having an organized government? and, if I was fortunate enough to return from Africa with my skin whole, might I not also hope to hold my own in Arizona under the flag of my own country? My mind was made up. I would at once prepare to go into Arizona.

Upon reaching New York, my first step was to provide myself with a map of the Pacific coast states and territories, and the states of northern Mexico. I then considered carefully the additional stocks of merchandise I would require in my new undertaking, what route I was to take, and what method of travel. As I was already well acquainted with California, Nevada, Utah, and the west coast of Old Mexico, and knowing the difficult approaches into Arizona at that time, I felt that the transportation of merchandise by a train of pack mules would be my most certain method of reaching Arizona in an independent manner.

The next question was, from what railway point would I begin my overland pack-train journey? After weighing all pros and cons, I came to the conclusion that my best course was to ship my merchandise to some western intermountain point. So I settled upon Ogden, Utah, a point almost two thousand miles from New York City, which was then the terminus of the Union Pacific Railroad. At Ogden I would purchase animals, saddles, tents, and camp supplies, then hire two or three reliable packers and begin my journey into Arizona.

As to the route to be taken, I could go southward from Ogden through the entire length of Utah, or I could cross the Great Salt Lake

Desert into Nevada, striking the chief mining camps and ranch regions of that state and trading my way into eastern California. There I would skirt along the east base of the Sierra Nevada mountain range, trading southward until I reached Owens Lake. From there I would go across a two-hundred-mile desert to Mojave Station on the Southern Pacific Railroad, where I would have shipped a quantity of merchandise for the Arizona and Mexico legs of my expedition. Mojave Station is about sixty to eighty miles from Los Angeles. From there I would go with a newly loaded pack train down the sinks of the Mojave River, thence across the desert to the east, crossing the Colorado River into Arizona at Hardyville. Upon reaching Arizona, I would plan my route into Mexico as conditions would best direct.

These plans laid down, I began my work. The merchandise was chosen according to the requirements of the inhabitants of the region into which I was going. For Nevada and eastern California, for example, where there were then five men to one woman, I would have to have a stock suitable for white mountaineers, ranchmen, Mexicans, Indians, and white inhabitants of mining camps. In New York City I sorted my merchandise accordingly, both those obtained in England (largely colored cotton piece goods) and in New York. I divided them into lots respectively for shipment to Ogden, Utah, to Eureka, Nevada, and to Mojave Station for those to be taken into Arizona and Mexico.

It was ten days after my arrival in Ogden before the shipment of merchandise arrived. This time I employed in securing men for my service and in procuring pack mules and saddle horses. As Corinne, Utah, was yet an important overland freight station for Idaho, Oregon, and Montana, I went there, twenty-eight miles from Ogden, and procured two men who came well recommended for my work. One was Simon Lee Edwards, skilled as a mule packer, recently from Virginia City, Montana, but a native of Cairo, Illinois, and thirty-four years old. The other was Patrick O'Donnel, twenty-nine years old and a native of Ireland. Both proved to be excellent men. I agreed to pay them fifty dollars a month plus food and to provide boots or shoes during the time they were in my employ. They were to manage the pack train in every detail and do all the work of our camp, as a large part of the time we would do our own cooking and live an outdoor life.

Although at the time of this expedition I was in my twenty-fifth year and had passed through much frontier life, the nature of this undertaking was an unusual one. It was that of an explorer, gold and silver prospector, mountain and river trader, and the country I was going to pass over had never seen such an expedition. By this I mean that no white trader ever organized such an expedition wherein trade was to be carried on with both whites and Indians and the goods traded being similar to the ones I was bringing.

My next step was to secure pack mules. These, fourteen in number, I obtained from a Mormon bishop named Layton, who lived some twelve miles southwest of Ogden.[3] Three excellent saddle horses of the hardy California halfbreed blood I obtained from Charles Nelson at Ogden. The rest of the equipment I purchased in Salt Lake City, including three saddles, bridles, blankets, and fittings for three saddle horses. The mules and horses had all been broken to the saddle, pack train, and to wagon harness. After five days of packing and sorting the merchandise, we were ready to start on a very interesting and not uneventful undertaking.

It was about midday on October 12, 1876, that I took my departure from Ogden with my two companions, fourteen mules, and three saddle horses. The evening of the first day brought us to Farmington, halfway between Ogden and Salt Lake City. The next day, owing to the fact that we found it necessary to make readjustments in our method of packing, it was somewhat late in the day when we departed from Farmington. We continued our southern course through Woods Cross and Centerville, reaching the Hot Springs at the north edge of Salt Lake City, where we took a westward road to a crossing of the Jordan River and on past Black Rock at the south point of the Great Salt Lake. At that point the Oquirrh Range of mountains approaches near to the south shore of the lake.

The blue expanse of the Great Salt Lake, the inland sea of North America, was spread out to the north and northwest as far as I could see. Its waters were rippling and splashing along a gravelly shore. Back to the east lay Salt Lake City, the Mormon capital, situated at the base of the Wasatch Mountains. That evening as I looked upon it, the evening sun was casting its golden shadows through the smoky haze that overhung the city. Like an elephant amongst forty thousand sheep stood the huge Mormon Tabernacle among the other buildings of the place. Still farther to the east I saw the walls of the great unfinished Mormon Temple. Its gray granite reflected the last light of day. Even farther to the east some two or three miles I plainly saw the buildings at Fort Douglas, a military post that had then been established for some years at Salt Lake City.

Turning our faces to the west and traveling on, we were soon near the little town of Stockton on the shores of Rush or Stockton Lake, where are smelted the silver ores taken from East Canyon and also the Honorine Mines to the east some three or four miles. East Canyon with the mining camp of Ophir lies about ten miles to the south.

The town of Stockton was located and built largely by General Patrick Edward Connor, who about the year 1863 came with a military expedition into Utah. The Indians of the intermountain country at that time were in many localities on the warpath, and it was found necessary to establish the military post known as Fort Douglas, from which military expeditions put down Indian uprisings. There was a three-stack smelter at Stockton. Its chimneys sent their black holocaust up to heaven from the throats of their three high vents. I witnessed the hot liquid lead, gold, and silver being poured into the trough-shaped molds. To every ton of these ores there was about sixty dollars in silver, eight in gold, and the rest in lead. These furnaces ran night and day, winter and summer. The slag or dross from which the bullion is taken is cast into a pile that in time grows almost into a hill of black worthless substance, but at times is used as road metal on the highways nearby.[4]

As grass and fuel were scarce near the camp, we found it better to put our mule train into a corral and to take our meals and rooms for the night at the one good little hotel. As in all places of public entertainment at that time, wines, liquors, and cigars were sold at the bar in this little hotel. In such places the men employed at the smelters and other mining works around the place usually spent one-half or more of their monthly earnings, adding much, of course, to the profits of the house. Another part of their earnings went into gambling, such as faro and poker. These conditions as found at Stockton prevailed at almost all mining camps, both at the mines and at the nearby villages where the ore is smelted. The hotel at Stockton was kept by a nephew of General P. E. Connor who, by the way, was the pioneer worker in the mines of the entire Utah region.

Early the following morning, we continued through the little town of Tooele, county seat of Tooele County, Utah.[5] The town at that date was wholly or largely Mormon in population. It was a quiet little town, as then were all towns of Utah. The town lots were very large, containing one acre each adorned with fruit and shade trees. Streams of water ran on both sides of every street, from which ditches carried the water over the gardens and orchards. The apples were yet on the trees as we passed through the town. The dwellings of this little city, as all other towns of Utah, were neat and well built of adobe brick, or unburned clay. The simple inhabitants here spend their noiseless lives laboring and confident that the faith for which they came into these once gloomy spots is the only gate to eternal life.

The town of Tooele behind us, we were now fairly out of civilization. The American desert was before us with all its wild fields and plains of white dust and salt mingled with alkali. We had not gone far when we met a man who told us that we had taken the wrong road, that the one toward a small settlement to the west called Saint John's and passing over a mountain range to the west was not by any means the best road. We must turn to the south, he said, and then the southwest, crossing over the Skull

Mountains to Skull Valley until we reached Porter Rockwell's ranch, where we would find persons to put us onto the best road into Nevada.

We took the course he gave us, across the lonely valley covered with ragged sagebrush, rabbitbrush, greasewood, shadscale, and alkali dust for twenty-five miles until we reached the summit of Skull Valley Range. At this spot we rested the animals and cast our eyes backward and to the north upon the dreary yet sublime view that is spread out before the traveler. To the west rise the Lost Mountains, the Deep Creek Range, the broad waste of Skull Valley; and to the south the mountain ranges and valleys seemed to run out into infinity. To the east, the Oquirrh Range and, far beyond, the granite peaks of the Wasatch, while to the north and northeast over hundreds of square miles lay the vast bosom of the Great Salt Lake, its huge mountain islands looming up into the clear, cold heavens, and the farther mountains beyond the quiet face of its waters. The islands in the Great Salt Lake present a cold, rugged appearance. Grass of a bunchy nature grows upon them, and there are several springs of fresh water on the one called Church Island, called by some Antelope Island. At one time the officials of the Mormon Church had upon this area a large number of sheep and cattle, hence the name given it.

Gazing over the vast Salt Lake basin, everywhere lie visible the evidences of the old prehistoric floods and convulsions that wore and worked the mountains into their present shapes. Stratum piled upon stratum, and here and there on the mountainsides marks that show the ancient waterlines when Great Salt Lake was a freshwater lake 370 miles in length and seventy-five miles in breadth, having an outlet by way of the present Portneuf River into the Great Snake River, thence by the Columbia into the Pacific Ocean. At that time, according to the measurements or altitude of the highest of these present waterlines, the great freshwater lake stood 1,050 feet higher than the surface of the present Great Salt Lake.

The mountains themselves abound with marine shells, of course proving that long ago these mountains were far down in some old ocean. The high slopes of the mountains in these regions in some places are covered with areas of pine, fir, and balsam timber. In most of these canyons silver mines are worked. Ophir City, Bingham, Alta, Little Cottonwood, and Big Cottonwood are the chief mining camps of northern Utah in which silver, lead, and gold are produced.

Descending the west side of this mountain range, we soon arrived at a Mormon ranch run by an American named Arthur Melvin, who was married to a deaf Scotch woman. He proved to be an exceedingly fine man, well acquainted with the history of the surrounding country from the time of the entry of the Mormon people into Utah in 1847. As at

Stockton, we found it wiser to have him furnish our animals with supplies for the night and ourselves with food and shelter than to open a camp of our own.

After supper, I was sitting on the south porch of Melvin's house talking to him when we beheld a man coming up through a cornfield below the house. The man was almost naked, having on only a pair of torn trousers. As he approached, we could see that he was burned and blistered from his waist to his chin. His feet, around which he had tied the torn remnants of his shirt, were cut and swollen. His eyes were bloodshot and his countenance haggard. At first we thought him insane, but we soon learned that he was one of two who had started from Ophir three days before to cross the American desert. They were going to Deep Creek, about one hundred forty miles distance. They had a mule loaded with provisions, blankets, clothing, and prospectors' tools, with a small keg of water. Out in the desert they lost their way. Their water soon gave out and thirst overcame them. They grew bewildered and in their desperation they killed the mule and drank a large quantity of its blood. The blood, being hot, only added to their misery. They scattered their food, clothing, and money around the fallen mule and separated from each other. We gave the man a little tea and whiskey now and then until he fell asleep and slept without waking during the night.

Early the next morning the other came in a like state. Both, however, got well before the close of that day. One of Mr. Melvin's sons went out and found their blankets, provisions, and money, which amounted to about two hundred dollars, of which they paid him fifty dollars for his services.

We were now far out in the desert, and Mr. Melvin, who had in his employ quite a number of men, requested that we open up some of our packages of merchandise and supply him with a quantity of clothing for his men. To this request I acceded, and furnished him a quantity of goods amounting to $325.

We then continued our journey, which led through a body of timber in Skull Valley. It was once the spot where many fierce battles were fought between the old Indian tribes of the country, the Shoshones and Paiutes, who both claimed the place. They would meet their opponents upon this ground and knock each others' brains out for possession of it. Their liking for it no doubt resulted from the large herds of deer and antelope to which both tribes laid claim.

Leaving the Melvin ranch, we reached the old Overland Stage road that ran westward from Salt Lake City to Carson Valley, Nevada, over the Sierra Nevada, and down to Sacramento, California. Along this road ran the first telegraph line from St. Joseph, Missouri, to San Francisco. The line was still in use at the time of our journey. The road was not traveled to any great extent, though still in service, and was fairly good and hard, producing no dust.

Near nightfall we reached Porter O. Rockwell's ranch.[6] He was at one time chief of the Danites in Brigham Young's service in Utah and was said to have been in the Danite service under the Mormon prophet Joseph Smith at Farr West, Missouri, and later at Nauvoo, Illinois. Upon our arrival the grim old chief with some of his men were engaged in branding horses. I made myself known to him and informed him that I desired grain and hay for my animals and meals and beds for my men and me. He asked his foreman to assist my men in taking care of the animals, and stated that supper would be ready within an hour and that a bugle would call for them at that time. We went into his house, which was a plain one built of palisaded cedars.

When supper was ready, the men were called in and we were seated at the table. Porter Rockwell said Grace. While eating I noticed the hard old face of the man before me. He had been a frontiersman a great part of his life, and had served in the Nauvoo Legion. He was credited in those days with being the chief officer of the Danites, or Brigham Young's Destroying Angels, men set apart for avenging insults or injuries, real or fancied, to the Mormon people. He appeared to be about sixty years of age, by birth an American, rather uneducated, fierce in his looks, and wearing his hair in long braids coiled up at the back of his head. I do not know whether his humors were alike at all times, but the evening and morning when I saw him, he seemed morose and snappish. The whole world outside parts of Utah, he said, was made up of thieves, harlots, hypocrites, vagabonds, and scoundrels. Through the evening for two hours he would at times talk in an interesting way of early Utah history, life on the plains, Indian fighting, his experience as guide to government parties at different times, and early life back in Missouri and Illinois. These parts of his conversation were really interesting and instructive, but then he would break away into another line of talk, saying that all government officials in Utah were a band of knaves trying to assassinate him that they might obtain his property.

Seeing that it was foolish to argue with him, I listened to all he said. He told me that for the past few years the government had been endeavoring to lay hold of him, that he might be tried for murder, claiming that they had warrants out for him for having attempted to assassinate Governor Boggs of Missouri. "But," said he, "no matter whether I did or did not shoot Governor Boggs, they have no proof of such an act, and without proof you cannot convict a man in any court. And for anything that may have taken place at Nauvoo or on the plains or in Utah, there was practically a condition of war between the Mormon people and the United States government, so all those claims against me should have been dropped.

"Furthermore, when the officers of the United States Army were passing through Utah at any time and wanted a guide, whom would they try to find to lead them out of their difficulties? Nobody else but Porter Rockwell. Yes, by God, when General Connor in February 1863 wanted a man of nerve to lead him and his army up into Idaho to meet the Bannock Indians for a fight, whom did he call upon? Nobody but Porter Rockwell, myself. And in the face of one of the damndest storms that mortal man ever faced, I headed that army through frost and snow, leading General Connor and his soldiers into that Indian camp where one of the damnedest, hardest Indian battles was ever fought, where General Connor won the greatest victory of his life over the united Indian forces on Bear River. And what praise do they have for Porter Rockwell? Just gave him a measly five hundred dollars. That is the kind of man I am, and that is the measly reward they extended to me." He then talked of other incidents that had previously occurred between government officials and himself.

He was the father of a large family with many wives, and the owner of much wealth, and looked upon himself as one of the great men of his day. Many of the Mormon people look upon him as the Samson of their land, pious and virtuous, a gentleman along all lines. Gentiles in those days called him a robber, a horse thief and bigamist, a ruffian and renegade from justice. Personally, he treated me and my men very well. It is true that I paid him very well for all that he furnished us on that occasion. The next morning he furnished me with two men, four mules, and a freight wagon loaded with five barrels of water to be carried to a point twenty-five miles from his place out into the desert, for use of my animals and men. For this I paid him twenty-five dollars, plus twenty dollars for the accommodations of the previous night.

While talking to him on the following morning, I asked him if he wore his hair in that manner to avoid headache. He looked at me with a penetrating gaze and said, "No, nothing of that kind. Let me tell you, sir, that I wear it in this way because the Prophet Joseph Smith told me, or rather commanded me, to so wear it, and that by doing so I would never be overcome by the rifle, pistol, or knife of an enemy. I took his advice, and you see I am living yet."

I never saw this famous character again. Some one or two years after this, while on a spree in Salt Lake City, he went into the old Colorado Livery Stable as he was accustomed to do and was found lying dead in a manger the next morning. It was a fitting end for one whose life had been so wild, turbulent, and shady.[7]

We continued following the old telegraph line from Rockwell's ranch. For seventy miles we toiled over that accursed waste of salt, alkali, soda, and impalpably fine dust. No shrubbery or grass on which horses or mules of a traveler could feed, no water, save here and there a spring of salt or borax water. As far as the eye can see the land is blighted and forever the sun of summer shines down on a plain that is wild, wide, and worthless. Rarely does it rain in summer or snow in winter. It is shunned by these elements as though it were fit only for a council ground of lost souls.

At the end of the first day in the desert, we camped where we found the six barrels of water I had sent there by Rockwell's teams and men. We met the teams in the afternoon, or rather had overtaken them while on their way to this spot. Just as we arrived, we found them starting back to Rockwell's ranch.

Two days brought my party across the desert to the Deep Creek mountain range, where we were cheerfully received at Mr. Carney's ranch at their east base. His ranch consisted of a half-dozen bullrush patches, with as many springs, each patch containing fifteen to twenty acres. He had the country round about well stocked with cattle. Timber being scarce in the vicinity, his house and outbuildings were constructed of sod and roofed with bark and clay.

His wife was very handsome, with three equally handsome children. He boasted that his wife was one of the handsomest women that ever left the city of Limerick, a city in which he claimed all men and women were well behaved and very handsome.

The scene around was rather primitive and wretched in appearance, and yet he was getting rich. He was a cripple. I asked his wife what had happened to him, and she told me that they had once lived in the Apache country of Arizona where her husband was an army blacksmith. They were making money until one unlucky day a government mule kicked her husband in the groin, since which time he had been a confirmed invalid.

We stayed at Carney's ranch overnight, enjoying our rest very much, while I learned as much as possible of the history of the place. From stories told me by Mr. Carney and two of his employees who had been in the region for some twenty years, I learned that the locality had been a center of Indian depredations during the 1850s and 1860s. This region was occupied by the Paiute tribe,[8] whose country extended westward from the Great Salt Lake to the Sierra Nevada, and from the Snake River on the north to the Colorado River, including the area westward along the northern border of Mexico to the vicinity of San Diego, California. That part of the Paiute tribe dwelling in the Great American Desert and in the mountains to the west was amongst the most primitive and barbarous of our American tribes.

Unlike the Great Plains, there were but few large game animals to supply the Indians with food. The mountain ranges of the Great Desert do not rise to high altitude, and hence do not afford streams in summer that supply the desert with water for wild animals. Consequently, elk do not abound at all, antelope and deer are very few, bears do not exist, and the only animals the Indians could use are the jackrabbit, mountain rats, mice, grasshoppers, crickets, horned toads, and snakes. The seeds of certain desert plants and pine nuts obtained in the stunted pine groves of the low mountains are the only plant foods.

During the warm seasons, the Indians go almost entirely naked. During the winter, they wear robes of rabbit skins or in some places groundhog skins. Their feet are shod with moccasins of deerskin, and their temporary camps are simply shelters of sagebrush. Their weapons are bows and arrows of a very primitive pattern. They have but few horses, which they usually steal from Mexican inhabitants of southern California, and even those horses in time of hunger are sacrificed to the direct necessity of the kitchen.

For many years these Paiutes were the inveterate enemies of California immigrants. Murder and robbery were their professions, with but little opposition until General Connor's command came through from California, pursuing these ruthless bands and showing them no mercy. Seeing their numbers decreasing daily, they sued for peace. Their last battle with General Connor was near Hercules Gap in eastern Nevada.[9] At that point the Indians were almost exterminated, and the Paiute tribe since then has been peaceful in its associations with white men. They have taken in a small way to laboring for white ranchmen in outdoor work, the women becoming quite proficient in kitchen and laundry work as well as gardening and caring for domestic animals. From time to time in this narrative, I will find it necessary to refer to my commercial associations with the Paiute tribe.

We left Carney's ranch about ten o'clock the following morning, and three hours later we were on a summit of the Deep Creek Mountains. Away to our right and some distance down the mountain to the west stood a smelter for the reduction of silver ores. Here and there on the mountainside were prospect holes and ore piles where the hardy adventurers of the west had been striving after fortune. Their efforts had been largely in vain, inasmuch as the veins were small and shallow. The smelter at the time of our arrival was shut down and the mining camp deserted. This left the wild coyote to wander at will through the little town.

At that altitude we could see far back into Utah and far into Nevada to the west. Nevada is divided from north to south by several chains of low mountains. The valleys between them seemingly have no ending. The country is but thinly inhabited by a few cattlemen living near the occasional springs and roving bands of Paiute Indians. As previously stated, game is not abundant: no bears, a few deer, but hundreds of coyotes and hundreds of thousands of jackrabbits.

Down the tortuous road we toiled until once more we found ourselves in a low valley. A house was in sight, then a group of houses where a number of cattlemen had lived and where they seem to have united their small number to protect against Indian attacks. A few miles farther, we reached Deep Creek Valley proper, where we found a post office, a small store, and an overland telegraph office. As there were altogether about ten families and an entire population of about fifty souls, I was invited by two of the leading men to remain for at least a day and trade.

The leading citizen of this locality was a Mr. Cut Worthington, a prominent cattle and horse raiser.[10] I made my headquarters at his house, and in a vacant building nearby I had my men open up a quantity of goods such as the people desired to purchase. Instead of one day being spent there, I found it a business requirement to remain for three days. During this time I disposed of a little over nine hundred dollars worth of merchandise, including goods for women, men's clothing, shotguns, Colt's pistols, field glasses, spectacles, Waltham watches, and a quantity of rather high-priced jewelry.

Deep Creek Valley is about twenty-five miles wide and one hundred forty miles long. At the time of my passing through it, there were altogether about thirty to thirty-five families in the valley, almost all Mormons and cattle raisers. The locality is too bleak for successful farming. Short bunch grass and sage cover the surface of a large extent of the valley.

The following day we crossed another rather high chain of mountains to the west and reached Thousand Spring Valley.[11] While high on the last ridge of mountains we had a fine view of Jeff Davis Peak, rising far into the heavens to the southwest.[12] Its bald crest is covered with snow throughout most of the year, and on its sides lower down grow forests of pinyon pine in which the Paiute Indians gather pine nuts and hunt deer. Near its base in placer areas considerable gulch gold has been obtained in recent years, and a little town named Osceola, now abandoned, was built there.

The largest part of Thousand Spring Valley at the time of our passing was yet unoccupied. One man named Cleveland owned an immense farm on which he raised great quantities of grain and vegetables and employed about twenty white men and from fifty to one hundred Indians. He had thousands of cattle and horses running over the valley and mountainside. The produce of his large ranch was disposed of chiefly in the central mining camps of White Pine County, forty to fifty miles away.[13]

On the west side of the valley a few men lived, raising cattle and horses and producing grain. As there is plenty of water and the valley quite low, well supplied with wood, and very healthful, it is a most desirable place for an emigrant seeking a home. However, as it is far from railway communications and unadvertised by any newspapers, it lies almost entirely unknown. It is one of the few valleys of eastern Nevada that are of value for agriculture, and perhaps the best in White Pine County. With the isolated inhabitants of this mountain valley we carried on a flourishing business for a few days. The money in circulation amongst them was almost entirely gold coin.

We continued over the old overland stage road, crossing the next range through Shelburne Pass. All of these mountain ranges of eastern Nevada are rich in silver, lead, and copper ores, but the rather low grade of ores discovered up to that time and the high price of working them prevented their development. Shelburne we found to be a small, dilapidated mining camp. An old smelter with many houses occupied by mountain rats was all that remained of its ancient glory. No white inhabitants save one man, a Mr. Burke and his family, were then living there.[14] He practically owned the town: he ran a trading post, hotel and garden, and a feed corral. He was deputy sheriff of that section, a doctor, dictated to the Indians, and in short was lord and master of Shelburne Pass. We found him a most hospitable gentleman, and at his request we remained one day with him, selling him a quantity of merchandise to be disposed of at his trading post.

From Shelburne Pass we traveled down the western side of that mountain range until we came to the mouth of Duck Creek. At this point I found living on a mountain ranch Mr. Norton Kinsley,[15] a man with whom I have since spent many a pleasant evening. For a long time he had been a miner and prospector in the West, chiefly in California. He had been a soldier in General Connor's California Volunteers during their campaigns against the Paiutes and Shoshones in Utah, Idaho, and Nevada. After his enlistment he settled in the neighborhood where I found him. He was not married, but was enjoying life as few men can. He was in easy circumstances, having hired help, and worked but little. He had a very fine library, and spent his time in the study of polite literature. When I first saw him he was the most thoroughly read man in English poetry to be found in western America.

Standing at his home, one could look up and down the long expanse of Steptoe Valley, over whose long breadth grows the sagebrush common to all of Nevada. Steptoe Valley was named after Colonel Steptoe, a pioneer army colonel who with several companies of cavalry and infantry and a battery of artillery pursued Indians from Utah across this valley and northward into Oregon in about 1855. Here he was defeated by the combined forces of two tribes. Since he was cantoned for a short season in this valley, it was named after him. Steptoe Valley is a bleak and rather barren region owing to its elevation, and is exposed to bitter north winds through almost every winter month. At the time of our crossing, its inhabitants consisted only of a few ranchers and stockmen.

On the west side of the valley at the base of a mountain range stands the fair little town of Cherry Creek, its quartz mills rattling and hammering on the silver ores taken from the adjacent mountains. The silver thus extracted is taken daily on stage lines running north to Elko on the Central Pacific Railroad. It is one of the neatest and best-built mining towns in all of Nevada. Unlike most others, it is situated on a sloping plain, and its streets are clean and regular. It has abundance of water from adjacent springs and a mountain creek. Its inhabitants are industrious, tidy, and thrifty.[16]

We unloaded our merchandise into a local warehouse, took our pack train to a large feed corral, and went to a hotel kept by a lady named Mrs. Bates. Some three years before my present visit to Cherry Creek I had visited the town on mining business and occupied rooms in the Bates Hotel. I found a very pleasant welcome upon my return, and proceeded to arrange for a two-day business stay in that little mountain city.

I found Miss Mattie Bates in the parlor playing the piano and singing a piece of music of which I was very fond. While I was sitting there, the door from the parlor into the lobby of the hotel was open and I heard two men telling about a party who that day had unearthed far out in the desert an old safe stolen many years before from an old overland stagecoach. It was a rich find, said to be over twenty thousand dollars in gold coin.

After three days of very profitable trade in Cherry Creek, we drove our pack train to the mouth of the famous Egan Canyon, where a few gold and silver mines were being worked. I remained a day or two doing business, as about two hundred miners were employed there. The mines were owned by a New York City millionaire named Mr. Flood, and the managing director was General Rosecrans of Civil War fame, the hero of Stone River, a very polite and amiable gentleman.

Down the east side of the mountain toward Hercules Gap I came to an old stage station. It was kept by a widow whose husband still walked the earth. She was a fine, portly looking woman, quite able, one would think, to drag a cannon from Moscow to the Rhine had it been her fortune to share Napoleon's retreat from Russia.

Her house was at the intersection of the north-south stage road from Elko to Pioche and the old overland California road that we were then traveling, which passed east and west.[17] A half-cracked, half-wrecked, shiftless air rested on the surrounding scene. The woodpile near the house consisted of some few dozen knotty logs that no man could or would split. The barn below the house had a forlorn, ragged, and dissipated appearance. Its manger was no more. Its roof had more holes in it than there are in a riddle, while the whole fabric stood in that half-drunken attitude often held by neglected tombstones. Seven or eight old and spavined horses stood on the barren ground in front of the barn, each standing on three legs with head down and under lip hanging, eyes closed and careless, seemingly, to all things, save now and then one would raise his tail to brush away a gadfly. Down the hill to the east from the house was a beautiful spring. Its clear water ran down into a pasture below and east from the spring about two hundred yards. Between the pasture and the spring there were some pools of water in which ducks and geese were wading, quacking and screaming. Farther to the east, the old gray mountains we had crossed two days earlier arose high into the cloudy heavens.

Arriving at this, the Lady Killfor's[18] hotel or tavern, we found it necessary to halt for the night. Coming out to meet us on our arrival, the kindly mannered and corpulent hostess asked us if we desired accommodations for the evening. When I informed her that such were the conditions, she said, "You and your men, with all your pack and saddle animals, can consider yourselves at home as long as you desire." We planned to have our evening meal at the Killfor House, as the place was sometimes called, and as the evening was somewhat dusty and unpleasant, we concluded that it was best to sleep within the house as well as eat there.

After supper, as we were seated in the front room, Mrs. Killfor came in to inquire as to what part of the world I was then going. Learning the nature of my journey and my business into distant parts, she began to tell me her own past, as well as her present prospects. She said she began life in Ohio about thirty-eight years before and began to show great natural ability and personal beauty at a very early age. She was first married at the age of fifteen, again at twenty-one, the third time at twenty-seven. Her fourth marriage took place on her thirtieth birthday. From age thirty-one to thirty-six, she had three more husbands, the last of which, Colonel Killfor, she had divorced only six months previously. "Since then," she said, "I have done nothing but strive to beautify my home and cultivate my daughters' minds. My quiet and romantic mountain home here contains enough to occupy my time, and if I ever marry a man he will have to be a rich, cultivated, and refined gentleman. For if he is not, I would not marry him. I don't care if God made him from the skelp of an ash tree." She then made us acquainted with her daughters and sons, who had been out in the mountains after cattle. The whole family looked half-starved and only half-baked. Their clothes had been cut in the wrong way, and one of the girls was a natural winker.

A little later my lady friend asked me if I was fond of music. I told her that I was, whereupon she sent into an adjoining room and took forth an enormous accordion. She began to work it in order to produce music, and after the instrument had been complaining for a time she asked me if I could identify the tune. I could not. Once more her shoulders began to work. The accordion went into convulsions, and again she inquired if I had ever heard that tune. Again I failed to name it.

She next called my attention to a small room that contained her library and said that if I wanted to read I could step in and choose any book I wished. I discovered that although there were perhaps three hundred volumes in sight, to my surprise they were nothing but government agricultural reports and similar books sent out by congressmen to their constituents. After looking over this library that would never be read by any mortal man or woman, I asked her in what part of the world she had obtained such a wonderful collection. She answered that it was the accumulation of many years. Wherever she went, that library went also. Whenever she moved, an extra span of animals was employed to transport her library, which indeed was not worth the fire that would burn it.

The night wore away until it was almost midnight, yet the fair and hopeful widow played away on the accordion airs that none but she herself knew. Now and then she told a short anecdote of her many weddings. At last we went to our beds, yet for an hour longer we could still hear the widow laboring on the accordion or singing snatches of old forgotten songs to melodies that were so wild and godforsaken that their sounds would drive the angels out of heaven were they left to take their choice between listening or leaving. At length I fell asleep and did not awaken until it was broad daylight.

The next day we traveled southward, passing through Hercules Gap, a vast natural gate through a low mountain chain of limestone. The walls of Hercules Gap are so high and perpendicular that the traveler stands awestricken at the wild grandeur of the scene. We passed through it to the little town of Robinson,[19] which we found to consist of twenty-five to forty persons. In former days I knew a few residents of the place. There were some mines being worked there and it was a place in which money was usually very plentiful. I was warmly welcomed by the people, for I had with me merchandise they sadly needed.

While my pack animals were being driven into the corral, I heard a pistol shot and asked the cause. A man ran up to me and said that someone had just been killed over at the hotel. Leaving the animals to my men, I ran across the street to the hotel and there on the floor lay dead a former friend, Mat Gleeson, a man I had known for years, and as enterprising a miner as ever handled a drill or opened up a silver mine. He had labored for years to obtain the price of a home. He then had a good mine called the Shark Lode, which he was about to sell for forty thousand dollars in San Francisco. He had actually been on his way from the mine to Robinson and stopped to eat in his own little hotel when a man with whom he had had a trifling dispute a few days before found him as he was going in and shot him dead. This man, named Roach, some weeks later was tried in court for the crime and sent to the penitentiary for life.

My trading in Robinson continued for two days, then we went to the town of Hamilton, once the liveliest, wildest mining camp of the western slope. During the winter of 1869 and 1870, Hamilton was the place toward which fortune hunters turned.[20] Treasure Hill adjoining the town was thought to be one vast mass of silver ore, and, while the snow lay deep on it, wildcat silver mines sold for fabulous prices.

Hamilton was built up rapidly into a city of more than twenty thousand people. It stood on a broad flat to the north of Treasure Hill, but at the time of my visit the city was half abandoned. At the Henry Ward Beecher, the Treasure Hill, and the Big Smoky mines there were yet three hundred men working.

Responding to an invitation from the remaining residents of Treasure Hill the day after our arrival, I had my men drive the mule train up to Treasure City on Treasure Hill, where we planned to do business. We set up headquarters for two days in an unoccupied restaurant on the main street, owned by a man named Carmichael, a very fine fellow who also owned the only hotel, which was adjacent to the restaurant.[21]

There, far above the clouds, its wooden roofs bleaching in the mountain air, stood the old weatherbeaten town, storm worn and half-wrecked. We reached the main street, from the lower end of which there was a majestic view of the surrounding world; thousands of square miles of mountain range and valley slope lay spread out before us. Far to the south in the clear blue horizon there lay mountains that were barren and gray. The valleys were dreary and in most places unfit for cultivation. On the mountainsides there was in some places considerable bunch grass on which cattle may fatten, and the valleys in some places produce white sage that is exceedingly good for cattle feed.

White River lies about forty miles from Treasure Hill, and Duckwater almost the same distance, only more to the west. On these two streams are a few ranchmen or farmers who raise barley and potatoes and other vegetables. They cultivate the land along the streams, irrigating it by ditches.

Toward the southeast, Kern Creek flows out of a low range of mountains. On it live the famous Dick Barnes, Joe Saborn, and Alexander McCulloch,[22] who thrive and fight like Irish kings with each other, constantly contending and quarreling over water rights. The little mining camps of the neighboring mountains consume the produce of these Kern Creek ranchmen. The high and dry region is always healthful and invigorating. Their produce—potatoes, barley, wheat, carrots, and cabbage—is good, while the beef of their cattle is tender and juicy, so that a sober Nevadan is as stout and brawny as a Scottish highlander.

Looking up and down the streets of this half-demolished town, I could not help calling to mind what a hive of human excitement it once was. These streets, now almost deserted, once echoed to the tread of thousands of adventurers in quest of fortunes. Treasure Hill became a city. City lots up there in the heavens were worth their measure in silver dollars. Men thought hopefully that when the snows melted everyone owning a foot of ground would find it a mine of inexhaustible wealth. But the spring came, the ground thawed, the drills clinked and hammers pounded, and most found it was a delusion and a snare. Giving their curse to that hill where they had left their money, most packed their blankets and sought fortune elsewhere.

Other towns nearby vanished as quickly. Far to the west in a deep canyon was Sherman Town, and to the southeast was Eberhardt, now in ruins.

Two of the former mines were still being worked on Treasure Hill, the Eberhardt and the Henry Ward Beecher. As I was through with my work that evening, the mining foreman took me down into both. For three hours we examined ore stokes running along tunnels, down incline shafts, and up into side workings. There yet remained immense quantities of rich ores in these two mines, which continued to be worked for about three years after my visit. The ore is raised out of the mines by means of steam hoists and hauled down to the town of Eberhardt where it is crushed and the silver cast into ingots of from one to two thousand dollars each.

Leaving Treasure Hill and Hamilton, we journeyed for sixty miles to Keiser Springs.[23] These springs are situated in a desert and consist of hot and cold water. Around them is about two hundred acres of grassland watered by the springs. The grass is wiry but very good, and the spot is an inviting one after traveling across the worthless deserts which surround it. To the east rises Troy Mountain across a vast bed of sand, ashes, and alkali—desert forevermore. At the foot of Mt. Troy is Blue Eagle Springs, another ranch or stock range.

Here and there through the mountains of Nevada are springs that water more or less ground. These springs are all owned by men who either raise produce for those who work in the mines or else have horses, cattle, or sheep.

At Keiser Spring I found a Mr. Billy Runnels with his wife and baby. He was an industrious man. The grass that grows around the springs to the amount of about one hundred tons he cuts with a machine, and when the winter sets in he hauls it with his six yoke of bulls to a mining camp about sixty miles to the south. Those sixty miles are across country without water or grass, so the traveler must carry both for his animals. After remaining at Billy Runnels's place for the night and selling him and his men a considerable quantity of merchandise, we started for Tybo.[24]

It was then in its glory. The Tugee[25] mine was booming; the smelters in the lower end of the town were roaring and flaring in the small hours of the night when we reached the town. The camp is situated in a gorge on the east side of a high mountain range in Nye County. The mines produced both lead and silver.

Now there are two ways of obtaining the silver from crude ore. One method is by milling it or by crushing it in the batteries of a quartz mill, where by means of quicksilver, salt, and other chemicals the silver is drawn away from the crushed ore. Ore that can be crushed in a mill immediately after coming from the mine is known as free-milling ore, while ore in which the silver and gold are largely associated with lead, sulphur, and other minerals must be roasted in a furnace that the sulphur may burn out, permitting the quicksilver to act upon the gold and silver.

Lead ores that contain varying percentages of gold and silver are cast into a furnace with a quantity of iron ore and limestone in order to flux the ore properly so that the metal will not cake and choke the furnace, but smelt and run well. The furnaces of Nevada are fed entirely with charcoal produced in the mountains round about. These charcoal kilns are owned and run mostly by Italians who sell their product to the smelters at from fifteen to thirty cents per bushel.

When heated sufficiently in the furnaces, the ore discharges its metals, which run out into troughs where bars are formed of from one hundred to one hundred fifty pounds in weight. These bars of base bullion contain from five dollars to one thousand dollars worth of silver to the ton of lead bullion, and usually contain also more or less of gold. In most cases these bars are sent to New York, Omaha, or San Francisco, where the metals are separated.

The slag, or base matter from which the lead and silver bullion has been taken, runs into pots which are dumped down the mountainside, where a hill of it forms near the furnace. Each pot when empty then receives a wash of lime or black lead in order that molten slag may not adhere to its iron sides.

In milling ores, that is, crushing them and withdrawing the metal with the aid of quicksilver, the lead that may be in the ore is lost; only the copper, silver, and gold are retained. They lie in a mortar-like state until the whole mass is put into a furnace and the quicksilver evaporates. The metal is then cast into ingots and sent to the United States office at Carson City or San Francisco, where the bars are again melted and refined, each metal being cast into separate ingots.

The town of Tybo was quite lively at the time of our arrival. The mining companies had just paid their men, and every man who had a dollar or a thousand dollars seemed anxious to get rid of his wealth as soon as possible. There were three dry goods stores in Tybo: Trowbridge's general store at the lower end of town, Rosenstein's above his place, and Aunt Hannah's millinery and furnishing for ladies establishment. Next to that was Charlie Garrett's drugstore,[26] then the post office and Johnny Peebles's Palace Saloon. Next there were two lodging houses, three gambling houses, a dance house, a half-dozen residences, two livery stables, a meat shop, and two blacksmith shops. On the opposite side of the street there were several restaurants and a number of Chinese wash houses. Over on the side of the hill to the south there were a number of little residences, and farther up the hill stood miners' cabins, humble but clean, cozy, and comfortable.

That was a lively night. Men played faro and poker in the high-toned-looking saloon on Main Street. The music in the dance house was loud, furious, and there was plenty of it. The dancers were miners of all ages and the professional German and Mexican dancing girls imported by the establishment.

We go in. There is a large hall with a big crowd in it, nine-tenths of which are men. A man wanting to dance goes over to where the girls are seated, takes one and sails into the middle of the floor, and dances with those in the set. When the set is through, he takes the girl over to the bar, takes a drink of beer or whiskey, and the girl takes a drink of water. He throws fifty cents on the counter, twenty-five cents for the whiskey, which belongs to the bar; the other twenty-five cents goes to the girl for her dancing. This dancing continues night and day if the town contains much money, and until the stores and dance houses have drawn every dollar from the miners, after which things are quiet until the next payday. Few men save their money, and although they are well paid, at the end of the year they are no better off than at its beginning.

We rented from Charlie Garrett a storeroom just completed, and from there carried on a very profitable trade for four days. The prices obtained here were considerably over one hundred percent above the regular invoice prices, yet when we considered that my expense there for myself, men, and animals was about seventy-five dollars a day, I was fully justified from a commercial standpoint in selling at such inflated prices.

We left Tybo and journeyed forty miles over the mountains to Belmont, the county seat of Nye County. The road took us over a long, dry, and dreary waste of mountain and valley, wild and desolate as well as worthless. On the high mountain ridges grow forests of pitch pine and mahogany, and the climate is dry, pure, and healthful.

Our business was about the same in Belmont as in Tybo. There were many vacant storerooms, and we easily found a place to exhibit merchandise. The animals were sent out with a caretaker into the mountains nearby, leaving my two men to assist me in handling merchandise, and we did a successful business for three days.

Belmont was at one time a very prominent mining camp, with a population of from two- to three thousand. That was in 1865, when two Philadelphia mining companies opened up mines in the vicinity. In what is now known as East Belmont, one of these companies erected a quartz mill costing $500,000. It ran for one week, was proclaimed a failure, and there it stands today, a landmark, but of no use to the land on which it stands. The camp of Belmont no doubt possesses some good mines, but no great success has attended their working so far. The town looks weatherbeaten and old. A few lawyers, the county officials, a preacher, two or three traders, and the proprietors of two hotels make up the population. Although the town is dilapidated, it is in a handsome place. It is neatly built, and shows good taste on the part of the builders.[27]

Leaving Belmont, we took a northwesterly route over a steep hill, up through a canyon, and along a steep mountain ridge until we gained the summit and proceeded to the little mining town of Jefferson.[28] From the summit I looked down. Below me in a canyon on the west side of the mountain range to the west lay the dreary waste of Smoky Valley, running northward to the Humboldt River and south far into the wilds of the Amargossa Valley. Smoky Valley is about twenty-five miles wide and but very thinly inhabitated. It lies like most of Nevada's valleys, awaiting reformation of nature's work. This valley, together with the Amargossa Valley, is about three hundred miles long and yet is not worth twenty sections of land in the Mississippi Valley.

In the little town of Jefferson we remained one day, doing a very thrifty business. We then passed westward down into the Smoky Valley, where I found a white American living with a squaw of the Shoshone tribe. Outside the house in the open yard there were several Indians, men and women, with a score of children. These Indians were playing cards for small silver coins, five, ten, and twenty-five-cent pieces. These Indians, like the entire Indian race, are inveterate gamblers, and he or she who plays cards well, or any other game of chance, is sure to be the true possessor of glory amongst the other Indians.

Two days after leaving Jefferson, I reached Austin, Nevada, then one of the thrifty mining camps of the state.[29] I found it a handsome little city, very prosperous and rich through its mining industries. About twelve hundred people compose its population, exclusive of about two hundred Indians of the Shoshone and Paiute tribes that always remain or hang around the Nevada mining camps. The principal mine of Austin, the Manhattan, employed about three hundred fifty men. There was another, known as the Yankee Blade, that employed about two hundred men at the time of our visit. The veins in these two mines are wholly silver in value, but the ore is fabulously rich. The veins are narrow but go to great depth.

At Austin we made our home at Crescenzo's Hotel, in the sampling room of which we opened our merchandise; and we remained there five days. Board and room for myself and two men, and the care of horses and mules, together with a license for doing business in that county, cost me a total of seventy-nine dollars per day. We remained in the town just six days, gathering in trade $3,100 dollars in gold coin.

From there we passed on to the town of Eureka, another mining camp, where I had a consignment of merchandise shipped from New York many weeks before.[30] We picked up the merchandise at the railway freight office, and opened up business at a warehouse obtained for the purpose, and carried on a brisk business for four days.

Eureka and Austin were incorporated as cities, with a mayor, a chief of police, and a well-organized police force in each town. To be the mayor or chief of police in a Nevada mining town means something, for the men holding those offices have their lives exposed daily to the attack of the entirely too frequent desperado.

A few words here relative to the Paiute Indians of central Nevada. In most mining camps these Indians are tolerated to the greatest extent of liberty possible. Through the day they are employed in various kinds of work by the whites. The squaws iron, wash, scrub, carry wood to town on their backs, selling it for twenty-five cents a load, carry water, nurse babies, and sweep, while the bucks, as they are called, saw wood, split it, and help the butchers, blacksmiths, bakers, and merchants. The pay for men and women is the same, one dollar per day and all the *hogadie* they desire to eat, which means cold bread, meat, cake, pudding, chicken, potatoes, and such like.

At all hours of the day groups of them may be seen on the sidewalks playing cards. They dress in almost the same clothing as the whites, and some of them dress well, both men and women. The gamblers and fancy men around the town give the Indians suits of scuffed fine clothing, old tile or high hats, high-heeled boots; and they themselves buy white shirts so that some of them at times look neatly dressed. But an Indian when he does buy a white shirt will wear it until it falls to pieces before being washed, unless he has the misfortune to lose it along with the rest of his wardrobe at gambling. The squaws may be seen wearing old silk, satin, or poplin dresses given to them by white women, and their attire is as motley throughout as one could wish to see.

They have their little sagebrush shelters on the hillsides north of both Eureka and Austin. A friend and myself went over to see their dwellings without roof, which made merely a shelter to break off the north wind. Each of such shelters was surrounded with all sorts of old trash gathered from the white residents of the town, including old clothing, saddles, broken guns, bottles, sheepskins, old boots, broken axes, miners' picks, and playing cards scattered in all directions, pictorial newspapers, torn books, and broken dishes. Here and there around the little shelters were tied sore-backed ponies, with more of the latter far up on the hillside grazing on the scarce grass. Scores of dogs were in sight, some sleeping, others playing, or now and then one of them might be seen gnawing a beef bone. On crosspoles hung scores of skinned jackrabbits drying in the sun. Little Indian children, some of them half-dressed, others stark naked, played with the dogs, screaming, screeching, and running after each other in play.

Within the shelters sat Indians, men and women, playing cards, others lying asleep on blankets or in a bed of warm ashes before a sagebrush fire. Now and then a squaw was seen nursing a baby or mending clothes. These Indians, being from an Indian standpoint well clothed and well fed for savages, developed the highest possible amount of genius, many features of which seemed native to themselves; but their main sharpness lies in gambling.

We left Austin, traveling up the Reese River, one of the narrowest rivers in the world. It is two hundred miles in length and but from three to six feet in width. Its source is a spring in the San Antone Mountains. Springs here and there on its route keep up the supply that is lost by absorption or evaporation. It flows into the Humboldt River in the northern part of the state. Along the Reese River are many stock ranches, and a few farmers raise barley, potatoes, and vegetables.

Noon brought us to Judge Logan's ranch in Reese River Valley. I knew him previously, and he invited my men and myself to dinner. The judge's wife was a most artistic cook, an exceedingly good housekeeper, and very agreeable in her manners. His daughter was well bred, extremely well educated, and very handsome. The judge employed about forty men on his ranch. He requested that we stay there for the day, put up our tents, open our merchandise, and allow his family and his men to trade with us, which I was very well pleased to do. We were well treated, and the business carried on for the next twenty-four hours was very profitable. May they all live long and be happy, and when death overtakes them may they go to heaven before daybreak.

From Judge Logan's ranch, we went on to the little mining camp of Ione. There is little to attract the traveler on the route: sagebrush plains and ragged low mountains covered with cedars and scrubby pines, and in most places considerable bunch grass on which cattle and sheep feed. In Ione there were only a few families, with about sixty men working in three silver mines.[31]

At Mr. Bowler's[32] I found ample room for my pack train, and in his mountain hotel exceedingly good accommodations for the exhibit of merchandise in his large sample room. That evening and all of the next day as the shifts of miners were released from the mines, I carried on a very profitable trade in men's clothing, cutlery, pistols, and other lines of hardware that I kept in stock. I found the people exceedingly hospitable, very cheerful, highly cultured, and most profitable to me for the time we remained with them.

I was somewhat amused at the personal makeup of the Bowler family. Both father and mother were red-haired. They had three sons and four daughters, and it seemed to me that the hair on each child was much deeper in its red color than that of the father or mother, which is saying a good deal. Notwithstanding, they were people of the most agreeable and amiable temper.

From Ione, our course led across the bleak deserts of San Antone and Clover Dale Valley. Glorious Lord! What a wild, weird, and worthless scene is spread before the eye. In all directions desolation and misery are expressed. No grass, no trees, not even sage can be seen, only hills and plains that in formation are of the blue miocene. In other places broken blocks of lava and the cones of two old volcanoes loom up out of the plain to the south.

Along the road in places one may see some queer and rare volcanic formations, a kind of glass very black and hard, known to the learned world as obsidian, which is really a volcanic glass. It is quite abundant in this region beyond San Antone to the west and for ages was used by Indians for arrow points and lance heads, and it is the same substance used by the priests of ancient Mexico for knives for human sacrifice.

There is also in this region a fairly good quantity of jasper. This substance was used largely by the ancient Egyptians for scarabs and amulets, of which I collected quite a number while in Egypt. In the British Museum I once saw a skeleton of a woman embedded partly in a limestone slab found in a cave in Mexico, and on the breastbone there was an amulet of this green stone. The lime particles in the water passing over it long since formed a cement by which it had adhered to the breastbone after the flesh had departed, and had doubtless been worn around the neck, as there was a hole through it.

At the base of these volcanic cones I found a few specimens of float copper ore that rolled from some vein in the mountain above. I also gathered several exceedingly rich specimens of silver ore; but, owing to shortness of time on that day, I was unable to spare time for prospecting. Water being very scarce, my men and I did not have an hour to spend on account of the great distance between springs, and we were anxious to leave these dreary wastes behind us and penetrate into a better grassed and watered region that was said to lie to the west.

Away to the south we saw Crystal Peak, a noted landmark, which is capped with snow a great part of the year. The intervening land, about one hundred miles, is wild, silent, desolate, and worthless. But if bareness rests on the earth beneath, the sky is beautiful. It is forever clear in the summer and fall, and the dry atmosphere is rare and pure. While the traveler finds pure water and is not obliged to walk, the journey is invigorating.

Looking back to the east we could yet plainly see the old quartz mill of San Antone built twenty years previously to treat silver ores from the surrounding mountains. The company dug a very deep well and obtained fairly good water for use in the mill. Unfortunately, after the mill was built and the well was dug, at the cost of $400,000, it was discovered that it cost about five dollars for every dollar of silver extracted. The mines and mill were abandoned, and now the high chimney of the old mill rears itself one hundred fifty feet into the heavens. When we saw it, the old mill was going to ruin, and there were no voices heard from the place where almost $600,000 was sunk to be seen no more.[33]

After leaving Austin, we made it a rule that every evening we would prepare our own camp, setting up our two tents, doing our own cooking, and sleeping under our own blankets. At Ione I hired a Chinese cook named Sam Hing. He was recommended to me by Mr. and Mrs. Bowler, and I found him to be worthy of their recommendation. He served us well for many months. I purchased a California horse and saddle for him, and he at once became one of the force, and remained with us for the rest of the expedition.

We toiled across this dreary land until we reached Crow Springs, far out on the San Antone Desert. Little grass was available in this vicinity, and that which we did find was short, bunchy, and very scattered. The water from the spring, however, was very good. It flows out of red sandstone and is the only water available in the long stretch of eighty miles.

At this spring we unloaded our animals and gave them part of the barley we had brought with us, reserving the remainder for the next day, then hobbled them to graze on the sparse grass. We set up our tents and made a little fire out of pieces of broken-down wagons and wooden boxes we had picked up along the road. While we were eating our supper, wolves came near our camp and began to howl and yelp, and continued to do this throughout the night. That night was very cold, and, although we had fairly good mattresses and plenty of blankets, because of our anxiety about our animals we spent an uncomfortable night, and toward daybreak we caught the animals, ate breakfast, and departed from Crow Springs at an early hour.

How little we know of the future and what it may bring forth! This seemingly worthless desert which at that time was not known to possess any mineral wealth became a few years later the scene of great excitement when extremely rich gold and silver ores were discovered, and the great mining camp of Tonopah was built.

From Crow Springs we traveled over the same kind of country all day and reached the mining camp of Belleville that night. There were two mills at Belleville crushing silver ores taken from three mines a few miles away in the red volcanic mountains to the northwest. The town was situated on a little sandy flat surrounded by everlasting barrenness. The people I found to be a wild set of fellows. They were hard drinkers of a very inferior whiskey. They told me that their drinking of so much whiskey was because the water of the country was unfit to drink. There were about two hundred twenty men at the mines and mills, and possibly twenty to twenty-three women.[34] All food was brought in from Carson City, about one hundred fifty miles to the north. We remained in Belleville thirty-six hours, doing a fairly good business.

All the business done in Nevada, whether with white men, Mexicans, or Indians, was done on the basis of gold and silver coin. No paper money of any kind was used.

Our next point of business was Candalaria, a group of houses and one stock barn still in the desert. And behold, oh angels and men, what no other spot on earth could show: there were seventeen houses, and of those thirteen were saloons.[35] The fourteenth was a house for dancing with the seven German girls who lived at the one miners' boarding house. Candalaria lies seven miles from the Belle Mine to the north, and is the single resort for the prospectors and wandering humanity of that entire region, which accounts for the exclusive nature of society there.

We left Candalaria early in the morning and journeyed to Columbus, another mining camp and mill town. It is built on the northern side of a desert that is thirty-five miles across from north to south, and this desert is covered with water in the winter when there is any considerable snow or rain. This sheet of water is rarely greater than one inch in depth, and when dry weather again appears, a vast quantity of borax exudes from the earth, forming a crust of large scales two or three inches deep. When these are stepped on, they tinkle like broken glass, and the material is called tinkle.

The gathering of this borax and soda is one of the chief industries of this region. A field of about forty acres is formed and the water turned over it for a short time. When the water has evaporated, the still moist borax is raked into long windrows. This tinkle contains much sand and earth, but the whole is put into tanks to which water is added, which dissolves the borax. The borax solution is then boiled down in the same manner as salt, leaving a residue of pure borax. The borax from these fields has revolutionized borax prices since there is so much of it and so little is used except by soap manufacturers, chemists, blacksmiths, and other industrial users. The borax is shipped from these marshes to railroad stations by means of twenty-mule teams, each of which pulls two immense wagons, usually containing ten tons between them. The man who opened this industry in Columbus Marsh, Lydea Valley, and Death Valley is known as Borax Smith. He has become a millionaire many times over from the borax industry.[36]

The appearance of the country is forbidding. Were it not that the mountains on either side of these desert valleys contain small quantities of grass and springs of very limited flow, it would be impossible to work any of the gold or silver veins in those mountains. The valleys themselves, and for that matter the greater number of low mountains, are forever sacred unto desolation.

Northwest of Columbus lies Bodie, California, a large and prosperous mining camp rich in gold and silver. Still farther west lies Benton, named after Senator [Thomas Hart] Benton, where silver is mined.[37] A short distance from Benton lies Bridgeport, the county seat of Mono County, California, one of the more desolate and barren counties of California lying east of the great Sierra Nevada range, and on its east line taking up a part of the broad and utterly desolate desert.

The rock formation of the region is largely volcanic, interspersed with uplifts of granite and at times measures of limestone and slate, wherein we find silver lead veins in sufficient volume to make their working profitable.

The Walker River region and the Carson sinks contain very little territory that is not desert, with greasewood and sagebrush plains and alkali covering a large part of the country. West of Columbus, near the base of the Sierra Nevada Mountains, lies Mono Lake, whose water is so charged with borax that it contains no fish. The region around the lake is covered with fragmentary obsidian, pumice, and volcanic ash. Along the west shore of the lake there are rocky elevations of volcanic formations in which there are great numbers of ancient fire chambers and caverns, black, barren, and silent. For a great part of the year the shores of the lake and a few islands are white with seagulls that come over the mountains from the ocean to nest. The eggs of these gulls are very much sought by the little mining camps as far north as Virginia City, where they sell by hundreds of dozens for seventy-five cents to one dollar a dozen.

We spent four days in Benton and Bridgeport, then continued our journey across the borax deserts southwest of Columbus. After a cheerless and hard day's travel of thirty miles, we reached a ranch occupied by two brothers. One was a widower and by profession a Methodist preacher, and the other, an old bachelor, was very slightly demented. We learned they were brothers to Emma Hale, wife of the Mormon prophet Joseph Smith.[38] Although they occasionally ventured forth to preach, they informed me that preaching in that region was poor business; a very good preacher would be laughed at and called crazy and a poor preacher could starve.

One of these men was a pretty good hunter and had just come in as we arrived with two jackrabbits, three ducks, four blackbirds, four chipmunks, and a meadowlark, all of which went into a pot together and boiled long and well. Large game is not plentiful in this land. Sometimes a deer or antelope may be seen in the mountains, and coyotes make their living catching jackrabbits, chipmunks and desert mice. As we had made a long drive that day and were somewhat tired, and as our hosts had prepared a very good dinner from the game they had brought in, we had supper with them and breakfast as well.

The next day we made a long drive to Fish Springs, where two old brothers maintained a public house and feed station. We found excellent water, and the men harvested a crop of wild hay that our animals much appreciated. From Fish Springs the road led us southward into Round Valley in Inyo County.[39] Round Valley lies hugged up in the Sierra Nevada Mountains. About forty families live there, raising corn, wheat, and vegetables and cattle, sheep, and excellent brands of horses. They sell almost everything they raise for hard gold cash in Bodie, Benton, and Bridgeport. This valley is quite elevated and is cold, wonderfully so, in contrast with the climate about two hundred miles to the west over the range near the Pacific Ocean. Here the mountains rise up bold, barren, and abruptly on both sides of the mountain valley. The White Mountains are to the east and the Sierra Nevadas to the west. Mt. Whitney here is 15,000 feet in altitude.

We made our headquarters for a few days at the ranch of my old friend Thomas Williams.[40] I also found in this valley a number of other friends, the Parsons family, Abner Jones, David Samuelson, and a number of others, many of whom I had seen years before in Virginia City, Nevada. Money was very abundant among these people, and my arrival with an assorted stock of merchandise which they badly needed was a godsend. In looking over my daily journals of that time, I find I sold in four days $2,346 in goods for which I was paid United States gold coins, except for about forty dollars in what were called Carson silver dollars. These dollars were minted at Carson City and known as the trade dollar, having been made for the Chinese trade to displace if possible the Mexican dollar so long current in the general trade of China.

From Round Valley we proceeded southward to Bishop Creek, another farming and grazing district. It is watered by the snowmelt streams of the Sierra Nevada. Bishop Creek Valley is about thirty miles long, seven or eight miles wide, and fairly well settled, but it is cold and bears no resemblance to the land beyond the mountains which receives the soft Pacific breezes that call forth a hundred forms of plant life not found east of the mountains.

We remained at Bishop Creek for three days carrying on a considerable trade with the Paiute Indians who wander as far northward as Bodie, Benton, Bridgeport, and Columbus. We found them in other camps as well, with considerable amounts of money, mostly silver dollars, half dollars, and twenty-five-cent pieces, but rarely dimes and never any nickels or copper cents. We sold them colored cotton goods, vermillion paints, beads, Indian jewelry, butcher knives and pocket knives, mouth organs, Jew's harps, brass whistles, a number of shotguns, powder, shot, gun caps, and playing cards. We carried on this Indian trade after we had completed business with the white families in a rented warehouse.

Another day's travel brought us to the vicinity of Big Pine, where we stayed for two days at the far-famed ranch of the far-famed cattle and horse raiser Richard Hessian.[41] Locally known as Uncle Dick Hessian, he is truly a greathearted man with a very interesting family. Besides his own three sons, he employed about twenty white men and from ten to twenty Indians.

We continued to Big Pine, which is less than four miles away. It was then a small place that took its name from a gigantic pine tree that grew on the banks of a small mountain stream.[42] In the canyons immediately to the west grow heavy pine and cedar timber. The town itself contained one small store, a wayside hotel, and of course a saloon, with about a dozen families. The hotel and saloon, bar, and feed corral were run by the same man, a Mr. McMurray, a second-generation Scotchman about six feet four in height and easily weighing two hundred fifty pounds. We spent two days in Big Pine, and trade there was very profitable.

From Big Pine we continued southward to Independence, the county seat of Inyo County. At that time, the military post of Fort Independence, at which were garrisoned two companies of United States infantry, was located about two miles north of town.[43] We did a very profitable trade in both the fort and town for six days. We found no Indians at that time near Independence.

Our next stop was the town of Lone Pine, a small hamlet made up largely of Mexicans, two families of Jews, and about twelve families of Americans. Our hostess, the Duchess Du Barry, was indeed a kind lady, as much as I ever found in any land.[44] I found it more profitable and convenient to board my party at her hotel and feed my pack train in her corral than to set up our own camp. We did business in Lone Pine for three days. By now our stock of merchandise was pretty well depleted. All my Indian goods had been sold, as well as the firearms, carbines, shotguns, and pistols, and my entire stock of field glasses.

There was but one more point I was to visit, Cerro Gordo,[45] which was a mining camp high up near the summit of White Mountains immediately east of the famed Owens Lake, which in those days was an immense reservoir of borax water. In addition to the two days I spent in Cerro Gordo, it took one day to reach it and a half day to descend the tortuous road from the mining camp to the east shore of Owens Lake, where I had left part of my pack train with our Chinese cook at Tommy Passmore's station.[46] The few people I found at Cerro Gordo had an abundance of money in the form of checks made out on a type of paper very much like parchment. Each check was about seven inches long and four inches wide, made out to the bearer and drawn on a bank in San Francisco, and negotiable everywhere in Inyo County and throughout southern California.

The Mexican population of that area at that time was made up of pretty hard human material. A great many of them were horse thieves and highwaymen, occasionally a murderer, and most all of them had been run out of the country to the west and along the coast. Some of them came from as far as San Diego, Los Angeles, and Santa Barbara, and some even from Old Mexico. The women were very similar to the men, easy in their ways. I found it absolutely necessary to have my men keep a watchful eye on the parties coming in to trade, for they were universally quick-fingered. Although they all had a little money and trade with them was profitable, it seemed that to be able to steal a few articles during their trading was glory to their souls.

The Mexicans of that region are largely of Indian blood, from fifteen to eighty-five percent Indian and the remainder of Spanish origin. As elsewhere in those days in California, they were fond of cockfighting, bull baiting, and of course gambling, at which they played away everything they possessed, from the horses they rode to the clothes they wore, when the necessity of a Monte game demanded.

When I finished selling my merchandise to the few Mexican miners at Cerro Gordo, I purchased a quantity of placer gold amounting to about nine hundred dollars in value, as I had been doing on this expedition whenever I had an opportunity, since I usually was able to make a profit of about one dollar on each ounce of gold purchased. The gold I had obtained on this trip from Deep Creek, Utah, to Cerro Gordo, California, amounted in value to a little over $4,500. When I reached Mojave, California, I shipped it to the San Francisco mint with instructions to have payment for it sent to my commercial headquarters at New York City in the form of exchange on United States Treasury gold payable to my broker.

Descending from Cerro Gordo, I arrived at the little station of Swansea on the east shore of Owens Lake and prepared for the two-hundred-mile journey to Mojave Station, California, over one of the most desolate regions in the world. In addition to the food we took for ourselves, we packed a ton of barley for our animals, and a number of ten-gallon waterbags for the most difficult stretches.

There is little about that journey of six days that I find necessary to record. The region is absolutely a desert. The freight road was then controlled by a man named Nado, who had what were called home stations along its length at distances about forty miles apart.[47] These distances constituted two days' travel for loaded mule trains and one very long day's travel for empty ones. We found the waste of sand that covers that region far better for the use of pack animals than it would have been for wheeled vehicles, convenient though the latter would have been in many respects.

At those home stations, water was sold at twenty cents per head for each animal. Hay and barley was $2.50 per night for each animal, and hay per ton was $150. Meals were $1.50. Our pack train pastured at night on such desperately rough feed as the desert afforded. Fortunately, my merchandise was all gone and we were able to supplement their diet with the ton of barley purchased at Lone Pine, and we had our tents and food supplies for our own camps.

The first home station south of Owens Lake we found managed by a man and his wife named Raymond, who were indeed fine people.[48] We were compelled to purchase an inferior kind of grass for our animals, for which we paid one dollar and fifty cents; but the Raymonds were so amiable and agreeable that I did not envy the money paid for horse feed.

The next day carried us over a dreary, dusty, cheerless road for thirty-nine miles to a station known as Fat Mack's, though its correct name was

Indian Springs. It was kept by an Irishman named Mike McMahon, who had a very handsome wife of his own nationality.

Day followed day as we continued our march across the desert, until the evening of the Saturday following our start from Owens Lake we reached Mojave Station on the Southern Pacific Railroad, where I found the freight shipped from New York. I thought it best to have our animals given a rest of five to ten days, for the two hundred twenty desert miles had been very hard on them. I was able to have them fed on alfalfa hay at Mojave for very reasonable terms. I placed the freight in a local warehouse.

I told my men O'Donnel and Edwards that I would give them a short vacation by taking them west across the desert to Santa Barbara. My Chinese cook obtained work at the local restaurant at Mojave Station for as long as I wished him to stay, or until our return.

Santa Barbara is the Naples of America. What a beautiful spot! How odiferous and how welcome the town and surroundings to one who has been wandering through the dry, lonely, and cheerless deserts of the interior for months. The first strange realization felt is the peculiar odor that comes with the sea breeze, and the eyes rest with pleasure on the fair flower gardens. Here and there the groves of olive and lime, the neat and pleasantly situated homes of the inhabitants all fill the wanderer's breast with happiness to know that he is once more in the bosom of civilization.

In the little town we found a private hotel and secured quarters for a few days. At a barber shop we were washed, shaved, scrubbed, bathed, pomaded, and lastly dressed in style. Then we sat down amongst some of the whitest people on earth to one of the best suppers I ever paid for.

What a noble effect the soft, mild climate of southern California down near the sea has on the inhabitants. My companions at supper that night were as good, smiling, and happy people as if they had been created during a carnival and endowed with eternal health and unfailing wealth. I tore asunder the conspicuous portions of a well-roasted hen and threw the pieces on my plate where they soon became well acquainted with several respectable looking, well-baked potatoes, whose breasts were well coated with rich gravy. Although my tongue was quite loose that evening, my jaws did honor to the purpose for which my Creator intended them, crunched and hashed a good single share of all the meats, roots, gravy, pies, breads, cakes, and snaps that graced that well-stocked table.

I well remember that when I went out to count the stars before going to sleep my steps were as high, proud, and light as those of a Cochin China rooster marching at the head of his family. A little later I went to sleep, and oh what a nice, cool place for the weary traveler. The soft feathers gave way, my head wooed the downy pillow, and I was asleep.

I arose the next morning and began to take a general view of the little town. A half-tropical appearance rests on everything in Santa Barbara, and a balmy atmosphere braces up the weary traveler, making him a new man. The wind was blowing from the sea and sniffed of the salt waves.

The inhabitants of the town at that time were a pleasant, good-natured set, made up of Americans, Spaniards, Mexicans, Irish, French, Italians, Germans, and a few Chinese. Until 1870 the population was mostly Spanish Americans and brown Mexicans, but since then other nationalities have settled there, made beautiful homes, and turned the old Mexican rookery into a little paradise.

After a few days at Santa Barbara, we mounted our horses and started back to Mojave Station. Our road took us down to San Buenaventura, whose orange groves and vineyards add a strange interest to the place. We continued on to Los Angeles, where we spent three days, then went north to San Fernando, another of the old missions now in ruins. From there we went to Elizabeth Lake and remained all night with an American married to a Mexican woman.

Upon our return to Mojave Station we began preparations for our expedition into Arizona. After five days of hard labor, our pack train started across the desert by way of a little-traveled wagon road to the Mojada, or Dry Lake, and Buckhorn Ranch. We were somewhat nervous about attempting such a wild journey to one of the loneliest countries of the world, but we were booked for the trip, so why should I fear? We had animals that were in their prime. Our fourteen mules were packed with merchandise consisting of men's clothing, silks, household goods, provisions, guns, ammunition, and extra clothing. Personally, I had a carbine slung to my back, a pair of pistols at my side. My men were armed likewise. A five-gallon water keg was on each mule along with his other load and about twenty pounds of grain.

Time passed slowly while traveling from Mojave Station to the Mojada. The road was dreary and the country thoroughly desert. The palm or date cactus called Joshua grows in its pride on all these weird plains. Noon brought us to the Mojada, or Dry Lake, a broad, bare spot in the desert. In the wet season it is a lake, but it was now dry, and its cement-like bed flat and smooth as glass. It is about five miles wide and four miles long. We nooned there, watering our animals with the water we had brought, then continued on.

As night fell, we found ourselves within sight of Buckhorn Spring, where we camped for the night. The place was much like the Mojada. We soon had a cheerful fire going from the dead Joshua trees lying around. We fed our animals with the barley we had brought, then hobbled them out on the thin desert grass, a sort of wire grass that grew for about ten acres around the spring. We ate heartily ourselves, for the dry air of the desert as usual gave us an excellent appetite for the supper prepared by our Chinaman.

Our baggage and merchandise was piled up in the little house that we found there, as I did not want to expose it to the possible attack of Mexican plunderers who might be in our wake. The cabins and small buildings at this now-abandoned stock ranch were built from the bodies of dried date cactus. The place was a strange-looking habitation. The Joshua or cactus logs were set into the earth as palisades, roofed over with other cactus logs, with a fireplace and chimney in one corner and a dirt floor. A few years earlier these buildings had been put up by a cattleman who grazed his herds over this area, but now all was abandoned. We spread our blankets within the cabin, not bothering to put up our tents. I sat on my bed for two hours and read by candlelight a volume I had with me, *Telemachus*, in French, then went to sleep.

The next day we faced a journey of fifty-one miles to the next water, over a country that will never know inhabitants other than the few wild animals that wander over it. Joshua cactus to the height of twenty to thirty feet grows over most of the route. Our course lay east southeast toward Sanders Ranch on the Mojave River at the forks of the road leading either to San Bernardino or Los Angeles. We traveled at a good gait, yet we were overtaken by night, and camped where there were some date trees, which we burned in order to cook our supper. As we were in a wide waste of sand where there was no grass for our animals, we tied them to a few date trees for the night.

Three hours travel the next morning brought us to the Mojave River, which at best is but an insignificant stream rising in the mountains of San Bernardino to the southwest. A few cottonwoods skirted the river. Here and there were thickets of arrowwood. About a mile beyond the river I saw the long-wished-for ranch of Mr. Sanders, who also kept a station for travelers.[49]

We crossed the shallow river and were soon at his house, where we turned our animals into the corral and unloaded our merchandise into a vacant building. Although we erected our tents, I concluded that we would take our meals with Mr. Sanders and let our Chinaman assist with other work.

I was much pleased with Mr. Sanders, his wife, and daughter. They were Mormons who had left Utah for San Bernardino and lived there for some years before coming out to this green spot on the river to open a ranch. I was there but a short time when I ordered a couple of chickens killed and a good dinner prepared, to which we did ample justice. We remained there for two days and traded a good deal with the Sanders family. The place was so pleasant and cozy that I was loath to depart, for the family was so kind that it seemed like leaving a relative's house; but business was business, and the caravan must go forward.[50]

Our road took us eastward. It was a high road from Fort Tejon and San Bernardino to Arizona, and it pleased me to be once more on a well-beaten road, although it was very bad in places and but few dwellings line it for 250 miles.[51] When traveling an old beaten road, you feel as though men have passed over the same route and you can do likewise, unlike when you are taking beelines across a lonely desert. After toiling through sand and dust all day, we came to the ranch and station of a Mr. Mathias, and although we had only made sixteen miles, we decided to remain there for the rest of the day for purposes of business.[52]

I found the lady of the establishment a very nice person of about forty years, and with her was a daughter, a Miss Blackburn, a girl of sterling virtues and great beauty. Good Lord, how refreshing it is to see a handsome woman after wandering over the deserts two or three weeks. It is sunshine to the gloomy spirit. A monk or anchorite may no doubt live in a state of hopeful existence in the deserts by drawing largely on the imagination; but it is only in anticipation of a rich reward that even they could be induced to remain in so accursed a land as that between the Mojave River and the Buckhorn Ranch.

The territory around Mathias Station is barren and poor. The hills on either side of the area are of wash gravel, and the drifted volcanic matter is dry and brittle. There is but little rain throughout the year. The rolling waste looks black and worthless. Of course it could be cultivated were water abundant, but only a small stream runs in the Mojave River and it is so charged with alkali that it is unfit for almost any purpose. There is a coarse kind of grass called Gietta that grows on the hills and valleys, but it is so coarse and woody that it must be cut with an axe or hoe, for no scythe nor mower could ever prostrate an acre of it. When green it is quite fair for livestock, but when dry it is worse than feeding them dried fish bones. Wood is also scarce and poor, consisting only of sagebrush and greasewood. The river runs eastward past the Mathias Station, but as our journey continued down to its sink, we will here make small mention about it, as we will have reason to make more notice of its unclassic shores.

After spending the night at Mathias Station, we continued on to the next station, which was run by Mr. McConnell, a whole-souled little Irishman living out in this dreary wilderness, raising cattle and keeping travelers when they come along.[53]

His house was a long log building with three apartments. The floors were of earth. Chairs were made from slabs of stripped cottonwood. His table was formed from four planks, the bedstead of frames of cottonwood poles with green oxhide stretched between them; when dry, these were so solid and tightly drawn that one could rattle it like the head of a bass drum.[54] Six or seven muskets or rifles were hanging on the wall. On a rawhide stand near his bed were several newspapers and a few books. At the side of the house near the door was chained a small gray fox, a common species in the dry wastes of the southwest. About two hundred yards north of the house was a thicket of arrowwood.

Our host had been a soldier in the American army for five years and had settled here after his discharge. For five years since then he has herded cattle and sheep, with neither wife nor child to cheer him. I sold him a suit of clothing, a variety of household goods, and a Winchester rifle and ammunition.

The next day, February 9, we continued for twenty-nine miles over a poor, dry, sandy road until we reached Camp Cady. Those were long, weary miles. Were Henry Ward Beecher or Dr. McGlinn to spent three or four months wandering through these deserts, I verily believe that it would evermore affect their preaching, for they would no longer doubt the existence of a Hell.

Camp Cady from 1861 to 1869 was an important military post where a company of United States soldiers held the surrounding hills against the Paiute Indians.[55] During that period, the Mojave route was the main highway of travel towards Arizona, New Mexico, and southern Utah, and was one of the most lonely, dangerous, and inconvenient stretches in the world.

When we arrived there, the old fort was occupied by one Mr. Brooks, who owned a band of cattle in the surrounding hills. He was a bachelor about thirty-five years of age. After our tents had been put up and we had our supper, I went over to Mr. Brooks to read a few old papers that lay there on the table. After he had eaten, I entered into conversation with him about the old fort and talked the good man asleep. When I left him about one o'clock in the morning he was sitting in his chair asleep. I gazed about the old adobe walls that looked so bare and cheerless. A mouse came to the mouth of its hole above the cupboard, looked about anxiously, and started back noiselessly when he saw me. When I went out to my tents, the old crumbling walls of the fort stood up like huge black monsters. The patches of arrowwood along the river called to mind the early days when the savages skulked there to bathe their hands in the blood of murder. Down below the fort their victims rest in their graves.

We spent two hours the next morning trading with Mr. Brooks, then continued on down the Mojave River, crossing it frequently that day, and in the afternoon reached the cliffs that at one point overhang the river. A band of ten thousand sheep had passed through this pass a few days previous. Feed was very scarce, and they were dying alongside the road by hundreds.[56] It has been said that it is a poor wind that favors no one, and the wolves and foxes that had been imploring heaven for a square meal were now rewarded for their devotions, as this march of mutton left them rich indeed.

That day, February 11, 1877, we reached Caves Station[57] on the banks of the river, where we found two or three scoundrels playing poker for a horse that one had stolen from San Bernardino, as well as about one hundred dollars piled on the table. We camped there all night, our tents in place and our carbines by our sides, as it was a place notorious for highwaymen and horse thieves. One of our number remained on guard until midnight, then I kept the second watch until six o'clock in the morning.

The next day, a few miles farther, we came to the Domes, or carved rocks that very much resemble the domes of a cathedral. Red as blood, they are older than the hills and majestic, as the works of nature ever are. We gazed in admiration on those vast formations far above us. Here and there were the channels cut into them by the streams of old storms, and far above all sat a coyote happy in contemplation as he watched our caravan trail its way through the miserable region. At one point in an abundant grove of arrowwood we encountered nine graves of men murdered by Paiutes years before.

Twenty-two miles from the Caves we came to Soda Lake, or the sinks of the Mojave, a vast valley of sand in the center of which is a lake that receives its water from the Mojave River.[58] Far as one can see lie sheets of white alkali. The water is brown and unfit to drink. Around the valley rise mountains which are low, bleak, and bare, but many of which are rich in gold and silver. Ivanpah and Ivanwap lie to the north and northeast.

We found Mr. Al Blackburn keeping a station at Soda Lake. A spring near the house furnished brackish water, but Mr. Blackburn hauled water in barrels from a much better spring of fresh, sweet water about three miles to the northwest. Around the station lay many dead cattle, each of them a dried-up mummy. Near the house were three of them that looked as though they were but lying down to rest; but they had been dead for three years. So dry is this climate that a dead animal, if not eaten by coyotes or foxes, will soon desiccate and remain entire for years.

At Soda Lake we met a Frenchman, Colonel Jean La Bruyere,[59] who had some years previous befriended some Paiute Indians who told him where he could find a rich vein of gold. When we met him, he had just arrived from his mysterious and somewhat distant mine. He had with him six Indians, and all seven were mounted on mules. The Colonel told me confidentially that he had taken almost $600,000 in gold from his mine during the last four years. He was on his way to Mojave Station where he would take the train to San Francisco to deliver his gold to the mint. He gave me some gold specimens from his property, but refused to allow me to visit the site. He did not expect the vein to continue producing more than another year, and I later learned that he himself died of pneumonia shortly after our meeting, while I was in Mexico.

While riding behind our cavalcade the next day I saw far ahead four men walking.[60] As a man on this road always prepares when he sees people are ahead of him, we each looked to our carbines and pistols. We threw cartridges into our weapons and traveled forward ready to speak to the travelers in a peaceful way. When we came close to them, I found them to be four Paiute Indians. One of them was the famous Black Jim, a well-known murderer and thief. They were all well armed with new muzzle-loading Springfield muskets. Like all Indians of this hot region, they were black as Negroes. They asked us for water, which we gave them. Four more villainous-looking rascals never walked over the dead. One of the four was Black Billy, for whose capture there was a reward of $3,500. I did not want the money. After we had given them the water and two loaves of bread, they left us, and we watched them until they were far away.

Our desolate highway led up a long slope of thirty miles until we reached the summit of a high ridge.[61] Here we rested and looked out onto the deserts that seemed to run out to infinity. Date cactus grows far and near over these slopes. They are quite large trees and some of them are as thick as the body of a man. The bark near the roots is like that of an ash tree, but the upper part is much like a palm, except that the branches are not so broad and are more brushlike.

When we reached Mountain Springs,[62] we found another band of free and easy gentlemen who were remaining overnight. Some of them were herding cattle in the mountains around, two others were prospectors, one of them kept the station, and the other was a mail carrier.

The next morning we passed on to Rock Springs. Water was available there for the stock at twenty-five cents per head, which we of course gladly gave. The station is an old one, with a half-dozen graves near a rock house.[63] An old man named Joseph Bentley whom we found there was a match for the country. He was old, perhaps seventy-five years, toothless, and baldheaded. His language was very profane, much as we would expect from the mayor of Sodom or Gomorrah. "Beautiful contrast," I said to myself. "Such men and such a country." But one thing I must say to their credit: though very ragged and desperate in looks, they appeared to have an abundance of money. The men at Rock Springs spent with me between four hundred and four hundred fifty dollars for clothing, guns, ammunition, field glasses, spectacles, miners' glasses or magnifying glasses, Sheffield cutlery, and twenty-five decks of playing cards, all of which they paid for in gold coin.

The buildings at that old station were made entirely of stone from the granite formation nearby.[64] This rock formation at that point was compact and barren, showing no sign of gold or silver. The next morning we left that old rickety rookery on that high point with the poor old wreck of humanity who managed it, and moved on toward Arizona.

We did not camp that day for noon, for we had with us no water but that in our canteens. Quite early in the day we reached Paiute Hill, where stands an old fort, once occupied by American army troops.[65] It was built on a volcanic shelf in a pass that leads to the Colorado River. At Paiute Hill we found a man known as Dutch Charlie, who told us to our delight that it was the last station until we would reach the Colorado River.

Dutch Charley was a squaw man, which meant that he usually kept around his house a squaw from the surrounding bands of Paiute Indians. He was a veteran and had spent many years in southeastern California, northern Mexico, and western Arizona. He was very hospitable and gracious in his manners to us. Poor fellow, he was fast approaching the grave, which he found about a year and a half after we saw him, after succumbing to one of the diseases of that country.

A few miles from his house, we saw a number of human skeletons lying in the sand a short distance to the left of the road. Dutch Charley told us they were the remains of three men killed for their money by one Thompson and two of his companions. I asked why they had not been buried, and was told they had not been discovered until three years after their murder, and the bones had been scattered by that time. He said that Thompson and one of his associates still lived farther down on the Colorado River.

Very late in the afternoon of the next day, from a high bluff, we came in sight of the Colorado River. Perhaps fifteen hundred feet below us rolled that wonderful historic stream. After such a desolate region as we had been crossing for many days it was pleasant to see that rolling river with groves of cottonwood trees and willow along its banks. After yelling "Boatman!" for an hour and firing off our carbines, we saw a white man and a naked Indian come down to the shore from their cabin. I was watching them with my field glasses. When we reached the river, they came over in their boat. It was a small ferry, but sufficiently large to take my entire stock on board, and in a few minutes we were on the soil of Arizona.

We had now gained the farther end of a long and desolate march, beginning at Mojave Station and ending thus at the Hardyville crossing of the Colorado River. The distances from one conspicuous point to the next along that route are as follows: from Mojave Station to Sanders' Ranch at the forks of the road, seventy miles; from Sanders' Ranch to Camp Cady, fifty miles; from Camp Cady to the Caves, eighteen miles; from the Caves to Soda Lake, sixteen miles; from Soda Lake to Marl Springs, thirty-six miles; from Marl Springs to Desert [Rock] Springs, twenty-two miles; from Desert Springs to Paiute Hill, twenty-five miles; from Paiute Hill to the Hardyville crossing, twenty-eight miles.[66] The total distance from Mojave Station to Hardyville is thus 265 miles. The entire distance is a desert and one of the most disagreeable roads in the entire desert region of the United States.

Now that we were in Arizona a strange and novel spirit had come upon us. The fact that we had landed in Arizona after a journey of almost one thousand miles from Ogden, Utah, led me to feel that reaching the east bank of the Colorado River in Arizona was to have gained another milestone in my life.

Hardyville was a little trading post consisting of seven or eight adobe houses. The Colorado River at this point is broad and deep. Its waters are muddy but quite healthful to drink, and it contains an abundance of fish. The place did not seem so desolate as previous stations on our route. A number of large cottonwood trees grew nearby, and there was a small vegetable garden. The buildings included a mail station, blacksmith shop, a sort of restaurant and lunching house, and store. These were all kept by Mr. William Hardy, son of old Governor Hardy of Arizona. I found him a very agreeable man who was desirous of accommodating me and my men in every way.[67]

The country round about consisted of exceedingly fertile soil that reaches from the river for more than a mile to the east. A great part of it is covered with arrowwood brush, but anywhere water can be taken out on the land vegetation of all kinds common to the semitropics thrives luxuriantly. Sugar cane, yams, sweet potatoes, grapes, peaches, figs, lemons, and raisins are produced in the mild climate where frost rarely occurs. There was no great cultivation at Hardyville at the time of my visit, but Mr. Albright Wilson, the Indian Agent there, informed me that the government intended opening up a farm of two hundred acres south of Fort Mojave where they expected to give the young Mojave men a thorough knowledge of agriculture as carried out in southern California.

Around the house there were three or four Mojave girls or women. They were almost naked except for short skirts made from strips of cottonwood bark that reached only to about six inches above the knee. I had never seen any members of this tribe before, and I was taken by surprise because they were really beautiful. They are of an olive complexion, with exceedingly mild eyes with soft and tender expression, something I had never seen amongst the women of other tribes. The expression of the eyes is common to both men and women.

Hanging near the door of the trading post was a large earthen jar containing about ten gallons of water. That method of keeping drinking water is quite useful, as the water is always cool. Vessels of this kind doubtless were used for centuries in all of Mexico and Arizona, as we see their broken remains, along with those of metates and stone axes, in every old ruin of those countries. They are usually called *ollas*.

Within the trading post there was a card table in the middle of the room at which four men were playing poker. On another table there were newspapers, and behind the bar on one side of the room there was a stock of liquor, from mild to infernal in flavor.

The proprietor was a fine fellow, somewhat loose in his way of living, but I found him a gentleman in every other way. I told him my business in that country and that on the morrow I would come over and have a business talk with him. He kindly informed me that he was at my service and would gladly assist me.

We spent all the next day trading with Mr. Hardy, who purchased $350 worth of merchandise. The following day we prepared our pack train and rode down to Camp Mojave, where two companies of United States infantry were stationed guarding the Mojave Reservation and the highways and mining camps to the east from molestation by Apaches.[68] The Mojave Reservation at that time extended along the Colorado River for about sixty miles, and contained the finest land on the river. Mesquite and cottonwood grow over much of it, serving as fuel, fencing, and house construction material.

Camp Mojave is certainly one of the most comfortable abodes in winter for soldier life to be found in America. Although the country round about is sandy, within the camp the grounds are well beaten down. The buildings, both officers' and men's quarters, are well constructed and suited to the requirements of semitropical life. The officers of each company were neat and well-dressed men, very sociable, and most agreeable in their manners. Some of the soldiers, however, did not look so well, as I afterward found in many of the military camps of Arizona, owing no doubt to the too frequent associations with the Mojave and other Indians along the river.

We spent one day at Fort Mojave doing business with the few families there and with the post trader, Mr. Benson Riley. The next day we drove down to the Indian agency, where we found a number of Indians cultivating the soil in small patches. Here and there they put in corn and melons, sweet potatoes, cabbage, carrots, and other vegetables. These Indians work quite well and make very good servants when they are well treated.[69]

Down near the river and west of the agency, I saw a number of little shelters made from willows and arrowwood. There was no roof on any of them. In many localities round about there were many more pretentious structures with flat roofs made of stringers running from wall to wall and covered with tules and mesquite branches, then coated with thick adobe clay, which when dried is impervious to rain.

Inside these little residences, we found the Indians chatting, gambling, and dressing their hair. A number of the women were grinding mescrew and mesquite beans in metates. Little naked children of both sexes were playing together outside each dwelling. Several dogs were sleeping in the sunshine, and in some baskets of Indian workmanship were quantities of fish drying in the sun, on which legions of flies were devoting their attention.

Just as we reached these open-air Indian dwellings, two young Indian men came up from the river bearing with them a large quantity of soft mud. This mud they spread upon their heads, matting it into their hair until at a distance they seemed to be wearing grindstones on their heads. This practice is common to both sexes. Applied to the head in this way it is allowed to remain for two or three days, when they go and plunge into the river and in this way remove it. It is very effective in cleaning the hair of all dirt and impurities and of vermin, and after having bathed in the river the men and women come out having their hair in a mass of curls, caused by its having been held in this condition the previous days.

As near as I could learn, this tribe numbered about twenty-five hundred. They are said to have numbered more than four thousand about one hundred years ago. They are a handsome people, and if they had been Christianized as the Indians of the California coast were by the old Spanish missionaries and trained in the mission style of life no race of Indians would surpass them in labor, industries, or usefulness to the country.

They go almost entirely naked in the summer, the women dressing only in cedar or cottonwood bark. They yet receive rations occasionally from the government. They are a very hardy people, naturally very healthful, and capable of great physical endurance. They will carry government messages on foot from one military post to another, traveling at from five to eight miles per hour over distances of from fifty to seventy-five miles. When a journey is done, a handful of flour, some sugar, or a few handfuls of parched corn satisfies their hunger. They receive from two to four dollars for such a journey and seem perfectly satisfied with the pay.

Situated as they are on the flats of the Colorado River, they are warm throughout the year, so they pay but little attention to building substantial shelters, skulking here and there amid the arrowwood and mesquite groves of the Colorado bottoms. They are fond of swimming, and at any time of the day you can see numbers of them swimming and paddling up and down the river. They catch great numbers of fish, many of which they dry in the sun for food. Their implements for farming are quite primitive, consisting merely of a sharpened stick and a shingle-shaped slab. With the former they plow the sandy soil and put in the seed, and with the flat piece of wood they stir the soil around the seeds. They raise melons and corn in little patches, carrots, onions, and sometimes a few sweet potatoes.

We remained long enough amongst them to learn that they have no particular system of religion. Like most other American Indians, they believe in good or evil elements and spirits. But these Mojaves bother themselves very little about the future state. God has made them a beautiful type of the American savage. The women are beautifully formed, and their dispositions and features are truly winning. Their large, soft, dark eyes bespeak a voluptuous soul and tenderness native to the daughters of European civilization. Some of the men are as nobly formed as the Grecian Apollo. They are agile as the wild deer of India, and have the endurance of the bravest and toughest sportsmen. These are natural gifts of heaven to these wild sons of humanity. But what is their real condition?

The beautiful squaws are filthy and given to looseness to a frightful degree. The men have become adepts at gambling, idleness, and the vices common among American frontiersmen. In warfare they are usually armed with clubs, spears, and sometimes bows and arrows. Their special weapon is a biscuit-headed throwing club three feet long. At present they have few arms amongst them.

Their marriage ties are not very strict. Women are bought and sold among them, but the women yet enjoy more freedom than we find among the members of any other Indian tribe. The marriage ceremony consists of buying the girl and then catching her, which is usually not hard to do. The mothers among them cannot be said to have a large percentage of maternal love, for it is common for them to kill their children. This they do in all cases when the child is of white and Mojave blood. No woman will raise a child that she has obtained from association with a white man. I have known instances where these women, finding themselves far gone in pregnancy, lie flat on the ground and have some other woman stand on their abdomen, and so crush to death the unborn infant. Can anything be more shocking?

Their present condition is one from which they might become a powerful arm of America were they but taught to be virtuous, made to work, taught properly the art of husbandry, and made to live on a hardy fare. But their prospect is not a bright one. Idleness, gambling, and sexual diseases are putting them beyond the possibility of long continuance, and no doubt one hundred years will leave but few of them alive on earth, much to our regret.

After a few days at Hardyville and Fort Mojave, we continued our journey. Twenty miles the first day over a very difficult road brought us to Union Pass, where we found a very primitive travel station run by a native of east Tennessee named Willis Anderson.

In the latter part of the evening two men rode up. They had with them two pack animals in addition to their saddle horses. They camped close to us and went to sleep before my own party turned in. After reading for a time and writing in my journal, I rolled up in my blankets and presently was sleeping soundly. I think it must have been about midnight when I was awakened by loud voices. My men and I found our landlord and his wife outside our tents in great excitement. One of the men in the other party came running up and said that his companion had committed suicide by shooting himself in the head with his pistol. We took a lantern down to their camp and found the poor fellow weltering in his own blood.

In the morning we learned from his companion, whose name was Henry F. Miller, that the name of the dead man was Charles Williams; and to my surprise I learned his people were ranchers near Benton, Mono County, California, whom I had met some two months before. These two men had come to Arizona to mine and prospect for gold and silver. They had with them a little over three hundred dollars in gold, all of which belonged to the dead man. The money and their animals of course fell into the hands of the dead man's companion. It was a sad affair, and I believe to this day that Miller killed him while he was asleep.

At about nine o'clock in the morning my pack train departed from Union Pass and traveled eastward into Sacramento Valley, a vast body of open country about thirty miles wide and fifty miles long. It was fairly well covered with gietta and grama grass, with juniper trees in places and an abundance of organ cactus, palo verde, cholla, and gigantic prickly pear cacti. At that season that country was really beautiful, with grass and flowers abounding. The gravelly soil contains great quantities of placer gold, but, in the absence of water to wash the gravel, very little mining has been done. This area is one of the most fertile in Arizona, and is well suited for grain and vegetables and fruit of the temperate and semitropical regions. But, since there is no water for irrigation and the wet season is very short, no doubt it will lie unoccupied for centuries to come.

We killed a number of quail that day, and we even saw a couple of mountain lions near a small group of junipers. They immediately ran, and

I began shooting at them with my six-shooter, but the shots fell short and only raised dust behind them. O'Donnell fired his carbine and seemed to have wounded one of them, as it winced, jumped to one side, and fell to the ground, but then it arose and with increased speed got beyond our range. When we came to the junipers, we found a deer partly eaten by the lions. It appeared not to have been killed more than an hour or two, and Sam Hing at once skinned and dressed the hind quarters to have with our quails for supper. As it was half past eleven o'clock, we stopped there and prepared an excellent meal.

We continued on at half past one and reached Mineral Park shortly after sundown. We found a hay corral and feed yard owned by one James Haas and made our camp there. We put up our tent in a large open space within the corral and did not take time to prepare any supper as we were all very tired after the long day's ride. The thundering of a large quartz mill at the lower end of the little camp kept us awake for a time notwithstanding our weariness; but at length we fell asleep and did not awaken until eight o'clock the next morning.

Mineral Park was typical of the mining camps we found throughout northern Arizona.[70] The buildings were largely constructed of stone and wood, though a few were of adobe, and their roofs composed of clay over a Spanish sword-grass bedding. Most houses had hardened clay or gravel floors. Gray, blue, and green lizards were numerous around every home, running up and down the walls after flies, and bats were secreted in the dark angles. There were about twenty-five families in the town, all white people, very nice and easygoing. I obtained a trading license from the sheriff, Mr. Comstock, for one month's business in Mojave County, although I did not expect to use it for more than two to three days in that little city. I would make use of it later down on the Big Sandy and in Greenwood.

The mines around Mineral Park are chiefly of silver, but the ores are very rich. The most prominent mining properties are the Keystone, the Lone Star, the Texas Girl, the Arizona Belle, and the Martha Washington. Because of the milling company's high prices, $100–$125 per ton of ore, only the very richest ores were being treated. The prices charged by the cormorants running the mill were so exorbitant that one-half the ore was left on the dump because it would not pay to crush it. The expression on the faces of those men owning the mill suggested that they regretted they could not charge the poor miner for the light of the sun and the stars by night.

I was very amused at the way in which men were rated according to the value of their mines. If a man had one that would produce from two to three hundred ounces per ton, no matter how much ore he had, he was considered to be a man of easy circumstances. There were quite a number of miners working little rat holes with small quantities of ore that would run from two to five hundred ounces per ton, and about once a month they would bring from two to ten tons of ore in on pack animals, for which, after milling, they would receive one to three thousand dollars. For a week or two they would be classed as rich men, drinking, gambling, horse racing, and loaning money to their friends. After a week or two, they would return to their mines as poor men, working for another stake to repeat the process.

Silver ore was discovered here about 1869, and the little camp opened while the Apaches and Hualapais were still fierce and savage. Many a poor fellow had his head split open and was left to the crows on the mountainside during Mineral Park's early days. It seems that Arizona's ancient inhabitants mined around Mineral Park for silver, but perhaps more so for turquoise, as considerable quantities of the latter have been found in the mine shafts. The silver deposits were rediscovered by a Mr. Bob Upton and others, who cleaned out a shaft which ran to a depth of about one hundred eighty feet. They found a small seam of turquoise running the entire length. The stone had been gouged out in places from eighteen to twenty inches deep. At the bottom of the shaft the turquoise ran out, and the miners found lying on the ground a number of stone axes. This old turquoise mine was located by James Haas and sold for ten thousand dollars.

The Mineral Park miners did not seem to be as happy as they might be because of the high milling prices which consequently gave small returns to the miner. Nevertheless, it was marvelous to me the amount of ready money that circulated in the camp. Food in the form of beef, mutton, and venison seemed plentiful, but men's clothing was extremely scarce. In other words, it seemed easier to obtain greenbacks than clothing. Consequently, during our four-day stay we did an exceedingly good business, especially in men's clothing, but also in Colt's pistols, shotguns, field glasses and other optical instruments, and women's supplies. There was a goodly number of Hualapai Indians with money, and we sold them beads, paints, Indian cutlery, red shirts, yellow and blue cloth and red calico, and very short skirts in goodly quantities and at extremely profitable figures.

The citizens of Mineral Park were certainly a festive people, and they had one or two balls a week. It was truly surprising the way in which the fifteen or twenty ladies composing the female population managed to dress. I do not wonder that there were one or two shooting scrapes each month because of the jealousies arising at those delightful little evening parties.

Groups of Hualapai Indians were seen playing cards or telling wicked stories of the good old times when they wreaked murder against the white men who fell into their clutches, who, after having their eyes put out, were tied to a cactus and burned alive. During the last day of my stay I was visited by Captain Charlie, better known as Hualapai Charlie, and a number of his band, who came to buy cards and other Indian trade goods. A more daredevil rascal never faced an enemy. He was about forty years of age, short, slim, and with one drooping eyelid. He no longer ran amongst the mountains in quest of murder, but played a good hand of poker. For fifteen years he skulked over northern Arizona killing prospectors and travelers until General Crook broke the tribe's power, after which Captain Charlie became the leader of Indian scouts in Crook's command. He will soon be among the fallen savages, the last of a ruthless, restless, heartless band of incarnate devils.[71]

Since the Indians around Mineral Park are no longer hostile to the whites, they are not prohibited from remaining in the district. They make money by cutting grass with hoes or axes, which they bind into bundles of from twenty to fifty pounds and sell for fifty cents to one dollar per bale. They also herd stock. The squaws carry wood on their backs and do domestic work.

These Hualapais are on friendly terms with the Mojaves down on the Colorado River, though not so much as formerly because of jealousies between the women of the two tribes that led to bloody warfare on occasion. For this reason, the Hualapais who had been living adjacent to the Mojaves moved northward to Mineral Park and into the country still farther north toward Temple Bar on the Colorado River.

We left Mineral Park just as day was breaking on a very clear morning and journeyed eastward toward the Big Sandy. Our first stop was a little mining camp called Hackberry. There was another band of Hualapai Indians there. We did not remain long because of the lack of business.[72] There was only one mine we could examine, a silver lead mine owned by a Texas cattleman named Bud Grounds.[73] He was capable of turning his hand to any human industry. Prior to his arrival from Texas with a herd of cattle and horses, he knew nothing about mining. Although he did not know a silver mine from an ash heap, he inadvertently ran onto a mineral outcrop which developed with a little work into a really wonderful mine. I never saw a finer-looking body of ore than his. It would mill two hundred dollars per ton in silver, with from forty to sixty percent lead.

During the day we spent in Hackberry, we met a widow named Baker from Oregon. She had a daughter, Ida, and a son named Moses Franklin. Some weeks after our departure, Ida Baker and Sam Crosier, part owner of the rich mine, were joined in matrimony by a wandering preacher. This

Mrs. Baker owned two dogs, a speckled coach dog she called Speckle, and a rather indifferent-looking cur, though highly intelligent for his appearance. When our caravan left at daybreak, these two dogs, who had not previously known my men or myself, followed us, and in spite of all protestations and threats on our part seemed resolved to join fortunes with us. They caused us to be suspected of persuading them to join us, and caused us more or less trouble by their frequent battles with other canines. We called one Hayes and the other Wheeler, the names of the successful Republican candidates in the presidential election of the previous year.

Our course from Hackberry led south until we struck the Big Sandy, a tributary of Bill Williams River. We reached Cane Spring just as it was getting dark. I recognized this spot as the probable locality mentioned by Padre Garces, who in 1776 worked as a missionary among the tribes of this region. He had crossed into this locality from the Colorado River, and his journal is so graphic in description of this country that I felt certain Cane Springs was one of his resting places.[74]

When we reached these springs, we and our animals were deathly thirsty, and imagine our grief when we found the stream plugged with the carcass of a Texas steer which was now decomposed. It caused us considerable difficulty, but water is water, especially in a desert. We hitched two mules to the steer and drew him forth. We cleaned out the spring, removing gravel and sand and some dead wood that had been thrown into it, and forced ourselves to wait for an hour for the water to clear. We then resolved that we must drink it or die ourselves.

We had just set up our camp when we were joined by a party of four men with saddle- and pack horses who were on their way to Silver Reef, Utah. They were jolly good fellows, and wilder devils never yelled in the mountains. They sat by our fire and cooked their supper, singing songs and telling hard and naughty stories.

As we were then in a country of skulking and plundering Indians, we hobbled our animals near camp. One of us kept watch until midnight, and another from midnight until dawn. The remaining members of the party gladly went to sleep, as we had passed a weary day in travel.

In the morning we parted from our Utah-bound friends and continued southward until we reached Russell's ranch on the headwaters of the Big Sandy. The family was from Oregon and consisted of Russell himself, his wife, and one boy.[75] The boy was a poor, sore-eyed example of fifteen years; but Mrs. Russell was a very intelligent-looking woman. To this day we remember that she was extremely handsome. I say extremely so, for one to be found in the wilds of Arizona.

She and her husband were wonderful contrasts in appearance. Russell informed me that his wife had run away with other men some seventeen different times in fourteen years, but every time she returned to his fireside after a few weeks of convivial life abroad with some vagabond that chanced to suit her tastes. Russell himself was not very prepossessing in appearance because part of his nose was missing, his pallet was partly gone, and his face otherwise disfigured. Doubtless his present appearance caused his wife's carelessness in taste, though she was a neat and clean person around her home. During that day I sold to the Russells and to a party of Mexican freighters a total of about $375 worth of wearing apparel, guns, field glasses, and cutlery.

Our road continued along the banks of the Big Sandy. Above the riverbanks were large columnar cactus and a great variety of minor cacti. The Big Sandy itself is an insignificant stream whose waters sink in the sandy bed at one time, then return in a booming current perhaps a mile downstream. The soil on either side of the river is largely sand and decomposed vegetable matter. Devilwood, mesquite, cactus, cottonwood, ocotillo, willow, arrowwood, and underbrush lie along the banks.

Nightfall brought us to the ranch of the famous Mickey Dolan. Had this humble but high-minded Celt lived in the days of Troy, Homer would have panegyrized him in immortal song for his gallantry, chivalry, bravery, and his hospitality.

His home was a double log cabin plastered with mud, roofed with rushes and mud, and floored with mud. There were two rooms, one of which was a parlor with a fireplace in its northeast corner before which were three or four stools. Near the door there was a table made from two halves of a cottonwood log, and under the table was a wicker-covered keg of whiskey. An old rifle hung over the door. There were a few novels and government reports on a shelf above the fireplace. Near the fireplace stood a blackened coffee pot, a large iron pot, and a skillet or oven. On the wall hung two spiders, or long-handled frying pans. There were two sacks of flour, a sack of sweet potatoes, and a sack of beans. On the wall hung two smoked hams, and another, half-devoured, was lying on the table. On another shelf on the east wall stood a half sack of dried apples, half a sack of sugar, some pepper, salt, and other cans said to contain cinnamon, black pepper, and allspice. In the second room, which was his bedroom, were six bunks made of mesquite wood with oxhides stretched over the frames.

Mr. Dolan met us with a happy handshake and asked us to make ourselves at home. With him were his assistants, Mr. John Dawson, a man named Murphy, and a very tall man named Dan McCarty. They were eating a supper of Spanish beans, bread, bacon, and coffee. As we were very thirsty and tired, I told my men we would eat with Mr. Dolan before setting up our camp. During our time at Mickey Dolan's, he told us many stories of love adventures in Mexico, escapes from the Apaches, and pugilistic victories such as I had never heard and never expect to hear again, which is saying a good deal.

Dolan's ranch consisted of about seventy acres of red sand and sandy loam. That year he had planted a considerable quantity of barley, sweet potatoes, onions, carrots, lettuce, turnips, beets, and strawberries. The barley sold for fifteen dollars a hundred pounds, sweet potatoes for twenty dollars per hundred pounds, onions for one dollar for three dozen, large carrots for seventy-five cents per dozen, small carrots for forty cents per dozen, lettuce for thirty cents per pound, large turnips for thirty cents per dozen, and small turnips for twenty cents per dozen.

Dolan had been a soldier in the U.S. Army. He had served in Texas and Arizona, after which he drifted a while, then settled at this place. He sold his produce at the little towns of Signal and Greenwood, ten miles downriver. He had at this time perhaps a little over ten thousand dollars in Signal and McCracken mining checks, having no fear that these companies would ever fail.

We left Dolan's the morning of the second day, after trading with him and his men for three hours, obtaining a little over two hundred dollars in good American money. In this region we began to receive considerable numbers of Mexican dollars, which were worth at the time about eighty-nine cents in American money.

Our next stop was Greenwood, a small mining town with a large suburb extending from one to three miles north and south of the town itself. We stopped in the northern suburb, where we ate dinner with two Oregonians, Tom Despain and his wife. He had four men in his employ, and they prevailed upon me to remain with them for three hours, during which time I sold him $175 worth of merchandise.

We made another stop for two hours at the Modoc Ranch run by Mr. Killworth. We sold him two shotguns, a pair of field glasses, and four suits of summer underwear. His wife bought four bolts of striped calico and twenty packs of playing cards. The entire lot totaled $279.

We eventually reached Greenwood about sundown.[76] It was then a roaring camp. Very rich ore was being brought down from the Signal and McCracken mines seven miles distant, and a thirty-stamp mill was thundering and pounding away.

Feed being scarce, we placed our animals in a corral for which we paid two dollars a head to feed them on gietta grass, much of which was three years old. It will be observed that I must have expected exceedingly profitable business in that camp, when my first act in residence was to cost me almost thirty-five dollars per day for animal feed alone.

As it was far in the evening when we arrived, we set up our tents, fed our animals, then went over to a large and lively looking rookery built of mesquite and cottonwood, and roofed with mud and mesquite branches.[77] There were about seventy-five men eating supper. To one side, two tables were reserved for special guests, and we sat down at one of those. The table was mesquite with bullhide stretched over it, and the chairs were empty nail kegs. The two waiters wore leather aprons. They placed upon my plate almost a cartload of pork and beans and a half loaf of bread from a dish containing perhaps twenty loaves. We were each given a quart cup half filled with coffee. The price for this meal was one dollar fifty cents.

Supper over, I sent my men out to take care of the camp while I prepared to inspect the locality and its people. Let it be here stated that from the beginning of our expedition it was a rule that my men were to avoid making acquaintances among the people we met. The nature of my business was well known among those with whom I associated, but a certain isolation was necessary. My men were permitted to give no information as to the amount of business I transacted from day to day, nor were they permitted to visit any gambling houses or questionable places. Our weapons were kept constantly ready for use. As I was doing business legally, I had no fear from any law enforcement officials; but I aimed to keep prepared to meet attacks from thieves, thugs, and highwaymen. I had proven the character of the men I had with me before leaving Utah, and I found them in every way dependable. I always found it perfectly safe to leave my camp with all its merchandise and animals in charge of the men.

The people in Greenwood were about like those in any mining camp of the old days. They were largely mining men and adventurers from the old mining camps in California and Nevada, though some were from Texas and New Mexico. Some were Americans, Germans, Irish, French, and Mexicans. All in all, the men were more or less desperate in character.[78]

The town was laid out with some degree of regularity, but scattered. There were about six hundred residents, with about seventy-five women. The women were of all ages from twenty to sixty years, one-half of whom, or perhaps more, were divorced widows from Nevada and California. I saw seven or eight Mojave squaws dancing for miners in front of a saloon.

The saloon was filled with Mexicans and various other nationalities. There were two or three circular tables around which men were gambling. The floor was of hardened clay and the bar was made of rough planks. Most of the persons there were wild and reckless fellows who played away the four dollars per day they received as wages, usually within two or three days after payday. There was a faro game going on, and a monte game patronized by Mexicans. About $290 would buy all the clothing worn in the whole camp, including a pair of overalls, a shirt, and worn-out shoes for every male, and a calico dress for every woman.

I was witness to a double murder that evening. In Mineral Park I had sold a double-barreled shotgun to the sheriff, Mr. Comstock. A few days later, prior to my arrival at Greenwood, he had sold the gun to a man on the Big Sandy, who worked at the quartz mill at Greenwood. I shall call this man Green, though that was not his name. Two men named Fatty Smith and Poker Smith ran a large stone saloon on the east side of Main Street.[79] On the evening of our arrival, these two men, who were quite fancy or well dressed, purchased fifty decks of playing cards from me at the wholesale price, one dollar per deck. As I was walking up the street, Green went into the saloon, and for reasons unknown, the two saloon proprietors vowed they would kill him.

Green went back to his cabin, got the shotgun, returned to the saloon, and shot one of the partners. The other partner got a pistol and approached Green, thinking to get a sure shot at close range, but Green fired first and killed him also. I never saw so complete a clearing out of a business firm in all my life. Green himself escaped into the arrowwood thicket on the riverbank.

We stayed in Signal and Greenwood for four days, doing a very profitable business. I had to take a large part of my proceeds in mining company checks, but also received a good number of Mexican dollars. As there were few other likely business prospects in Mojave County, we then turned our course to the east. Prescott, the capital of Arizona, lay one hundred forty miles in that direction over a mountainous region with rocky washes, broken water courses, volcanic lava beds, and up steep cliffs and down tortuous windings that would have made the brains of a billy goat reel.

We left Greenwood at four o'clock in the morning and traveled about thirty miles the first day. As the sun was going down we camped in a grove of cedars where there was good grass, dry wood, and a small stream of excellent water, a tributary of the Santa Maria River. I remember the occasion so well. Never did I eat a meal that I enjoyed more fully than that evening meal. I always made it a rule that while camping my men and I would have the best foods that we could procure in the country through which we were passing.

While the men were securing the camp for the night, I sat down beside the fire to read, and soon became intently interested in the wanderings of Telemachus. My concentration was broken by the sound of approaching horses and the howling and barking of our dogs. In a moment three men appeared, dismounted, and called for something to eat.

In a few minutes Sam Hing had coffee and a good supper placed before them, and never did I see men, civilized or savage, eat with such wild and ravenous appetites. They quit after an hour, and then only because the gallon coffee pot was empty. They told me they had not eaten for three days.

They left to set up their camp, then returned to our fire. The one most ragged and talkative of the three looked at my outfit, then at me, and asked "Who in hell are you, and where in hell are you going?" As he asked me these questions, I observed that he had his coattail torn off.

I told them we were on a prospecting expedition and rambling through the mountains. He looked into the fire as if he were weighing the truth of what I told him. His two partners seemed as curious about us as their loquacious leader. The three men appeared as poverty-stricken as Lazarus. They were well armed with carbines and six-shooters, but their shirts and trousers were in tatters. They looked truly desperate. They turned out to be the famous Buckskin Charlie, a gambler, horse thief, and stage robber; Tim Mulnix, a gold prospector; and another desperado named Rawhide Steve.

When they had had all they wanted to eat, they obtained from me in addition about fifty pounds of provisions to carry them for two or three days. Then they spread their blankets and lay down, but they spent a good part of the night talking about their past three days without food and how fortunate they were to have spotted our campfire. Buckskin Charlie told several wild stories of his past life. Tim Mulnix, the most ragged of the three, seemed the most dissatisfied about the recent turn of affairs.

In the morning, I shot three jackrabbits with my shotgun, and Sam Hing prepared them for our collective breakfast. While we were eating, the chief robber went over to where my baggage and merchandise were piled, and observed that we had men's clothing with us. He swore by all that was high and holy that they would have to clothe themselves, for they were well able to pay for anything they obtained from us. Even though it was apparent that our bandit visitors had abundance of money, I did not desire to open up our merchandise at that point; but, as I also did not desire to be killed on that occasion, I complied, and the men purchased more than three hundred dollars worth of merchandise. I was pleasantly surprised to see that we were not to be drawn upon for a forced loan, as I knew at least two of the men to be highway robbers who had just plundered a stagecoach down near Wickenburg. No doubt our treatment of them had the favorable effect of prompting them to purchase, rather than rob, our goods. I was much pleased when I saw them preparing to leave us, inasmuch as I had laid away in one of the bales of merchandise five thousand dollars in cash and mining company checks.

After they departed, I found myself in a very strange sort of mental trouble. During the night, the three highwaymen had discussed visiting a German named Jacob Valentine who was working some small placerites nearby. Buckskin Charlie told the others that the man must have four or five thousand dollars in gold dust by that time, as he had not been to Wickenburg for some six months. I felt certain that they would not hesitate to kill him if they could not obtain his gold dust in any other way. This compelled me to decide that after the robbers left, I would take a shortcut on horseback to Valentine's camp and warn him. I instructed my men to travel at a slow gait toward Kirkland Valley about seventy miles away, and said that I would overtake them by nightfall.

It was seven miles to Valentine's camp by a route I had learned of from a man named Nat Small, in whose corral and feed yard we had camped in Greenwood. He had informed me that a faint trail southward from the springs where we had camped would lead to Valentine's camp if I should desire to trade with him. The route Buckskin Charlie and his men were following was some five miles farther than this shortcut, though over an easier route.

Spurring my horse forward, I reached Valentine's camp in about an hour, where I found him and two Mexican employees. I introduced myself and told him of his danger. He thanked me profusely and told me he would hide the considerable gold he had, leaving only fifteen or twenty dollars out where the robbers could find it, then when they had left he would follow me with his gold, trade with me at Marooney's station, and accompany me the rest of the way to Prescott.

I left and overtook my pack train before one o'clock that afternoon. I felt extremely pleased in conscience for having thus warned a man who I felt would almost certainly have been murdered otherwise.

It was almost sundown when we reached Kirkland Valley and arrived at the ranch of Mr. Malachi Marooney. The conditions around his home were simplicity itself. He owned there an unfenced ranch and claimed a squatter's right to 640 acres of land.

Mr. Valentine arrived in time to be our guest for supper. He informed us he had ridden hard to overtake us after being visited by Buckskin Charlie, who had ordered him to produce whatever gold he had or they would kill him. Mr. Valentine, who evidently was a man of nerve, told them that they were welcome to what he had, which was not much as he had had a poor season and had disposed of what gold he had taken out at Prescott. He told them he did have a little, about two ounces, which he had placed in large brass cartridge shells, and that they were welcome to that if they required it worse than he did. Buckskin Charlie had then told him that if that was all he had he had better keep it, as they would find richer men than he elsewhere.

Mr. Valentine spent two hundred dollars with me in much needed merchandise, which he left with Marooney. We related this story to Mr. Marooney, and suggested that it was possible they might visit him also. He said he feared nothing from them, as he had very little for them to take. He told us that a similar party had visited him some months previous, and that through a dream he had anticipated them and had hidden a few hundred dollars in gold coin in the rocks some miles from his house.

We did some business with Mr. Marooney the next morning, then continued in the company of Jacob Valentine along the Santa Maria trail. I was very anxious to reach Prescott, which was yet sixty miles away. I was doubly anxious, as we were in bandit-infested country and also in a region where there were yet straggling Apaches watching that they might waylay and murder solitary travelers. We traveled that day over an extremely rough country, over rocky ledges and cliffs, through brambles, and mile after mile of scrubby manzanita. Although we traveled continuously, we did not make more than twenty miles because of the rough and crooked road.

Near sundown we camped at an Indian spring. The evening was very pleasant, so we did not put up our tents. We piled our merchandise, made our fire, fed the animals, and lay down early. We prepared two watches for the night, one until midnight, then I myself to watch until morning. Our animals were hobbled. The coyotes in the hills were numerous, and our two dogs, Hayes and Wheeler, kept offering them challenge during the night if they desired to fight. While I was on watch, I grew uneasy because our animals seemed more or less excited, which indicated a possibility of Indians. Of all animals on earth, a mule is most afraid of wild Indians. The barking of the dogs and the howling and yelping of the coyotes kept everyone from sleeping that night.

A mile forward on our road the next morning, I killed a deer, which O'Donnel and Sam Hing quickly skinned, and packed the hindquarters with us. When we camped for dinner at high noon, Sam Hing prepared part of the venison with some corn bread. I had never eaten sweeter meat than that venison, and it was the first corn bread we had eaten since leaving Mineral Park.

In the middle of the afternoon I saw a queer-looking object near a cactus a short distance from the trail, and upon examining it more closely we discovered to our horror that it was the skeleton of a white man. It was tied to a columnar cactus. The feet had been burned away, the clothing removed, and a shot had been fired through the head. A thong of rawhide held it to the cactus. We lowered it from where it was hanging and buried it. It was, of course, the remains of some poor man burned alive by Apaches, but whether Mexican or American we could not tell.

We continued to a mountain ranch where we had hoped to find human beings, but to our great surprise we found only one man there, living in extremely simple conditions. A beef hide supported on four poles served as his shelter. His clothing hung on one of the poles, a sack of flour on another pole, and about thirty or forty pounds of jerked or dried beef was suspended in a sack from a juniper tree nearby. It was a young man who welcomed us, saying that he was extremely happy to receive company. As there was no water for many miles beyond the spring at his camp, we saw it was best to camp there for the night.

Our landlord, whose name was Louis Berenger, was clothed in the wildest rags. He told us he was a native of San Francisco, twenty-three years old, and the son of a French merchant. He had been very wild at home, and his father had banished him. After drifting in Arizona at length, after many adventures through the hills and across the deserts, he found a man who had a band of cattle in this lone district, and who engaged him to watch them for fifty dollars per month and board. His food was quite plain: flour, beef, sugar, and coffee, with all the game, such as deer, turkey, or quail, that might come within the range of his rifle or shotgun. He seemed repentant of his past, and out in this lone desert he talked to us like a philosopher. He had by him books which he studied, and seemed resolved to be a nobler and better man. We sat by his fire and talked half the night away.

Going to our tents and spreading our blankets, we lay down to sleep. It was, however, only a little while until rain began to fall, and soon a wild storm was raging without. Fortunately our tents were large enough to cover our large bales of merchandise, but the storm sadly treated poor Mr. Berenger's provisions. It was only a short time before the falling water was all around us. We were compelled to repack our bales of merchandise, as a stream of water was running through the center of one of our tents. However, no serious damage was done, and in the latter part of the night we slept soundly.

In the morning it was a wild sight to see torrents of water yet running down the sides of the mountains nearby. We realized we had experienced what is known in all mountain countries as a cloudburst, and even in the mountains of Arizona such storms will occur. Our young Californian fully realized that a single bull's hide made a very poor shelter during a mountain thunderstorm. O thou fair mortal designed as a wife for me, had you but seen me on that memorable night and morning, you would long since have withdrawn the thought of unity with such a pitiable object as he who was perched on a bale of merchandise waiting for daylight in those stormy hours.

Edwards and O'Donnel went out to look for the animals, and I to get a shot at some possible deer in the vicinity. Jacob Valentine helped Sam Hing prepare breakfast, and the young Frenchman put his own camp in order, or all of it that remained after the storm.

Two hours later we shook hands with the Frenchman and began our day's travel along the rough and scurvy trail, which we found worse than that of the previous day. It went up and down over lava beds, up and over and across old volcanoes; and then at last we came down to the north side of the far fork of the Santa Maria River. We traveled up its course until night, when we came to a lone tent. There was no one there, and in fact we never learned whose tent it was, but we determined to take possession of the site. We made a fire nearby, put up our tents, and prepared our evening meal, which, as we had killed no game that day, consisted of jerked beef with bread prepared by Sam Hing and butter in a can for which I paid two dollars per pound down on the Big Sandy at Tom Despain's ranch. These things with very good coffee served for our supper.

After supper we all sat outside the tents enjoying the moonlight in a country that even in midwinter is pleasant and mild. I will never forget, if I were to live a thousand years, that splendid night under an Arizona sky. Not being able to sleep, I left my men in their slumbers and went outside. I sat in the moonlight and enjoyed the wild, mild beauty of the moonlit sky at midnight. My mind was in one of its pleasant, happy, pleasurable states so that the moment made a lasting impression. There was a wild, pleasing spirit that haunted that mountain stream campsite, and I will state further on in this work how I came near to changing my life because of the romantic spirit I experienced there. Returning to my tent, I lay down to sleep and was called up later to keep watch until daybreak.

The trail improved somewhat the next day. The Santa Maria region of Arizona, the mountains on either side and the stream itself, have long been a scene of terrible murders. The hills are rich in placer gold, and many a fine fellow has had his head split open by Apaches along this same trail we were now traveling. The Apache, the Spaniard, and the American all strove for empire along the banks of this stream that was now voiceless save to my associates and myself. Little of this area is fit for cultivation, though there are occasional patches of forty to fifty acres that could be tilled.

On the fourth day after leaving Greenwood, we reached a small valley where we found another lone Irishman whose name, strange to relate, was similar to the previous one we had met. Instead of Marooney, it was McRooney.[80] We reached his camp weary and hungry, not having halted for our noon meal. I say we were hungry. Yes, hungry as yellow dogs of Constantinople. O hunger, what a leveler thou art! The stomach of a king becomes as pitiable in its feeling as that of a mendicant. I was never in a country where one could be in better condition to devour fifth-class fare than in western Arizona in those days, and never at any time felt as desperately hungry as on that evening when we reached McRooney's lone cabin.

His home was decidedly of a shiftless appearance. The little cabin was built of logs and Spanish bayonet and roofed with sods. The fence around the little place was falling in. There were some horses feeding at a distance from the house. Eight or ten pigs were rooting around the little hills nearby. The pigs looked as shiftless as the proprietor. There were two or three additional pigs loitering around the house. There was, however, one exception, a smart-looking old sow industriously prospecting for bugs and worms or corn grains in a pool of water near the door. Around her played seven little snow white pigs with all the innocent looks of infant pork. O snap and vim, I respect thee in man or hog. That sow called to my mind many a poor virtuous mother whom I have seen washing and scrubbing for everyone who came, that her children might not suffer. The word "whiskey" might explain all.

Mr. McRooney met us at his door, stated that he was delighted to see us, and invited us inside. He asked us in an Arizona expression, "Where in hell we had come from." As I explained our journey, I began to observe conditions at his house, which were characterized by a certain derelict sameness. Here was a human ruin, a man whose hopes evidently were blasted, whose prospects proved to be like eggs that have failed to hatch, simply love's labors lost, surely to the hen.

He had about twenty bushels of corn piled up in one corner, and a roll of blankets in another. Ashes from a fireplace were spread all over the cabin floor. An old Sharp's carbine whose lock was frozen with rust hung on the wall. Rust had also crept into its bore, and wasps had built a mud house on its stock. A side of old government bacon hung on a wall, and mice had tunneled into its interior and made a home. What a field lies on the floor of that cabin for the student of future ages! He will be able to follow stratum after stratum and tell the food of the occupant throughout all seasons. For example, when a pot of green corn was boiled, the corn was eaten from the cob and the cob thrown on the floor, there to rest forever more. When potatoes were to be eaten, they were peeled, and their skins left on the floor until the morning of the Resurrection. The bones of the wild turkey, the jackrabbit, or the quail, the seeds of the squash, the feathers of the wild duck, or the husk of the corn ears, all found there an open grave. The lord of the manor gradually found himself approaching nearer to Heaven as his drift of household garbage accumulated.

After supper, I returned to Mr. McRooney's residence. He was busy preparing a supper of fat government bacon and corn bread, the latter made with water and without salt or soda. With these two dishes, he had water to drink. I asked my noble friend how much we would owe him in the morning, as we might depart before he was up. "Why," said he, "God love your great American heart, you owe me nothing but thanks." I felt that he was quite poor, so I gave him a dollar for the water we and our animals had drunk from his spring and for a five-pound sack of salt.

Leaving Mr. McRooney's place, we soon reached Skull Valley, a dry little mountain district at the foot of the Bradshaw Mountains. There a few ranchers were striving with nature and winning only tolerable success for their labor. Wheat and corn are grown in that high region, as are sugar cane, carrots, turnips, and other garden vegetables, and potatoes also thrive. Skull Valley is one of four adjacent valleys, including Kirkland, Grass, and Williamson's valleys, which in ancient times were all cultivated by the lost people whose old walls and towers still stand on the hilltops, and whose stone cups, earthen dishes, and stone hatchets and axes were today plowed up in the fields. They were a brave people, who seem to have striven here for their lives against some fierce foe, but their fires went out and they are no more.

It was on February 20, 1877, that we stood on a high ridge of the Bradshaw Range and looked back over the region through which we had just traveled. Range behind range of ragged mountains, desert, and grassy plains succeeded each other until a waste of distance reached our feet. There among the tall timbers I could see one of the grandest views I ever enjoyed. The golden light of evening bathed every object with its rich flood. The juniper and pine hung and waved in the wind. Thankful for our good fortune, we continued on, and at ten o'clock in the evening we reached Prescott, the capital of Arizona.

At that late hour I thought it best not to set up our tents, so, after placing our merchandise in a warehouse run by Mr. Dan Hatz, my men and I took rooms at the Hotel Montezuma and slept until eight o'clock the following morning. My bedchamber seemed to me somewhat aristocratic and in wonderful contrast to my places of nightly rest during the previous three months. As I rolled over drowsily in my spring bed, I wished that it were possible to have such a luxury every night in that wild, dry country, for I had not enjoyed such creature comforts for a long time.

After breakfasting with my men at the hotel, I sent them over to put our pack train in order while I went out to look over the town and to deliver several letters of introduction. One of these went to the territorial governor, another to Colonel C. P. Head, a merchant; a third to A. L. Bashford, a wholesale and retail merchant; and a fourth to a Mr. Otis, the postmaster.

Prescott was well built in a beautiful spot, beautifully laid out, and surrounded on the south and west by pine forests, with open country to the east and southeast. It was wooed by gentle suns and balmy mountain winds, and was in a high, arid region. About a mile to the northeast was Camp Whipple, a post of the United States Army.

The town was made up of about fifteen hundred people. The buildings were of wood, stone, and brick. There were in all about thirty stores, each one apparently doing a good business. There were meat shops, blacksmith shops, barber shops, whiskey saloons and gambling houses, and half a dozen hotels, the chief of which were the Montezuma, the Hotel Prescott, the Hotel Dan Hatz, and others whose names I have forgotten.[81]

The people of Prescott I soon found to be lively and clean, made up chiefly of native Americans from the eastern and central states. Many of them were also from California. There were quite a number of Irish, French, German, English, and Mexicans. Many religions were represented: Jews, Catholics, Methodists, Presbyterians, Baptists, infidels, spiritualists, and heathens. The wealth of the town was considerable. A.L. Bashford, Colonel C. P. Head, a Mr. Campbell, Mr. Goldwater, Mr. Alexander, and a Mr. Peck[82] were the richest men of the place. Education was accommodated by a splendid public school.

Both public and private dancing I found to be one of the chief amusements. Public dancing is done in two dance houses at all hours of the day and night. For fifty cents the poor, rough-and-ready, tumbled-down miner could dance with some Mexican, German, or American girl. Private balls of an aristocratic and exclusive nature cost twenty dollars for admission.

The morals of the town were fair to average. Those that were not of a strictly moral order were as decent as their business would allow, and I bear kind memories of all people I met. There are a few episodes in my experience there which I will retain for a book of sketches which will show how mysterious society can move even in a small town like Prescott.

There was a beautiful plaza in Prescott, unfortunately denuded of its pine trees by an old money broker who was mayor for a time.[83] Why he and the town council ordered such a thing as destruction of the magnificent pine and juniper trees in that plaza I do not understand, unless it was to let the public have a better view of the mayor's old junk shop on the east side of the square. I can only say that I hope those who ordered that destruction may never know the happy shade of a forest grove in the world to come.

During that day I secured a newly constructed storeroom with shelves, counters, and tables for exhibiting my merchandise, and on the second day I was there I was doing business. I traded a total of five days in Prescott and did exceedingly well. I spent an additional two days trading at Fort Whipple after gaining permission to do so from the commander and post trader.

After eight days in Prescott, we departed early in the morning for the next leg of our journey, crossing Arizona to the south and down into Old Mexico. We took the old government road to the southwest, crossing the Bradshaw Mountains.

The first day, we saw nothing of particular importance. We passed through two or three little valleys of little value in themselves because of the scarcity of water. All the mountains of this region are not very high and receive little snow in winter and less rain in summer. Such snowstorms as come in the winter melt away, leaving very little water for irrigation, and what rain comes is so uncertain that men have almost despaired of ever making farming a success in many of the dry districts of Arizona.

As the sun was setting, we reached Mr. Jennings's ranch in Kirkland Valley, a fine large house and good barns. He had a handsome wife and a half-dozen children, and a corps of laborers on his farm. This proved that even there beauty, snap, and sinew were employed to good advantage. I traded all the following day with this good man and his dependents, selling them four hundred dollars worth of merchandise.

Before leaving his place the next day, Mr. Jennings told me about a variety of ancient ruins that lay scattered on the hillsides about two miles from his home. I determined to see them. Soon we came to a number of old walls on the crest of a knoll at the north end of the adjoining valley. They were of brown sandstone and built without mortar or cement of any kind; and, save for the fact that the builders showed some little respect for right angles, I saw nothing of which to boast. In an appendix I will treat more fully of these ruins.

We returned to the main road leading to Wickenburg over Antelope Mountain, a long sentinel whose top is quite flat and sloping to the north. Its sloping crest is strewn with decomposed gold quartz, and large veins of the quartz are found in many places on the mountain, all quite rich in gold. Water, however, cannot be procured on or around this mountain, this preventing millions of dollars in gold being taken from it. Without doubt it is said to be one of the richest gold localities in America.

Near the south base of Antelope Peak we found a travel station kept by one Yaki Wilson,[84] an old man some called a gentleman of the first water. His life had been passed in the wildest scenes of various adventures, and his arm was always ready to aid the oppressed. Others say that he is no more or less than an old pirate of the Barbary Coast of northern Africa, a robber, a born filibuster, a man whose hands used to be raised against everyone, and everyone's hands were raised against him. When I saw him he was an old man of about sixty-five years of age. I found him agreeable in his manners, kind and gentlemanly towards me and my men. In addition to his travelers station, he also keeps a trading post for American and Mexican miners, and buys some gold dust. We remained for that day and night and did about four hundred dollars worth of business with him, for which he paid in gold dust which I accepted at fifteen dollars an ounce.

From there to Wickenburg the road crosses the plains of the Hassayampa for less than twenty miles. The entire plain is strewn with decomposed and broken quartz, all of which is more or less gold bearing. For ages it has been carried down from the mountains to the north by storm waters, and it could be profitably mined if water could be brought to it. But water is scarce and always will be in this region, thus leaving this gold to rest forever in the gravels. The Hassayampa itself is a small river that flows in the wet season across this region and empties into the Salt River. When I reached it, it was dry. The high road ran along its bed in some places until we reached Wickenburg. In the song and story of Arizona for many years the Hassayampa has become famous as a region where a taste for the marvelous seems to enter into the soul of the traveler. It is said that when a man once crosses the plains of the Hassayampa and drinks three times from the river, he or she will never again tell the truth. It is a wonderfully interesting region. In climate it is a paradise during the winter and little short of Hell for heat during the midsummer.

We found Wickenburg to be a dilapidated old rookery inhabitated by about seventy-five Americans, including fifteen families, and from eighteen to twenty Mexican families. In the old days between 1858 and 1868, Wickenburg was a lively town with a wild and fast population of almost one thousand. Here stood the great quartz mine reducing the ores from the Vulture gold mine, working night and day reducing about forty tons of rich gold quartz. The town was then the liveliest camp in Arizona. Here in the desert all the luxuries of three continents could be found. Champagne, whiskey, beer, and Mexican wines were as plentiful as the waters of the Hassayampa River. Everyone gambled and there were playing cards enough to sink a warship.

But times changed. The mine at length failed to pay, and the town itself literally went to the devil. It is now a sepulcher of its former glory. The old mill has gone to rust, the miners have long since packed their blankets for other scenes, and the fairer portion of creation that beguiled the lonely gold miners is no more.[85]

We drove our pack train into a corral owned by John Peebles,[86] who had earlier made a rich gold discovery on Antelope Peak, and erected our tents near the river. We piled our merchandise in a warehouse owned by

Mr. Peebles, and we were ready for business in that ancient-looking, half-obliterated town. To become better acquainted with the locality, I told my men that I would not that evening eat supper with them but would go over to a *fonda* kept by a Mexican family. It was only a short distance from our camp.

When I heard a steel triangle sound, I entered the *fonda* and was soon seated at the table. The meal consisted of Spanish beans, boiled jerked beef, Mexican bread, Costa Rican coffee, and California honey. Most of the dishes outside the coffee and honey were flavored with chili colorado, or red Mexican pepper. The food was served on tin plates. The table and chairs were made of oxhides stretched over a mesquite framework. Of course such furnishings have a sound like a bass drum, but what odds when one is hungry? The doors and the beds in the sleeping compartment were made of the same material, as was the cradle where Mr. Peebles's daughter rocked her baby.

While I was eating supper I took particular notice of a somewhat strange-looking individual seated opposite me. It seemed he was a young man, but was quite feminine in appearance. He had long hair and looked quite boyish. I was not long in finding out that this apparently young man was a woman dressed in men's clothing. She was very handsome but extremely talkative, and on the mining question she was deeply interested. I learned that she was Molly Monroe,[87] once the proud daughter of a Massachusetts banker. She was then beautiful, highly educated, and wooed by many a worthy youth in her native city. She made a tour to Europe and Asia, returned to her home, and shortly after gave her heart and hand to a man who proved in time to be a noted counterfeiter. She thus felt herself so disgraced that she flung herself away and thereafter was a ruined woman. She went to California and dwelt in San Francisco as a star of the underworld. Later she went to Wickenburg and established herself as the queen of a very beautiful structure there. She had numerous female companions, and the gilded life she led was the envy of every weak woman from Wickenburg to Chihuahua.

In time the gold ores gave out, the miners departed, and the Apaches again roamed over that locality. This famous woman's mansion was soon in the dust, and she changed her style of living. Putting on male attire, she rode through the hills of Arizona with prospectors, soldiers, gamblers, and men of all sorts. It is said by some that she was for a time the boon companion and partner in a band of stage robbers and highwaymen. Be that as it may, she became a splendid shot with either rifle or pistol, and to see her out riding, dressed in rough clothing, the legs of her trousers thrust into her bootlegs, her hair flowing over her shoulders, a couple of six-shooters in her belt, and a Henry rifle at the pommel of her saddle, she was a strange-looking being. She was often the mark for an Apache's arrow, but always escaped.

It was hard to look upon her and contemplate the beautiful, innocent girl she had been. Since I saw her, I learned that she grew so thoroughly demented that she was sent to a California lunatic asylum. When I saw her in Wickenburg, she claimed to be a thorough spiritualist, with spirit communications with the dead almost daily.

An hour-long conversation with Colonel Peebles enabled us to become very good friends. He invited me to his house that evening, which was in the rear of the principal saloon. He seemed very proud of his saloon and told me he prided himself on his brands of whiskey, brandy, beer, and Spanish wine. Upon learning of my business, he requested that I by all means remain in his town the next day, for he himself wished to trade, and he said he would do all he could to help me gain the good will and wishes of Wickenburg's varied inhabitants. When we entered the town, I was taken for a greenhorn, traveling with men as green as myself. I was looked upon as a defunct catfish, and was at first taken for the leader of a gypsy caravan. When it had been established that I was a trader with a varied stock of merchandise, a new spirit was shown to me at once.

There was one feature in that old town about which I marveled. Every man I met seemed to take pride in trying to make believe that he was a desperado. One old man, the owner of a restaurant and saloon who seemed to have known military service, told terrible stories about the Mexican War of 1847–1848. His stories were bloody enough to put snakes into the boots of old Homer, the ancient poet.

Conditions in that half-desolate town were truly desperate. The place looked as if it had been sacked and blown to pieces by bloodthirsty warriors of ancient days. The houses built of mud bricks were going to pieces. The whiting was washed from the walls, the roofs of most let in a view of the stars, and the few that were yet inhabited held a wonderful variety of humanity. Among them were a few families of exceedingly nice Americans from New England, Ohio, Missouri, and Texas. A few equally nice people were from France, Ireland, and Germany. There were a few families also of the better class of Mexicans.

In one half-wrecked old structure I found one rather interesting Mexican family named Reverado.[88] There was the old gentleman himself, a very distinguished-looking old Mexican. His wife, now somewhat up in years, was equally interesting. He had two sons who recently had been working on a lease in the Vulture Mine. Most interesting of all was his daughter, an extremely pretty little Spanish beauty whose name was Dolores. She was certainly, I do not hesitate proclaiming, the flower of Wickenburg.

While doing business the following day, I became quite well acquainted with this Reverado family, and especially so with the girl Dolores. Although her people were truly as poor as rats, they were respectable people, and she was as pretty as an angel. They were from the state of Sonora. They had come to Wickenburg to work in the mines, but only the two sons could secure work. The old gentleman thus sat down in the sunshine, while his wife and daughter had to earn their bread by washing the bulletproof shirts and overalls of Arizona adventurers at twenty-five cents apiece. Their home was a dilapidated old rookery originally built of adobe and cactus. Its white walls looked like the face of a smallpox victim, and the food they ate would give the devil himself a wind colic. Let me see what it was; I can easily call it to mind: first, stewed red peppers with mutton suet; then stewed turnips with boiled carne seca, or dried jerked beef; finally, Mexican cakes and more jerked beef prepared in a different method. As I sat down, Dolores had a steak of the latter in her hand, and the long strings she pulled from that stewed jerked beef would have made strings for the fiddle of Beethoven.

I spent the next day trading with the people of Wickenburg. I became somewhat filled with love for that most interesting ramshackle town.

We left the next day and followed down the Hassayampa riverbed, which was about twenty yards in width during the wet season. It is sometimes a booming river for a few hours, but at most times in most places in fairly good weather it shows only a dry riverbed. However, anywhere along its course pure palatable water may be found at a depth of from one to twenty feet by digging into the sand.

As before stated, this celebrated stream flows across a wild, weird, desolate, rich, and historic region. It was infamous for generations because of murder and robbery carried on by the ruthless Apaches. We might deem it worthy of being called the "American Calabria," because there one can almost always find trouble of one kind or another. In the groves of mesquite and cottonwood along the river the Apaches would hide and await the coming of unfortunate travelers, murder and rob them, and leave their bodies to the vultures. How many men lost their lives on the Hassayampa will never be known, but a reign of terror existed there for more than twenty years, from 1845 to about 1868.

Over the vast region of the Hassayampa one beholds great numbers of the giant cacti looking like steamboat smokestacks or like the spectres that aroused the fancies of Don Quixote when he rode in quest of adventures. There is such a variety of wonderful cacti, perhaps more than twenty kinds, from the gigantic columnar cactus to the miserable cat's claw, the savoia, the tuna, the Spanish bayonet, and the huge melon cactus that in times of hard pressure will provide water for the wandering prospector. On the crest of the columnar cactus in the early spring blooms a tuft of yellow or pink flowers, which a little later develop into a fruit about the size of a small banana, sweet and delicious. The Mexicans call this fruit *pita haya*, and prize it as a god-given luxury. After a period of years, these monsters die and fall to earth like one of Napoleon's old war horses. Their long ribs are then used by the Indians for lances, for roofing adobe houses, fencing, hen coops, and fishing rods.

A few hours from Wickenburg we came to Smith's quartz mill, where ores from the Vulture and a few other small gold mines were reduced. We found a small town there, made up of English, Irish, Germans, a few French, and quite a number of Mexicans. A more unprincipled lot of scoundrels and rascals I never found in any community. Each of them kept a Mexican mistress to cook and wash for him. Mill workers were paid seventy-five dollars a month and board, and the Mexican women would get most of it. The whole band, men and women, were thieves of the worst type, and so far as my memory goes, my feeling towards them was such that I felt like saying, "May the forked lightning split in twain all such towns as I found at Smith's Mill."

It is not worthy of the name on the map of America. Picture to yourself a low sandy flat by the side of a waterless river, a high, dry region surrounding it, a mill in the center of the flat, a miners' supply store on a little knoll about one hundred yards away from the mill, and a boarding house for the workmen near the store. The boarding house was made of cactus and willows covered with dry mud, with a dirt floor. There was a long table made, of course, from rawhide, on which were placed thirty or forty tin plates, a great number of tin cups, and six to eight pans filled with bread, beef, and beans.

To this coarse fare there sat down as hard looking a lot of reprobates as ever graced a frontier dinner hall. Some were cutthroats who had been thieves from their mothers' breasts. Some of them had been for years in Mexican prisons for theft, murder, arson, rape, highway robbery, and horse stealing. These men would not hesitate to follow you out and murder you for what money you might possess, strip your body of its clothing, and leave it to the crows. As I sat there contemplating them that evening, I recalled an enormous mosaic I had seen in the museum of the Lateran in Rome. It depicted a number of the old gladiators who used to fight in the Colosseum. There were Gauls and Germans with unforgettable facial features as depraved and desperate as one might expect to see on the faces of fallen angels in the dreary regions of the damned. As I looked on that piece of work, I never expected to see anything so repulsive in human nature; but, when I entered this dining hall at Smith's Mill,

I found them duplicated there in those desperate, fiendish, depraved, and repulsive expressions.

The manager of the mill was named Smith.[89] It was he who had relocated the Vulture gold-mining property when the former owners had not secured a proper patent and had allowed their rights to lapse. The property itself was yet worth many millions of dollars because of its value in gold. Smith himself was somewhat desperate in character and was said to have killed his man on several occasions. He was making, at the time of my visit, an immense amount of money each month by means of cheaper and more modern methods than had formerly been applied to the rich ores. He paid his men both at the mill and mine in gold bullion at fourteen dollars per ounce.

Notwithstanding the villainous makeup of the men in and around the quartz mill, we carried on a profitable business with them; but we kept a constant watch each time our merchandise was exhibited to keep those fellows from robbing us. They would deliberately steal anything from a pocket knife to a suit of clothes, or from a double-barreled shotgun to a silver watch. I found it necessary to erect the larger of our two tents to hold our merchandise, then erect a counter across which we would transact our business, not permitting more than three persons to enter the tent at a time. I found the Mexican women living there even more persistent in thieving than the men with whom they were living. Nevertheless, I managed to dispose of a little over four hundred dollars worth of merchandise, receiving in exchange gold bullion cut up into small blocks of from five to twenty dollars each in value, allowing fourteen dollars per ounce for all bullion so taken.

When my trading was finished, I asked permission from the superintendent of the mine and mill to visit the mine, which was about twelve miles away. He gave it to me in the form of a letter to the submanager at the mine. Leaving my men to watch our property, I took my saddle horse and rode to the mine.

It was one of the largest bodies of medium-value ore that I had ever examined. There was then fully one million tons of gold ore in sight. The work had been carried down to a depth of six hundred feet. The lode was eighty feet in width, and since it was largely free-milling ore, the proper kind of quartz mill would have left no waste in the entire body of ore I examined. I was there in February, 1877, and the mine had produced off and on at that time, since its beginning in 1863, an estimated twenty million dollars. There was no water in the immediate vicinity. The mine is situated on a sloping plain at the south base of the Vulture Mountains. For many years after its discovery those attempting to work it were compelled to keep an armed guard against the Apache Indians, and even at the time of my visit there was still a danger of occasional raids on freight teams and workers who might be exposed at some distance from the mine.

It was late in the evening when I returned to Smith's Mill, and I found it necessary to remain there for the night. When we continued down the Hassayampa in the morning, the weather was extremely warm and our animals, which had been bred in a more northerly latitude, suffered very much. The water we had taken from the Hassayampa River bubbled and steamed in our canteens, and the sweat blinded my eyes in that month of February to a greater degree than I had experienced elsewhere in any part of the world.

The Hassayampa plains were fairly well covered with gietta grass, columnar cactus, and mesquite. Red-eyed rattlesnakes were numerous. At many points on either side of the road we saw the bones of dead Apaches who had been killed in fights with the military or in attacks against travelers. Almost hourly, little groups of from three to ten coyotes would cross our way.

Night brought us to a little station known as Agua Fria. It was a very desolate spot. The station keeper, Eccles Burchard,[90] and his wife were only making half a living. They were very happy to see us, and told us that they knew not why, but no one had passed that way for more than a week. They had a well of exceedingly good water at a depth of about sixty feet, and after that exceptionally hot day's travel, the well and its owners were welcome sights to us and our animals. Our two dogs, Hayes and Wheeler, must have suffered greatly from the heat, so I bought for them all the half-trimmed bones and scraps of bread that Mrs. Burchard had to sell.

I did not expect to do any business with those people, who seemed to be poverty stricken. However, to my great surprise, just as we were about to retire for the night, Mr. Burchard came over and said that they would regard it as a favor if we would open our merchandise for them. The truth of the matter was, I did not think that they had enough money to make business with them worthwhile. This judgment proved to be greatly wrong, for within three hours I sold them about $350 worth of merchandise, for which I was paid in gold dust.

On the evening of the following day we entered Phoenix, Arizona.[91] In those days it was a long string of adobe buildings of one and two stories on both sides of a long street. The buildings were flat-roofed after the Mexican style, with verandas around some of them on two or three sides. In front of them were scores of Mexican children playing in the open streets, many of them climbing up on the flat roofs. Their mothers and fathers were sitting in the doorways smoking cigarettes and talking.[92] The town was built along the north bank of the Rio Salado, or Salt River, one of the chief rivers of Arizona, and the delightful shade afforded by the stately cottonwood trees made the place a most inviting spot to the traveler coming off the burning plains of the Hassayampa. The deep green of the trees, the adobe houses, the interesting American and Mexican population, and the cool breeze made the spot a place of happy, dreamy enchantment.

The population consisted of about one thousand people, mostly Mexicans, and about half of the few Americans living there were married to Mexican women. Mexican women seemed to fit well into any white society of those days. Those dark-eyed daughters of the south possess an air of voluptuousness and a happy-go-lucky expression that win the goodwill of almost any nationality.

We left our animals in a feed corral owned by one John Lynch, an Irishman with a rather prepossessing wife, and set up our tents in an open area also owned by him. Sam Hing prepared a meal for us at eight o'clock, and an hour later, while smoking some cigars and discussing our experiences with the scoundrels and reprobates at Smith's quartz mill, we all felt the good fortune of having reached Phoenix.

We remained in Phoenix for four days doing business. So good was my trade, in fact, that I found I now had more mules than I needed to carry my remaining merchandise. Consequently, I sold six of them to some Mexican freighters for $995, which cut our traveling expenses by more than one-third. I thought it wise to retain all my men, however, as their company afforded protection.

Near Phoenix there are many interesting ancient ruins which I will describe in my account of my third Arizona expedition.[93] It is enough here to state that along the east road out of Phoenix towards Hayden's Mill, I observed a number of mounds, ruined walls, irrigation canals, and one very well defined but low pyramid. It stood on the north side of the road, and measured about three hundred feet in length by 150 feet in width, with twelve- to fifteen-feet-high walls sloping at about forty-five degrees. It appeared to have been designed as a perfect pyramid approximately 125 feet high, but it had not been completed. Tremendous quantities of broken pottery and ruined stonework such as walls, roadways, and stone monuments could be seen on either side of the road east of Phoenix. It was fully evident that at one time there had been a dense population in the Salt River Valley, and the great quantity of broken pottery was evidence of lengthy occupation. These remains over almost all parts of Arizona must be those of a superior race who died out long before the arrival of Columbus.

Along the road east of Phoenix were ranches owned by Mexicans and Americans. Irrigation ditches watered numerous fields in which wheat, corn, potatoes, cabbage, sorghum cane, and melons were produced in great quantities. It was also a good region for lucerne or alfalfa.

The great drawback to progress in the Salt River region was the fondness of drinking, gambling, and idleness. But God pity us all—they have only their share of vice and misery. I shall never forget a statement made to me by a clergyman in Phoenix who was laboring there as a missionary. I told him it was a great pity to see the looseness of morals and the utter carelessness regarding a future life. I particularly regretted the intemperance I had observed and the general love of gambling.

"Oh, well, yes, it is too bad," he replied, "and yet I do not know but that taken all in all, the people here will average up regarding goodness and charity with people in other regions. I do not know that people in other places are any more or less virtuous than the people of Phoenix. They just serve the devil in another way."

We did not leave Phoenix until one o'clock in the afternoon, and we took so much time investigating the ancient ruins that we did not reach Hayden's Mill until sundown. The man Hayden who had erected a grist mill sixteen miles east of Phoenix I found to be a very pleasant and agreeable citizen.[94] He was sharp in trade and was doing a very profitable business. Many people around him regarded him as a "heartless old cormorant" who was getting rich through avaricious ways, but I found him to be a very worthy man of about sixty years of age, and fairly well educated. His wife was young, agreeable in manners, and a woman of considerable culture. A native of New England, she had taken to southwestern ways, and when I entered their home she was sitting in a mesquite-and-rawhide rocking chair smoking a very long cigar. She asked what type of merchandise I was carrying, and then requested that we remain for two days to trade with her and her sister who was married to an officer at Fort McDowell.

Hayden was truly a man of business in the old style. He sold a variety of goods to the local inhabitants at the high values common at that time. He obtained his workers at very low wages. His mill was very busy, and he shipped his flour over much of Arizona and even into western New Mexico. He was fast building a colossal fortune. The Mexicans in the valley looked upon him as a power in the land, as he was their supplier of calico, tobacco, whiskey, clothing, and other merchandise.

The Salt River Valley is about seventy-five miles long. The river rises in the mountains of south-central Arizona and flows westward to its confluence with the Gila. Its irrigable bottomlands extend about four miles on either side of the river, but much more territory could be utilized to the east by constructing a system of dams and reservoirs. This region will become one of Arizona's fairest spots. Semitropical fruits can be grown here, such as as figs, limes, oranges, peaches, apples, and grapes. At present, though, the inhabitants grow only such basic crops as corn, sweet potatoes, rather inferior potatoes, alfalfa and lucerne, and a few other vegetables.

There are many Mexican inhabitants and white adventurers who marry Mexican women and settle down to an agricultural life. I love to meet such people. There are many things I love, but one thing I do not love is a woman who marries some old weatherbeaten wreck of sixty or seventy winters simply because he has money, for there is no love in such a place. It is a sort of legalized prostitution: she sells herself for a sum of money and becomes a cold-blooded, cold-breasted speculator. Her heart shrivels up like the rind of a government bacon. The harpies of old were not less repulsive than these human beings of either sex who swap age for money.

Upon leaving Hayden's Mill, our next objective was the famous town of Florence, about eighty miles south of Phoenix. At the end of the first day we came to a little travel station kept by a German and his wife. It was a desolate spot, and the couple lived in a cactus-built shanty with about ninety cents worth of clothing among the man, his wife, and a baby. Of course the climate in that region is hot, and people do not require much clothing; and, outside of Prescott, where everyone dressed well in recently purchased clothes, everyone elsewhere wears clothes that seem to have done service for many years. It seemed remarkable to me, in view of the amounts of money I found all over Arizona, how few of the people were well clothed. Furthermore, I found very few fat people. Many, in fact, were either slim or even skinny. Just why, I am unable to tell.

We set up our tents and enjoyed one of the usual excellent suppers Sam Hing had grown famous for furnishing. We were fortunate in eating much better, because of Sam Hing, than the usual Arizonan, who ordinarily ate the same thing three times a day. Prices for meals at Arizona travelers' stations were always good. They were never less than a dollar, and rarely more than two dollars. A chicken dinner would cost $2.50 anywhere, and if wine were served with the meal the price would run up to about $7.50. If the wine was exceedingly good and a whole bottle served, the price would be ten dollars. Few persons in Arizona in those days drank a full bottle of wine with any meal unless they were successful gamblers or highwaymen.

The German at this station was named Henry Schwartz, and his wife was named Caterina. Their child was a beautiful girl about six months old. They had two cats, one a black one with a very short tail, and three dogs. To all appearances they had very little with which to support themselves. Their food that evening consisted of dry bread, jerked beef, black coffee, and a single dish of stewed dried apples. The animals were watching their owners intently, fearing no doubt that there would be nothing left for them. However, much to my surprise, as at the other poor travel stations, the family purchased almost two hundred dollars worth of goods, paying me in Mexican gold doubloons and some few Mexican silver dollars.

The next evening brought us to a little station called Sacatone, on the Gila River.[95] Water was brought to it from a spring some distance away by means of wooden pipes acquired from miners. A man from Georgia named Amos Carroll ran the station with his very handsome Mexican wife and family of three girls and two boys. They were well-mannered people who provided water, gietta grass, and meals of Mexican bread, jerked beef, Mexican sugar, and Costa Rican coffee. The coffee found in Arizona and Mexico, incidentally, is universally of good quality.

This station was at the border of the Pima Indian reservation, a small sedentary tribe long native to this region. Carroll and the Pimas carried on a sort of contraband trade; that is, he sold them wine and whiskey and playing cards and other means of gambling, contrary to the wishes of the nearby Indian agent. The agent also told me that Carroll purchased horses, mules, and donkeys furnished to the Indians by the government, paying them not more than one-third of their value and reselling them to travelers or Mexican traders at high prices.

I had a double reason for camping at this point. First, it was very late in the evening when we arrived. Second, I wanted to spend a few hours the next day studying the Indians, as I had heard much about them in Prescott and Phoenix and knew that some ethnologists claim that they are descendants of the ancient people whose ruins we had seen.

The agent whom I met the following day I found to be a rather overbearing kind of man. When he learned that I had stayed the previous evening with Amos Carroll, he said, "I suppose that you know more now about the history of this Pima tribe than I do, and also as to how I am treating them and carrying on my work as the Indian Department in Washington expects that I should do it. This man Carroll and his wife are constantly sticking their noses into my affairs. They are telling everything they know and a great deal that they do not know."

I replied that as to that I was not prepared to say. He was the official representative of the United States government, and I expected to learn from him the official information about this interesting people. He then seemed to grow more mellow and in the course of an hour became quite willing to give me all the information possible.

The Pimas[96] are a semicivilized tribe who were Christianized by the Spanish missionaries led by Padre Kino about two hundred years ago. At the time of my visit they were rather indifferent Catholics and were being waited on in a religious way by Presbyterian missionaries.

They have irrigation canals drawn from the Gila River. They grow potatoes, carrots, corn, squash, pumpkins, and melons. They also raise a considerable amount of lucerne or alfalfa which, strange to say, they are as fond of eating themselves as are any of their cattle. They gather the screw-shaped pod of the locust, which is high in sugar and which they grind into a meal in metates or hand mills. The loaves made from this meal look and taste very much like sugar and sawdust. They use mesquite pods in the same way. Other sources of food include quails, jackrabbits, and an occasional deer or wild turkey. At the time of our visit they owned about 1,800 head of sheep, about 1,000 head of goats, and from one to two thousand dogs, more or less.

The men and women go three-fourths naked, and the children entirely so until the ages of from eight to twelve years. The women are quite good looking. Both men and women wear long hair. As a race of Indians, they are quite chaste and temperate. The Indians are always on friendly terms with the whites, ever offering shelter to the Mexicans and Spaniards in the old bloody days of Apache domination. They have a school with about two hundred scholars. The Pimas are averse to war and claim to have always been on the defensive whenever compelled to go to war. Foot races, throwing the spear, shooting bows and arrows, ball playing, and dancing are the chief amusements among this simple people.

Their reservation contains about 64,000 acres, of which about ten thousand are under cultivation. They are, taken all in all, a good, industrious people. They manufacture a very good quality of pottery of all sizes from small cups and pitchers to immense ollas containing from twenty to sixty gallons. There is a striking resemblance in the pottery to that of ancient nations of Asia.

Their dwellings are constructed of poles, rushes, willows, and mud. They are cone-shaped and pleasant to live in, though in that hot country they are usually infested with fleas. Near each building stand two or three huge structures made of willows woven like baskets, which are in fact simply large baskets covered over with willow roofing and are used to hold grain. They are supported on legs or short columns of stone to prevent rodents from getting in.

After leaving the Pimas, a few hours' riding brought us to the village of Florence, the county seat of Pinal County.[97] We found it to contain a motley population of Indians, Americans, and Mexicans. They were living in all kinds of houses, from the adobe house to the slender shelter of a single Mexican blanket. Verandas or sun shelters extended around the east, south, and west sides of many of the homes. Under those verandas hung large ollas containing water, which was usually cold and extremely delicious for drinking in that hot climate. The town was well supplied with water by means of two canals from the Gila River, the waters of which are pure and potable. Part of the town contained gardens. A few orange trees were planted here and there, and shade was furnished by cottonwoods and mulberry trees.

High-throned Jupiter, how hot it was the day after our arrival in Florence! The little streams running through the town were in places green with floating plant life and almost boiling with heat. The people were either playing cards, drinking Mexican whiskey or wine, or eating native fruits. Others were telling old Apache stories or discussing the richness of the silver and copper ores over in the Globe district and those adjacent to Florence.

I liked Florence. I liked the people, at least some of them, who were kind to visitors and travelers. We remained there five days, trading very profitably. We were treated fairly well, allaying our thirst with an excellent lemonade and cheering our nerves with a good quality of Mexican cigars.

Understand me: I am praising only a part of the people of Florence. As to the others, I would simply say, "O ye scoundrels and degenerates, do you think for a moment that Christ shed any of His blood to regenerate you? Do you think that the cross-eyed, bowlegged, foul-mouthed, spindle-shanked, gin-soaked reprobates that line your streets will ever be transformed into angels of light to live in happiness amid the fields of high and holy immortality? Or more simply stated, do you ever expect to arise from the chaos and ruin of all things that we now see around us? Surely if you do, then there are happy possibilities of lesser sinners. For, to tell the truth, I found you and your town hotter than I would wish Hell to be were I able to send there my worst enemies, you, the wicked ones of Florence. You were dishonest and grasping enough to make your neighborhood the chosen paradise of all robbers and thieves. And two of the five hotels in Florence and three of the many lodging houses I found to be the winter quarters of all the fleas, gnats, spiders, and cockroaches on the face of the globe."

Florence stands on the south bank of the Gila River, an interesting old river that rises in the mountains of western New Mexico and crosses the entire territory of Arizona, flowing into the Colorado River north of Fort Yuma. It has seen the coming and going, the rise and fall of half a dozen now-extinct races. Here are the ruins of reservoirs, aqueducts, old temples, mounds that once were pyramids, knolls that once were dwellings, and white, limey dust piles that once were human bones. The traveler asks who these people were, and our answer is that we do not know.

Before leaving Florence, I visited the Silver King and some other mines about twenty miles northeast of town. These mines, and cattle and horse raising, are the chief supports of the town of Florence. Around the town and down the river to the west there is a little farming, but the greater part of the population have nothing and live on hopes. A very considerable part of the population are gamblers who also practice highway robbery at times.

The houses in Florence are similar to those throughout Latin America. They are of dried brick, flat-roofed, one story high, and some of them are oblong and quite extensive in size. The better ones are quite neat within, with whitewashed walls and a sort of cement floor. The walls are decorated with six-shooters, shotguns, Bowie knives, and Winchester rifles, as well as gay-colored shawls, cheap pictures, and collections of ore specimens, saddles, or spurs.

Like all towns in the Southwest, Florence was wedded to the custom of dancing. It is not too much to say that at least one third of the people's lives are spent in dancing. They dance by day, they dance by night, they dance in summer, winter, spring, and autumn. They dance at weddings, they dance after the birth of children, they dance after funerals, and I do not think there was ever a man or woman who did not dance three days before death.

The day after leaving Florence, we arrived at Casa Grande, a prehistoric ruined fortress on the plains of the Gila, and about which even Baron von Humboldt writes. The country round about showed signs of having once been cultivated for a considerable distance on both sides of the road. We crossed an old aqueduct about thirty feet wide which ran its curved course across the plain from the Gila River far above where the town of Florence now stands. At various points there are remains of lateral canals that watered a vast region. Broken pottery and other ancient articles lay scattered in every direction.

The soil is a drab gray and spongy in texture, but very fertile. A light, bushy vegetation furnishes excellent food for sheep and goats. Mesquite grows along the water courses, but there is little cactus beyond an occasional columnar giant.

The ruin itself is a wonderful old structure, afar and alone in this arid region. Silence is around it, and antiquity upon it. It was constructed of a grayish concrete, and nothing remains of the wood partially used in it, but holes are visible in the walls where wooden joists supported its floors. These holes now look like the portholes in the sides of an old fortress or in the sides of an old man-of-war. On one wall, twenty-eight of these holes are visible. It was once an immense structure, and all that remains stands forty-five feet high, fifty-two feet long and thirty-two feet six inches on the inside, and sixty-one feet long and forty-seven feet wide on the outside. The outside walls are much worn and uneven. Judging from the foundation and for some feet above the foundation, the walls were six feet thick.

Interior walls show there were as many as a dozen apartments. The concrete is of a coarse gravelly nature, and its consistency is quite compact and firm. The entryways, which were on the north and south sides, are quite ragged and uneven. There are several irregular openings on the interior walls. The walls themselves were coated with a cream-colored cement. Inside the rooms is an immense amount of accumulated debris, which if searched would no doubt bring to light many old relics. I struck the floor at several points, and it gave forth a hollow sound, causing me to believe that there may be a subterranean passage to some point of exit now hidden by debris. To the south there is a ground plan of another large building, and on all sides are remains of lesser structures constructed from the same material as the main building.

Fortunately for us, four Mexican trade wagons loaded with fruits and vegetables from northern Sonora passed by while we were there. As each of the wagons carried two barrels of water, we obtained enough for ten dollars for ourselves and animals to enable us to camp at Casa Grande for the night. After setting up camp and eating supper, I spread my blankets and resolved to sleep that night within the old structure that knew so many years of weird existence on the lonely Gila plains.

Twilight was upon the world as the moon arose and shed her soft light along the plains, lighting up the old ruins as I lay down upon my blankets for a while until the moon would rise higher. Then I arose and went out to gaze upon my environment, which was clothed in the very romantic moonlight. The light had now filled every nook, crevice, and corner of the broken walls, seeming to restore the ragged angles until the weather-beaten, time-worn fabric stood as an honored queen of the silent plain.

Never, even in the Colosseum in Rome or in the ancient Egyptian ruins of Karnak and Luxor, did I realize a more melancholy and yet happy contemplation than on that wild lone plain in Arizona. Those who reared this structure, who built the now buried city around it—where are they now? In the dust. I imagined I could see their phantom forms rise and fly back to their old industries. Who were they? I repeat that we do not know. They may have been Aztecs, they may have been Toltecs. They may have been a people who became extinct as their last blood was shed around these walls. They may have been the ancestors of the Pimas.

This old ruin was first discovered by Padre Eusebius Kino about 1682 or 1683.[98] He was a German by birth, and reported his discovery to his famous scientific countryman Baron von Humboldt, who in turn reported it in his famous books on North and South America.

Having satisfied my curiosity regarding the Casa Grande ruins, we departed the next morning for the famous old city of Tucson, about forty-five miles south of Casa Grande. We had just left when we saw to the south what appeared to be a train of white pilgrims, with five burros quite well packed. We found it was a party of fifteen adult women from twenty to thirty-five years old. Their burros carried all their personal effects, including food, blankets, and cooking utensils. They also had two small tents with folding poles. They were travelers, laundresses, or all-around useful Mexican women going up from Mexico into the towns and mining camps of central Arizona. They were just such women as we found many days previous at Smith's Mill on the Hassayampa and elsewhere.

They were seeking companionship with prospectors, miners, cattlemen, or whosoever might desire to employ them as companions for work and play for six months to a year. After separating for these purposes for a season in the mining camps, they would again find each other and return for a visit to Sonora of Chihuahua, to return to Arizona or New Mexico the next year. Sometimes these ladies were *gambusinas*, or women placer miners, who would pan gold themselves with wooden bowls. They thus lead a sort of gypsy life, except that such parties never include men.

These women were dressed in plain dresses made from white or brownish cotton domestic, or unbleached cotton, each wearing over the dress a cloak of the same material. Each wore broad-brimmed straw hats and light shoes, though two wore sandals. Each had a staff about five feet long, two of them carried lightweight double-barreled shotguns. When they met us, they wished us all God's blessings and questioned us about our origin and destination. Then they asked about the business conditions in the towns we had visited. They assured us of their goodwill, praying that we might not be robbed or have our throats cut while among their countrymen farther to the south.

We spent one night out on the desert; then the second day from Casa Grande we reached Tucson, which is two days' journey north of Mexico. Tucson possesses many points of interest. For more than a century and a half it was a central point of trade among surrounding Indian tribes, and there was a small presidio occupied by Spanish or Mexican soldiers. After the Treaty of Guadalupe Hidalgo, Tucson became an American military post.[99]

The town stands on the west bank of the Santa Cruz River at a junction of roads and has always been a point of commerce. During the Civil War, Tucson was captured by a small Confederate force under Kirby Smith, a famous cavalry officer. After the war, Tucson became a rendezvous of Mexican bandits, American cutthroats, and wandering desperados; but, by the time we arrived, the city was halfway respectable on the part of two-thirds of its inhabitants.

Tucson was at that time but an average-looking town even for Arizona, and a far cry from recent years when Apaches used to raid into its streets and the best man was always the bloodiest. I secured a storeroom to exhibit my merchandise from a lady of Spanish blood named Señora Arcadia Valdes, who, in addition to milking a few goats, owned a hotel. She had a son named Jose and a daughter named Maria. She herself was a tidy little creature. Jose was fairly well educated and employed by the local merchants, Lord & Williams. Maria was as handsome as a cluster of ripe grapes, and as industrious and virtuous as she was handsome. I carried on trade there for nine days.

Overwork had left me somewhat run-down in health as we left Tucson and visited the old ruined mission church of San Xavier del Bac, built by the Jesuits and Franciscans more than two hundred years ago. It is a beautiful structure. The tooth of time has not yet entirely defaced its fair proportion, and although the Apaches time and again shed blood within and around its walls, it is still a temple of God and the best specimen of Gothic Moorish architecture in the United States. It was begun by Padre Kino, who labored in northern Mexico and Arizona from 1687 to 1711, converting the Papagos, Pimas, and other tribes, and met martyrdom by a small party of rebels among his Indian converts.

The interior of the church is decorated with a number of good paintings, and the altars that are now plain and unassuming once glittered with more than $100,000 worth of precious metals. The country around it once had a flourishing community of Mexicans, Spaniards, and Papago Indians, with beautiful fields of corn, wheat, beans, melons, and fruit, while sheep, cattle, and horses fattened in the mountains. Its prosperity ended when the wild Apaches overcame the Christianized Indians and the white inhabitants and looted the mission.

I measured the building and found it to be 115 feet in length by seventy feet in width. Its plan is that of a Latin cross. On the timeworn front of the church may be seen the coat of arms of the Franciscan order—a cross around which is a coil of rope and the naked arm of Christ—and that of St. Francis of Assisi. South of the church is a convent of the Sisters of Mercy, who run a school for the Indian children.

I went inside the church and examined the beautiful paintings that seem so strange in this region where barbarism is thought to reign supreme. There are festoons and garlands on the walls, and four large frescos representing the Annunciation, the Visitation, the Nativity of Christ, and the Visitation of the Magi. There is a grand old altar once covered with gold leaf. In niches around the walls are statues of the saints.

The arched ceiling, fifty feet high, was once covered with scriptural paintings. Back of the main aisle are two large paintings of the Last Supper and Pentecost. The mason work was done by two brothers named Guana.[100]

Up three flights of stairs, we gained the top of the west tower, from which we could see far out over the quiet and hazy valley. Rarely does the traveler in any country see a lovelier sight than from this old church tower. There are four bells in the tower that yet chime well, though they are green with age and fastened to their places by means of a score of strips of bull hide. One of them is dated 1604, and the other three bear no dates. The 1604 bell was no doubt cast in Spain and the others made in some part of northern Mexico. While we were standing in this old tower, a hawk flew above us in a circle. When he was directly above me, I drew my pistol and shot him, which the Papagos who saw it from below thought was a great feat of marksmanship.

We spent the night with a Mexican family nearby, then continued on our journey southward through the town of Sapori and on to Altar in old Arizona. Altar is really only a large rancho consisting of a trading post, post office, and a *fonda*, or wayside inn. As this all belongs to one family, it is a sort of monopoly. The Gutierrez family owns it, and it covers mountain and valley for many leagues in all directions. The vast cultivated area produces various grains and semitropical fruits, and they never bloomed in a fairer home than we found there. There were oak, ash, walnut, and mesquite growing to goodly proportions and each producing an excellent quality of wood. Such timber as this in such quantities is rarely found west of the Rocky Mountains, and nowhere north of Altar because of the great aridity.

The evening we reached Altar there was a ball, and I received an invitation. I had my men open a bale of clothing where I had a very fine suit which I carried for just such occasions as this. One of my men was to accompany me. We went to a barber shop and put ourselves into proper trim for a dress parade. There was a Mexican officer and his sister in the house near to where we camped, so we asked the honor of his company as well, and were soon with them at the fandango. His sister was a daisy regarding neatness and beauty, although not as white as he.

There certainly was some tone in that ballroom. Many of the men, or hidalgos, wore six-shooters, and, while we were dancing and smoking cigarettes in the ballroom, in an adjoining room there was a faro or monte game in full blast, to and from which members of the dancing party went as luck or whim prompted.

My lady at the ball was indeed a bewitching little creature by the name of Chata Galupa, and, although I found her in a little ruined town amongst a band of horse thieves and murderers and other vagabonds generally, I marveled at her intelligence. She seemed warmhearted, well educated, a good singer, and in every way ladylike, all of which speak very much for a woman of southern Arizona. Her brother was present at the party and very much to my liking. The ball broke up at twelve o'clock, and I took my fair companion to her home and bade her and her brother adieu for the night.

I left that rascally little town while she and the other members of her family were still no doubt sleeping. In a few hours we reached the Mexican line, where we paid our respects to the officers of the government custom house. As the law demands, we exhibited our merchandise, giving our bills of lading, and paying the custom duty required by the Mexican republic.

We continued on our route toward Hermosillo, the capital of the state of Sonora. The country is yet in a primitive condition. At five points on the highway where there are trading posts, I did some business with the merchants and families dwelling there. The presence of Indian blood among the inhabitants shows its effects on Sonoran civilization, for frequent civil wars have demoralized the people. The rather imperfect state of the law places Sonora among the semibarbarous districts of the world.

At Hermosillo, a beautiful little city, we found all the common vegetables and fruits of the semitropical and temperate zones thriving in the largest sizes and the sweetest flavors. The greatest variety of flowers also thrive here. Every court is filled with them, and in the windows they bloom beautifully. The passion flower is very common, and the Egyptian water lily grows to its largest size in the soft sunshine. The air is laden with the rich perfume of the orange and lime, and a drowsy, luxurious feeling pervades the atmosphere.

There are quite a number of Mexican stores where merchants are satisfied with a moderate amount of business. Money is rather scarce. A few Mexican silver dollars and the copper coinage of the country comprises all the *Moniada Alfiada* in circulation, with a considerable quantity of Mexican paper money.

Many people seem to have no fixed occupation. They live in tiny adobe buildings, and their furniture consists of a few heavy chairs, a table, a looking glass, a half-dozen mats, a few earthen jars; and the walls are decorated with pictures of the saints. The ceilings are further decorated with strings of chili colorado, or red pepper. There are two or three beds, in one of which invariably lies a hairless dog during the day and three or four children and a dog at night. At night, festive little parties of young caballeros and señoritas sing and dance in the gardens, vineyards, and other open areas. They waltz away the early hours of the night.

The soil is very rich, but agriculture is in a rude state. The plow of the scriptures is still in use; that is, a forked tree, one branch of which is armed with a steel snout, and the other serves as a tongue. The main shaft serves for a handle to steer with, holding the plow in the furrow. Wagons are all two-wheeled carts made by crossing two pieces of ash or oak by means of a mortise. They are mounted or bound by a binding of wood dressed into as circular a shape as possible and equipped with a rawhide tire. The wealthier farmers have iron wheels; but they have to be guarded closely, for they are valuable for making spurs, knives, and other articles necessary to Sonoran housekeeping. Most Sonorans are too poor to have wagons, and instead use small horses, mules, and donkeys. All these Mexicans are expert packers, and in every street one may see such animals laden with merchandise of all descriptions.The streets of most Mexican towns are rather quiet, and business is not extensive.

I found the Germans in Sonora quite powerful. They import goods from abroad, engage in manufacture, and are made law officers. They marry Mexican women and seem well contented with the country. As in all countries, white men are foremost in every aspect of society. The old Castilian blood still predominates although Mexican society is republican in all things. The Spaniard is a white Mexican, and is classified as *gentes do sangre azul*. There are three classes in Mexico: those of white skin, called blue bloods; then the mestizos, or mixed white and Indian blood; then those wholly of Indian blood. The law does not distinguish much as to color, but society is full of castes.

Money is everything there, as elsewhere. There is much luxury among those of landed wealth. Their sons and daughters are taught French, Spanish, Italian, Latin, and music. Although the men like to gamble, many condemn it. Monte is played everywhere at all times by both sexes. It is the strongest temptation the devil can lay before a Mexican, for they will play away their horses, money, land, homes, jewelry, clothing, and the last dregs of virtue before they will leave the gambling table. They will bet on anything—bullfighting, cockfighting, bear fighting, and horse racing. These are enjoyed by all classes.

All classes meet at the bull ring, and there the young lady of wealth and culture hopes to meet the glance of her gay admirers. The town *alcalde* there bows to the wealthiest men, and everyone looks around to meet the gaze of some friend or foe. What black, lustrous, and winning eyes these young Mexican girls have that one sees at bullfights. Happy manners are displayed at Mexican balls. There seems to be something in the atmosphere that sets the soul at rest with the world and prepares the heart for the reception of surrounding pleasures.

There are fetes or holidays for every victory ever won by a Mexican general. There is another feast for every Mexican saint, and after Lent come the Sabbath festivals, which are seasons of great pleasure and innocent enjoyment.

The men all have a hankering for military renown. They also search the mountains for rich ores that will place them on easy street, or hope to make fortunes from lottery tickets or the rise of national stocks. Very few of those who pretend to be educated have any desire to come down to manual labor, and a horse thief or highway robber if successful is thought more of than if he were an honest tradesman.

Domestic life is quite happy. Husbands and wives seem quite fond of each other. One feature I do not like is that women of public infamy are often welcomed into virtuous houses. A lady in Hermosillo to whom I spoke of this replied that in the United States a man of profligate character often associates with people of high moral character, and should not a similar woman do likewise? I replied that women are somewhat different in this respect from men, and, if I had a sister whom I saw in the company of a harlot, I would soon cease to respect her. Her answer was that different people have different ways and that I might expect to get a wife in Mexico who would be all I could desire in virtue and affection. That I do not doubt, for they seem to be excellent women well treated.

A young gentleman wishing to court a lady does not have all things his way, for it is difficult amongst the best families for him to meet her and to talk with her alone. In the higher social circles, daughters are ever guarded by their mothers or a lady older than themselves. Such courtship that takes place must be of a very dry order. If at length, after a reasonable term of courtship, all things look favorable and the young cavalier has sufficient nerve, he calls at the home of the young lady, calls her family together, and asks to marry her. If they look upon him favorably, they then ask for a prominent member of his family to present a formal proposal. If the proposal is accepted, the lovers do not meet until the day of the wedding.

It is difficult to weigh the virtue and vice of the Mexicans. I found much that was vicious among them, and I also found much to admire. We must remember that for almost fifty years civil wars raged in that country, and that, of all wars, civil wars most lower the moral fiber of a country. Among the lower classes, morals seem lowest; there are many petty thieves amongst the men, and the morals of the women are also low. Morals vary from one locality to another, as well.

One social feature I would stress in Mexico is the obedience of the children, which exceeds that of any country I have visited. In California, by contrast, it is easy to find a fifteen-year-old who is hoodlum and rascal enough to plot a murder, robbery, or arson. In Mexico, speak to a little boy and he will remove his hat and bow and reply with as much courtliness as if he had been trained in the most polite court in Christendom.

I found the Mexican cookery in restaurants, hotels, and private homes much to my liking. My Sam Hing was an excellent cook in the American manner, but the meals furnished me by Mexicans I always found more satisfactory. This especially refers to their way of cooking fowl, mutton, beef, and pork. It is true that one may at times imagine Mexican cookery to be a trifle too highly seasoned with chili colorado, but one grows accustomed even to that, and when hungry whispers to himself, "God bless Mexico and all Mexican cooks."

Good old Sonora. What a land for sleep—that soft, voluptuous, refreshing, dreamless sleep we often so enjoyed in Mexico.

When I arrived in Hermosillo, I carried letters of reference from American bankers, lawyers, clergymen, and merchants introducing me to the governor, the Bishop of Sonora, university professors, prominent merchants, and wealthy rancheros. These letters were so many passports into the most prominent circles of the city and the state of Sonora, enabling me to carry on a most prosperous trade. Yet at the same time I was under a heavy strain and compelled to spend money like water. Although I was handling merchandise of superior quality and unfamiliarity among Mexican merchants, I was unable to sell it at prodigious figures beyond what I had paid for it in New York and England. Under favorable conditions I might have made my Mexican journey most profitable, but my daily expenses for rent, upkeep of my men, licenses, and special taxes kept me from realizing much profit. But the experiences of being in Mexico were of great value to me. As I was also, in addition to being a trader, an employee of a New York brokerage and investment company to look after its mining investments in the United States and Mexico, and also a correspondent to the *San Francisco Chronicle* under the *nom de plume* of Don McDuff, I had very few hours of leisure.

One evening when I had about completed my labors in Hermosillo, I was visited by a man named Manuel Gonzalez and his wife, Margareta Coverubius. They had ten large, perfect pearls of wonderfully beautiful color which they desired to sell. They said they had obtained them in the Gulf of California some distance north of Guaymas, and were asking the ridiculously low price of seventy-five dollars for the lot. They said they were in need of money to return to their home in Guaymas. Realizing the pearls were worth much more, I asked why they had not sold them to others in Hermosillo. Gonzalez said there were no pearl buyers in Hermosillo who were willing to give him a fair price, and that he thought I would do better by him. I bought them and asked him if such pearls were easily obtained at Guaymas. He told me I could get considerable numbers of them at from four to thirty dollars apiece from friends and relatives of his there, whose names he gave me. This information aroused my avarice to such a degree that I concluded to run down to Guaymas.

After concluding my business the next day, I gave O'Donnel a letter to Don Antonio Pico, a friendly ranchero with whom I had done some business, and who had invited us to visit him for a week or month before leaving the country. I asked Don Antonio to furnish my men and animals such accommodations as they might want until my return from the coast. I then boarded a *volante*, or Mexican stagecoach, which, after a twenty-four-hour ride, landed me in Guaymas.

I had with me letters of introduction from the bishop at Hermosillo to Padre Eusebius Mora, another to an English merchant, and one from a banker at Hermosillo to a banker in Guaymas; but, although I was well received, I found I could purchase no pearls at favorable prices. There were a half-dozen Jews and eight or ten Germans at that time buying all the pearls available. No one knew the parties to whom I was recommended by Gonzales. I determined I would have to remain there for two or three years in order to develop sources for pearls, and I would have to compete with perhaps two hundred others. I remained two days studying the town, its trade, and shipping, but then took the mail *volante* back to Hermosillo.

I spent four days with Don Antonio Pico and his delightful family, then departed northward with my men. As I had considerable sums of Mexican coin, gold bullion, valuable mineral specimens, and a large quantity of Mexican opals from Queretaro, I resolved to make good time in leaving Sonora, for bandits had been inquiring about the nature of my business and my probable departure time. With four saddle horses, three well-packed mules, and our one remaining dog, Wheeler, we left the home of Don Antonio Pico. Also, the day after we left, I thought it best to disguise ourselves to appear that we were a lot of poor devils from Poverty Row.

Two days from Don Antonio Pico's, we reached a little wayside country *posada* and *tienda* kept by a widow, Señora Marguerita Alvares. About an hour before arriving at her place we were overtaken by a terrible rain and windstorm in which I irretrievably lost my hat, the only one I had. She laughed at my discomfiture and promised to find me a replacement before I left. But all she could come up with was an old brass and steel helmet once worn by one of the Imperial Guards of the Emperor Maximilian, the Mexican emperor executed some years before at Queretaro. She said it had been captured by Mexican soldiers some fifteen years before and left at her place. I bought it for three Mexican dollars.

Before leaving her place, we secured the Mexican gold and silver coins and bullion as well as possible in the bales of our camp equipage, and prepared to pass out of Mexico in as miserable plight as possible. I was wearing a suit of Irish frieze purchased the previous year in Ireland. I put it into a pitiable plight, tearing the legs off just below the knees and the coat into tatters, while leaving the vest buttonless. I put on a pair of United States Army shoes, cutting off the toe tips, slitting them up the sides, removing the strings, and drawing them onto my feet without socks. My men followed my example and made themselves look worse than I.

My dog Wheeler had grown sore-footed and seemed low spirited and discouraged since losing his companion Hayes some weeks before in Arizona. As he appeared to take a liking to Señora Marguerita Alvares, I traded him to her for an adult monkey that seemed to like our caravan. We placed this monkey on top of the pack of one of the mules, and with perfect evidence of happiness and contentment he traveled with us until we reached Wickenburg, Arizona, where I sold him to John Peebles as a gift for his wife.

The monkey was an interesting little rascal, but rather mischievous, and his conduct very much lowered my estimation of monkey intelligence. For example, when he was cold one morning while we were getting ready to break camp, instead of throwing more wood onto the fire, he threw on some knives, forks, tin plates, and a pair of overalls, not realizing the mistake he was making. As to the relative merits of dogs and monkeys, always give me the dog. I never knew anyone to get a monkey down to any useful labor or to train him to a point where he would indicate appreciation for what was being done for him. So, when I sold our monkey, Pedro, to John Peebles, I said to myself that he was my first and last monkey, and have kept my promise up to this time.

We continued to wear our tough-looking habiliments across the United States border, on to Tucson, and as far as Florence, where we felt we could at last afford to look somewhat more decent and civilized, and dressed ourselves in better clothing. I purchased a fairly good hat.

As we continued on to the Salt River region, we ran across a colony of Mormons who had just come down from Utah to lay the foundation of a city, locate farms and orchards, and take out an irrigation canal from the Salt River. I remained with them one night, and the next year visited with them longer on my second expedition. They gave their settlement the name Mesa, which it still retains.[101]

We passed through Phoenix and reached Wickenburg. Realizing that the country to the north along the Santa Maria and around Signal and Greenwood was infested with highwaymen, I resolved to change my plans. In the first place, I changed our course to the northeast toward forts McDowell and Verde along the Verde River. Secondly, I decided to forward some three thousand dollars to my brokers and agents in New York City. Even though express charges from Wickenburg to New York City were prodigiously high, I regarded the expense as better than the risk of robbery. The high rates were a result of the circuitous route of the express, which went down the Colorado River to Fort Yuma, then down the Gulf of California to the ocean, up to San Francisco, and across the country by rail.

Three days after leaving Wickenburg, we crossed the Hassayampa and the low mountains to the east, and another two days brought us to Fort McDowell, where two companies of soldiers were stationed.[102] We remained there one day to meet the commanding officer, Colonel Burnsides, and the post trader. They invited me back on a subsequent expedition to trade with them. As my route then led to Fort Verde through country with much danger from renegade Apaches, Colonel Burnsides offered to send a Lieutenant Thomas with me, with a detachment including a sergeant, a surgeon, and ten men. They would bring an ambulance and dispatches for the commander at Fort Verde and requisitions for certain medical supplies. I very gladly accepted the offer. Although the distance was seventy-five miles, it took us three days, for daily distances covered by the army are short, and the roads were in rather bad condition.

An unpleasant event occurred on this ride. My two men and cook traveled in the rear of the command with our three pack animals. On the morning of the second day, the sergeant and five men were sent ahead to prepare our noon camp in a cottonwood grove on the banks of a stream. My saddle horse, Billy, was very restless for some reason that morning, so I resolved to accompany them. As we reached our destination in Black Canyon, we suddenly came upon three Apache squaws and an old man who must have been seventy years old. They had five saddle horses which I assumed were stolen, loaded with buckskin and deer meat. They were about to ride off as we came up. The old man had been cleaning an old smoothbore muzzle-loading United States musket, and with him leaning against a palo verde bush he had a bow and a quiver of arrows. He also had three small cock-eared black dogs. As we came up, the squaws asked for sugar and tobacco.

While my horse was drinking, I dismounted and bent over to fill my canteen. While I was doing this, one of the dogs sank his teeth into my leg behind my knee. I sprang up, and since his teeth were still embedded in my trousers, I was able to throw him in front of me. With all the strength of my right leg, I kicked the dog with my heavy riding boot directly over his heart and killed him.

The squaws screamed, and instantly the old man seized his bow and let fly an arrow. It was deflected by a palo verde branch and, instead of hitting me in the breast or abdomen, struck my thigh. The incident took place more quickly than it takes to tell it. The sergeant shouted to me, "Shall I kill him?" Instinctively I said, "No, I killed his dog." But as I said this, the old Indian snatched up his weapons, sprang onto his horse, and the whole group vanished up a steep trail through some chaparral. I attempted to pull the arrow from my leg, but the head had stuck in the bone and the shaft came loose, leaving the head in the wound.

When the rest of the party reached us, there was temporary excitement. The lieutenant asked the sergeant why he had not killed the man at once and taken the squaws prisoner. The sergeant replied that I had requested him not to, since I had killed the dog. The officer shouted back, "You are not taking orders from Maguire. You know your duty. You deserve to be courtmartialed for neglect of duty." He then asked me if I was seriously wounded, and I asked if the surgeon would remove the arrowhead. The surgeon pulled out the arrowhead, disinfected the wound with carbolic acid, and put on a light bandage. He told me that as the Indians were obviously a hunting party, he did not believe the arrow was poisoned.

The lieutenant asked me to ride in the wagon, but I preferred the saddle, and we continued until nightfall. That night I experienced an excruciating pain for about an hour, but it then subsided and I experienced nothing more than an occasional stinging sensation for the next few days. Within ten days the wound was healed, but it left a permanent scar. Undoubtedly that clump of palo verde bushes saved my life.

We reached Fort Verde the next day and remained there another day, being kindly treated by Captain Gallagher, the post commander. My men and I then continued alone, stopping for one night at Kramer's Station, then reached Prescott. We stayed there two days, having our animals reshod, our laundry done, our pack saddles repaired, our guns cleaned, and writing letters. I paid my respects to Mr. Otis, the postmaster; Colonel C. P. Head; A. L. Bashford; Mr. and Mrs. Alexander; Judge Avery; and a few others.

We passed through Williamson's Valley on the way to Mineral Park. Far up in the heavens to the northeast towered the San Francisco Mountains, and to the north arose the long hogback ridge of Bill Williams Mountain. Day after day we traveled, passing Camp Willows and then Peach Springs on the old military road through lightly timbered mountains. Now and then we met a hunting party of Hualapai Indians, or two or three prospectors with their mules or burros. Everyone we met, white or Indian, was armed to the teeth. Almost everyone dressed in a few well-worn garments.

The third day out from Prescott we met U.S. Marshal Jeff Standifer with a deputy. They were trailing four stage robbers who had held up the Prescott and Wickenburg stage six days before and were thought to be heading for Bill Williams Mountain, a stronghold of stage robbers, horse thieves, and murderers. The officers were armed with Sharps carbines, and Standifer had in holsters on the pommel of his saddle a pair of extremely large single-shot English dueling pistols.

The fourth day we reached the station of dirty Mrs. Baker, a pioneer widow and kindly patron of wandering travelers.[103] She had three fairly good-looking daughters and four sons. The sons were excellent shots and good hunters and Indian fighters. The family came from Texas, where Mr. Baker had been killed in a gunfight four years previous. They owned four hundred cattle in the surrounding hills. In politics they were Democrats; in religion, hardshell Baptists. Mrs. Baker's uncle had been killed at the Alamo, and another uncle had been with Houston at San Jacinto when Santa Anna surrendered.

Her home and surroundings plainly indicated why she was known as "dirty Mrs. Baker." Her children, though, were nice, amiable, hospitable, and good-hearted people. She very much prided herself as coming from a fighting family and did not seem to have much, if any, fear of highwaymen or Indians who infested the region.

When we reached Mineral Park, I again met Bob Grey, Bob Upton, James Haas, Mrs. Wilburn, Brean, and Spear, and remained there overnight. From there we retraced our steps through Union Pass to Hardyville, across the Colorado River and the Mojave desert to Blackburn's station. There we found the sister and two nieces of Jean La Bruyere, the gold miner who had died of pneumonia, who had come from France to claim his remains. The relatives presented me with one of his pistols, a most beautiful weapon, and its mate to Al Blackburn. I still have the pistol and some gold quartz specimens La Bruyere had given me.

We continued retracing our route to Reese River, Nevada, where I had a second mission of a mine purchase to attend to for the same New York party. After that, I had no more business, either in trading or mine purchasing,[104] so we proceeded on to Salt Lake City, where we stopped at the far-famed Walker House and met my friend, General Patrick Edward Conner, hero of the Battle of Bear River. The next day, June 22, 1877, we arrived in Ogden.

The expedition had taken eight months and eleven days. We had traveled 4,793 miles, sold $31,341 dollars worth of merchandise, and purchased four gold and silver mines for my brokers in New York City. I wrote thirty-one newspaper letters and eleven magazine articles, for which I was paid $427. My net profit in trading was only $6,413, and I was paid $2,417 in purchasing and reporting on mines, of which my profit was $1,518 plus expenses from Mojave Station to Ogden, Utah. My total profit for the expedition was thus $9,247. In addition, I sold the pearls I bought in Hermosillo in New York City and made nine hundred dollars, though I afterward learned I could have obtained almost double that.

As to the three men who accompanied me on that memorable expedition, O'Donnel, strange as it may seem, returned to Mexico that same year and married Clothilde, the second-oldest daughter of Don Antonio Pico. I had surmised that something of the kind was brewing, as he often sang her praises. He settled in Mexico and being a good, trusty, and worthy man has made good. I received many letters from him in subsequent years.

Edwards went up into Washington Territory and settled. I had two letters from him, then heard no more. I never saw Sam Hing again nor heard from him after paying him off at Ogden on June 23, 1877.

The three mules and four horses I brought back I sold to Alex Toponce at Corinne, Utah.[105] Eight days after my return to Ogden I started by rail to New York City to prepare for another expedition into the southern country of Arizona and Mexico the following fall and winter. So ended my first Arizona expedition.

Don Maguire
May 24, 1883

Second Arizona Expedition

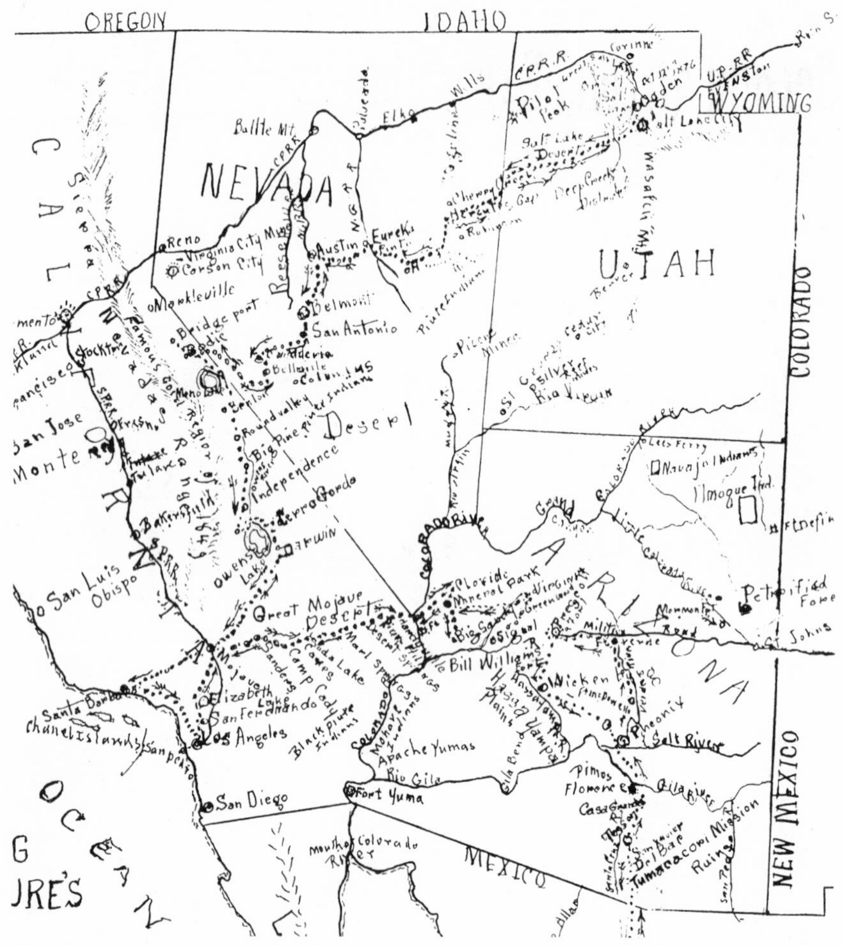

Portion of map of Don Maguire's first expedition. No map was found among Maguire's papers of his second expedition. USHS

2.

Second Arizona Expedition

WHILE TRADING THROUGHOUT Arizona and Mexico during the winter of 1876 and 1877, I determined to make a second expedition into that country the following winter. Consequently, during July, 1877, I went to New York City to purchase a stock of merchandise. The inventory I chose was well suited to the needs of the inhabitants of those regions. I purchased in the first place a considerable quantity of men's and women's clothing, mostly of superior quality, and in weight suited to a southern climate. I also bought a large variety of laces, ladies' underclothing, hosiery for both men and women, a stock of California-made men's gloves, and some high-class, American-made gold and silver watches. Trade in those regions also called for a stock of field glasses, magnifying glasses, spectacles; cutlery such as Bowie knives, pocket knives, butcher or skinning knives, and hatchets; double-barreled shotguns, Winchester and Sharp's rifles, and Colt's, Remington, and Smith and Wesson pistols. For Indian trade I bought Indian beads, paints, colored cotton goods by the piece, Indian jewelry, and several cases of South Sea shells. At a government sale in New York City I purchased five hundred condemned muzzle-loading smoothbore muskets for the liberal sum of seventy-five cents each.[1] As a unique feature of the Arizona trade, I purchased 2,500 decks of playing cards, 250 dice boxes, and a high-quality set of dice for each box. All of these goods were shipped so they would reach me in Ogden, Utah, about the middle of December, 1877.

Immediately after finishing my business in New York City, I hurried back to Ogden and departed for northeastern Idaho for purposes of mining and trade.[2] My mining investigations were carried out in the interest of Purbeck, Moses & Company of Wall Street, brokers, mine investors, and manipulators. For twenty-one days I traveled throughout the Boise basin, visiting the communities of Idaho City, Quartzburg, Centerville, Grimes Creek, Rocky Bar, Atlanta, and Garden Valley. Then I went into northwestern Idaho, to the communities of Mount Idaho, Lewiston, and Moscow, where the great Nez Perce war of 1877 drove white settlers before them. I had the honor of being among those who made the greatest speed to escape from the warlike horde.

I then went into Montana by stagecoach, traveling north from Missoula to the country known as Tobacco Plains near the Canadian border. My goal on this leg of the trip was to investigate trade possibilities, particularly in purchasing furs and peltries from white men and Indians. I soon learned that others had established a monopoly in that trade. I stopped at Flathead Lake, then the chief center of the Flathead Indian Reservation, where I met Major Peter Rognan at the Jocko Agency, with whom I formed a most agreeable acquaintance and who taught me much about the Flathead Indians and Father De Smet's mission among them beginning in 1840.

No region could offer a greater contrast to the Southwest than this part of Montana. In the latter, one finds beautiful green valleys, timberlands with hundreds of flowing waters, abundance of wild game, plentiful quantities of fish, and a climate which, though cold, is one of the most healthful and bracing in all the world. These features stood in bold contrast with the hot climate, trackless, sandy deserts, the Apache-infested mountains of Arizona, and the Paiute-controlled areas of southern Nevada and California, not to mention the coyotes, horned toads, green, blue, and black lizards, and the Gila monsters, and, lastly, the horrible red-eyed rattlesnakes on the plains of the Gila. I planned future visits to Montana, fished and hunted for a few days, then left by stagecoach for Corinne, Utah, passing through Butte City and Virginia City, where extensive placer mining had been done from 1862 to 1870.

Toward the end of August, 1877, I returned to Ogden, then continued on to Salt Lake City, where I had the pleasure or the pain of attending the funeral of Brigham Young, the great Mormon leader, who died in the last days of that month.[3] I entered the Tabernacle with the huge crowd, and, passing through the line, I was soon permitted to look upon the face of the dead prophet. He was dressed in his temple robe, which was a white robe with a white necktie at the throat, seemingly a very neat fit to his corpse, his hands crossed on his breast. He wore a cap quite similar to those we see in illustrations of the priests of old, and resembling those worn by bakers and plasterers. His was not a particularly handsome corpse, as it had a somewhat pinched appearance. On his face were many dark spots about the size of small tack heads. The face seemed to me wholly expressionless. Among his many relatives and family members, including many of his wives, I did not see any evidence of recent tear-shedding, although of course there must have been more or less of this on the part of some of them. I was much pleased to have attended this great event in the history of Utah, and the closing scene in the life of the man who had been conspicuous in the eyes of the world during the previous forty years.

There were about twelve thousand persons present in the great Mormon Tabernacle on that occasion, fully eleven thousand of whom were Mormons. A prayer and religious service followed the viewing of the corpse. The other leaders of the Mormon Church gave their experience and feelings on that sad occasion. The Mormon Tabernacle Choir sang appropriate hymns, and the great Mormon organ pealed forth the Dead March in *Saul*. Prayers were repeated by different members of the twelve apostles, and in due time the casket was closed and borne out of the Tabernacle by the pallbearers. It was placed in a grave on the hill northeast of the Lion and Beehive palaces just beyond the Eagle Gate. In this unassuming grave the great Mormon leader was left to rest until the morning of the Resurrection; and so closed the funeral of Brigham Young, at which I was an attendant, if not a mourner.

Three days after Brigham Young's funeral, I departed on another journey into Idaho and Montana, but returned to Ogden early in December, 1877, to begin preparations for my second expedition into Arizona. The merchandise I had purchased in New York City had arrived and was stored in an Ogden warehouse.

I found it best to undertake this expedition with wagons instead of packing a mule train. It was much more convenient. A greater amount of merchandise could be carried with much greater creature comforts to myself and my employees. My first step thus was to purchase four wagons, which I obtained from the firm of Burton, Herrick, and White Agricultural Implement Merchants of Ogden. These wagons were known as the Peter Shettler wagon, and were 3-1/2 and 3-3/4 inches in the skein of each spindle. They were well-constructed wagons built particularly for hard mountain service, and costing $145 for the lighter weights and $160 for the heavier. They were furnished with canvas covers, and the Ogden wagon makers had added additional high boards on the sides. They had also added cleats or barrel rests on the sides, and two boxes for holding hardware and other material were attached to the sides of each wagon bed.

As on my previous expedition, I purchased my draft animals from Bishop Layton, who lived southwest of Ogden. I bought twelve mules for $1,500. I purchased harness for them in Salt Lake City for three hundred dollars.

Amongst the overland freighting fraternity in Corinne, I employed two well-recommended teamsters: George Andrews, a Missourian about thirty years of age, and Peter McCue, a Californian of about thirty-five years. These men assisted me in Ogden in opening boxes of merchandise, repacking them into bales, lining the wagon beds with blankets, preparing our camping equipage and cooking outfit, and preparing our tents for a long journey. All this took up our time until Christmas. Between then and New Year's, I looked about for a third man to act as teamster, or assistant teamster swamper, and also for a Chinese cook. The latter I also secured at Corinne.[4] His name was Fong Kee, and he had come down from Montana for the winter, riding in a freight wagon. He was very good as cook and all-round camp man, thirty-two years of age, a native of Canton, China.

It was late in the day of January 3, 1878, when we took our departure from Ogden, and consequently only got as far as Farmington.[5] The next day brought us into Salt Lake City. We placed our animals for the night at the Colorado Stables, and I got rooms for my men at the unassuming Colorado House next door. I stayed at the Walker House, where I had a business appointment with Dan McGlinn, a California mining man. We were up until 2:00 o'clock in the morning discussing business and past experiences with some Salt Lake friends, including James and Thomas O'Reilly and Robert Walker of the Walker Brothers merchants.[6]

After breakfast, I met my men at the Colorado Tavern, where they had just eaten, and asked them how they had rested the previous night. One of them said he had rested fairly well except that he believed the hotel was a spook roost, and surely the loneliest spot on earth. He believed that it must have been built and occupied by spiritualists, for during the night he seemed to feel the disembodied creatures passing in and out of his room constantly. Strange to say, the other two men and the Chinaman also said they didn't like that hotel even a little bit.

We got our teams ready and proceeded southward until we rounded the point of the mountain twenty miles south of Salt Lake City and came upon the broad vista of Utah Valley with its beautiful freshwater lake and its then eight incorporated cities, Mountainville, Lehi, American Fork, Battle Creek, Provo, Springville, Payson, Spanish Fork, Pond Town, and Santaquin. The valley is thirty-five miles long and about the same in width. It is surrounded by high mountains, some of which bear snow during the greater part of the year. The chief among them is Timpanogos, twelve thousand feet in altitude. In ancient times the valley was inhabited by moundbuilders, a sedentary people, the remains of whose villages are yet found near the banks of the Provo River. The remains consist of foundations of buildings, granite and sandstone handmills, arrow- and lance heads of flint and obsidian, earthen pipes, and beads of bone, stone, and burnt clay. Some of the ruins hold earthen pots containing beans, Indian corn, human bones, and various little tools of bone and stone.

The little cities of Utah Valley were, like those to the north, constructed largely of adobe. For the first ten years of Mormon life in Utah, 1847–1857, all towns were walled about for Indian protection. These walls were usually about eight feet high, three feet wide at the base, and eighteen inches thick at the top, with watchtowers here and there. Heavy wooden gates were opened during the day and closed at night, while nightly sentinels guarded the walls. The walls were usually of unburnt adobe brick, though sometimes stone and mortar were used. There were no homes outside these walls until about 1865, after which, because of the dispersion of the Indians, country homes began to increase as elsewhere.

Provo, the county seat of Utah County, is a typical Utah town. The houses are mostly of adobe; the streets are very wide, with streams of water flowing in gutters on each side; and shade trees of cottonwood, maple, or locust line the sidewalks. Every block in a Mormon town contains ten acres, divided into one-acre lots for families of one man and as many wives and children as he can manage. In every lot there are apple, peach, and plum trees that bear teeming yields of fruit. Adjoining Provo is a very large area of farmland irrigated by the Provo River. The farms each contain from ten to fifty acres. Early each morning the men go out to work on the farms and do not return until evening. Cattle, sheep, and horses are taken care of by herdboys, who drive them into the foothills to graze during the day.

The people of these little cities are industrious, and very many of them are, in a small way, quite wealthy. The population contains a good number of English and Scotch, a very few Irish, a large number of Scandinavians, and a few half-breed Indians and Mexicans. The leaders, such as the bishops, are usually Americans or English, and occasionally Scotch. As we were detained in Provo for a number of days awaiting additional merchandise from New York City, I had time to become acquainted with some of the prominent people. Among those was a Dr. Riggs and his family, Isaac Bullock with his three wives and numerous children, and Benjamin Roberts, a veteran of the Mexican War, with whom my men and I stayed.[7] Benjamin Roberts's son Sam replaced my man Bernard Foley, who at that point changed his mind and decided to go labor in the Utah mines. Sam Roberts proved to be a most efficient and dependable young man for the entire period of my second expedition.[8]

All adult Mormons pay ten percent of their earnings to the church, whether it be in money, farm produce, or livestock. In every town there is what is known as the tithing yard and a tithing house for deposit of those offerings. The bishop then deducts ten percent of this for himself and sends the rest to the tithing house in Salt Lake City. There is, in fact, a double system of government in Utah: in addition to the county and state officers one finds elsewhere, there are the church officials and bishop's courts. It is in those courts that most civil cases are settled, except for murder, robbery, rape, or horse stealing. Utah has the death penalty for extreme malefactors but is humane indeed in offering the convict his choice of the gallows or the firing squad. A Sheriff Beasley in Provo told me no women had ever been executed in Utah, and were instead sent to the state penitentiary. He also said that Utah County to that time had only sent seven prisoners to the state penitentiary.

The art of dancing among the Mormons is carried to perfection. They will often commence dancing at 1:00 o'clock in the afternoon and continue until midnight, always beginning and ending with a prayer. While waiting in Provo, my men and I attended these dances, church entertainments, and other social events. But about the end of the third day it was gently hinted that, as I was a Gentile, if I continued to attend these functions where the fair daughters of the town congregated, my men and I might get rotten-egged.

Mormon life in Utah is almost military in nature. Their daily life is by rule and order with which other parts of the United States could have found little fault were it not for the vice of polygamy. Without polygamy it is not likely that the Mormons would ever have been compelled to seek an asylum in Utah. Most of their troubles then and since have arisen because of this vicious institution. It is based upon nothing but the old animal lust, and with slavery and cannibalism has been one of the practices that has reduced man to his lowest state of degradation.

Every Utah community has a school where reading, writing, and arithmetic are taught; but as a body the Mormons are, I think, the poorest lot of penmen and spellers in America. Among the wealthy, the girls are taught to play the organ, and a large number of them sing quite well. There is a theater in every town, to which admission is obtained by a quantity of farm produce.

The Mormons grow all their own food, and large fields of lucerne or alfalfa make excellent winter fodder for their animals. During the rest of the year the animals do very well on the bunchgrass in the mountains. Sorghum or cane in Utah produces fairly good molasses, while thousands of yellow-legged chickens produce ample eggs. Mormon butter is under somewhat of a ban in the Gentile world. Artemus Ward said that the Salt Lake House was strictly a temperance house, in that one could obtain nothing there stronger than butter, but that the butter was stronger than any whiskey. Mormon cheese would be excellent if all the milk or whey were taken out of it, or if the cream were allowed to remain. Consequently, Utah cheese does not enjoy much demand in other territories. Napoleon might have bought the territory's entire cheese output for gunflints.

The adobe bricks used for building material are larger than burnt bricks, and are of a dirty gray color. In a very dry country like Utah they do very well for twenty or thirty years, but are very inferior as a building material. The Mormon Tithing House, the President's palaces, the old Tabernacle, and the Salt Lake Theater are all built of these adobe bricks and plastered on the outside to resemble granite. Utah timber, which consists of red and white pine, mountain maple, birch, alder, haw, and serviceberry, is inferior for cabinet work and house construction. Yet Utah furniture is made from these woods and painted a reddish brown and then varnished.

Utah women attempt to dress as stylishly as in any part of the world when they can obtain the means; but more usually the contents of a Mormon lady's wardrobe is limited. Mormon male's clothing rarely fits, and I believe the worst lot of hats are to be found in Utah. A man will pay a dollar and a half for a wool hat, then for two or three years he will wear it to church and other special occasions. Then for the next eight or ten years he will wear it to work and to bed, in valley and on mountain, until it goes to pieces, covered with enough hair, glaze, dirt, and guano to fertilize a Dutchman's cabbage garden.

Mormon literature and learning are yet in their infancy. Orson Pratt is a man of some learning, partly college taught, partly self-taught, who understands Latin and Greek and something about mathematics. He is a staunch polygamist, but poor as a rat, although he dresses well and is the only man after Brigham Young whom I ever saw among the Mormons in Salt Lake City wearing a plug or stovepipe hat. He is now an old man and will soon fall into his grave, for his age is far beyond seventy. There is one Edward W. Tullidge,[9] who seems to be church historian in Utah, as he has written the lives of Joseph and Hyrum Smith, Brigham Young, and a general history of the Saints in Utah. He has given a good deal of his pen-work to the encouragement of peace between Mormon and Gentile in Utah. He seems to be a kindhearted sort of man and I believe has done much good by his attempts at literature.

No woman has ever written any work of great merit on any subject in the Mormon Church. How can it be otherwise, when so few of them have ever been favored by an education? Eliza R. Snow, who is credited among the Mormon people with being a poetess, has prepared one or two volumes in which there are poems of some merit, but to me her poetry is harder to digest than the victuals in a Russian tavern.[10] Mrs.

Carmichael, whose husband was connected with the army at Fort Douglas a few years ago, wrote a little volume of poems which had true merit; but it is long out of print.[11]

Eventually my merchandise arrived, and we made ready to leave Provo. We were well prepared for the journey. My men and I were armed to the teeth, each with two revolvers, a double-barreled shotgun, and a breechloading rifle. We had a complete camping outfit, two tents with folding tent poles, an abundance of bedding, and all other features necessary for a long journey across a broad stretch of wilderness. The mules I had purchased from Bishop Layton proved themselves so far to be excellent animals. One span of them was said to have belonged to Brigham Young, who used them with others in overland carriage journeys.

The morning we left Provo was sharp and cold. The roads were only fairly good, but we drove at a merry gait. The young man employed at Provo would call out goodbyes to his friends, telling them that he was departing for Arizona and Mexico. No doubt those were the happiest moments of his life, for he had never been out of Utah Territory.[12]

We drove on through Springville, Payson, and Spanish Fork, and night brought us to a little place called Santaquin, where we enjoyed the hospitality of the venerable and famous Brother Abel Butterfield,[13] who had been a servant in the house of Joseph, the Prophet, in Missouri and at Nauvoo. As Mr. Butterfield kept an excellent home place for travelers and an equally good stable, I thought it best not to erect our tents or to feed our animals in the open, so we decided to stay with him. Mr. Butterfield was a remarkable-looking man. He stood six feet four inches in his stocking feet, raw-boned, broad-shouldered, big-mouthed, Roman-nosed, long-haired, and lantern-jawed. By night or day he was as loquacious as a hungry duck, for he had recently taken to his bosom a huge Danish girl as a second wife. His former wife clung to a small dwelling close to the main house. In the morning, Brother Butterfield gave us a fairly good breakfast of potatoes, pork, stewed peaches, and a fair share of Mormon butter. His bill was very moderate, and upon our departure he also gave us his blessing. As he was a Mormon patriarch, he said his blessing would be a blessing in all days and nights of coming tribulations.

During the next few days, we passed through Nephi and on to Chicken Creek, crossed the Sevier River and Round Valley, and eventually reached Fillmore. We set up our tents each night, cooked our own food, and purchased oats and barley for our mules from nearby Mormon homes.

Fillmore was the capital of Utah Territory from 1850 to 1857.[14] It is situated in a broad, volcanic region. In the center of the valley rise two black volcanic buttes that were once active, and the entire country outside the immediate vicinity of the town is a waste of sands, gray sage, and black lava. As we entered Fillmore late in the evening, my eye fell upon a tavern sign to the right of the road which said, "FOOD AND REST FOR MAN AND BEAST," under which appeared the words "BY JOHN BOURNE," and under this a Masonic square and compass. I went inside and asked Mr. Bourne for permission to camp near his place and to purchase hay and grain for my animals. He welcomed me, and invited my men and me to join him and his wife and his four daughters, two of whom played the melodion and accordion, for an evening's entertainment when we had finished setting up our camp and eating.

We found Mr. Bourne to be a very sociable and interesting gentleman, though a peculiar one, of which there were a good many throughout Utah at that time.[15] He was an Englishman who had been converted to Mormonism while living north of Cape Town in South Africa. He was a tall man of goodly proportions, as was his English wife. They had at that time two sons and four daughters, ranging in age from a son of about twenty to a son of about seven. The four daughters were all comely but different in height and appearance. The eldest stood fully six feet in height, very rawboned, yet very attractive in the face with snappy, laughing eyes. Another was about five feet tall and very bunchy in figure. One would enjoy looking at her a second, third, or fourth time. The other two girls were of medium height.

Mr. Bourne asked me if I belonged to the Masonic fraternity, and I replied that I was not so fortunate. He said he had been a Mason for more than twenty-five years and was going to call his tavern "THE SQUARE AND COMPASS TAVERN," but the bishop warned him that there were few, if any, active Freemasons in the Mormon Church, and this would likely cut down his business.

The entertainment of the evening was a pleasing restorative, for the oldest daughter, Ophelia, played the melodion well, and another daughter, Marthena, played well on the accordion. The other two daughters, Jenny and Sylvia, sang such popular airs as "Annie Laurie" and "Comin' Thru the Rye." When they finished, my men and I rose, and I moved a vote of thanks. As we had been with them for an hour and a half, we began to say goodnight. At this, Mr. Bourne exclaimed, "Why good God, you are not going so soon. We are only just beginning to have a pleasant evening. Ophelia, bring in the cider."

Ophelia brought in a wooden pail filled with cider, a gourd dipper, and twelve large goblets which she filled and passed around. The cider was exceedingly good, with somewhat of a kick in it, but not to a dangerous degree. After his first drink, Mr. Bourne informed me that he had apostasized from the Mormon Church because it had not properly recognized his leadership talents and because he objected to tithing and blood atonement and his wife objected to polygamy. He had written to Brigham Young to that effect, and had afterwards been snubbed by him whenever he paid a visit to Fillmore.

The next morning we paid Mr. Bourne twelve dollars for our board, and resumed our journey to the south. We passed through Kanosh, a little Indian reservation, where I met Chief Kanosh, one of the most agreeably mannered and best-looking Indians I ever met. He looked very much like a well-groomed Frenchman, and received me at his tepee with great courtesy. He was chief over about three hundred Paiutes. When I told him I was on my way to Arizona, he warned me seriously to beware of the Apaches, who were famous for killing and robbing both whites and other Indians. I thanked him for his advice, and gave him some plugs of tobacco and other presents.

A few miles beyond Kanosh, near a rocky point adjacent to the wagon road, there are a number of very large blocks of lava on which there are shown a number of human footprints. No doubt they were cut into this rock by the ancient occupants whose remains we find at many points in this valley. The footprints are about the usual size of an adult human being. Why they were cut into the rock is difficult to decide upon. Possibly they were a monumental feature, or token of some event, but it is certain that the work was done long ago, for the black manganese oxide that covers these blocks covers to an equal degree the footprints. They must be at least from one thousand to fifteen hundred years old.

From there we passed on to Cove Creek Ranch Fort,[16] where Brigham Young or the Mormon Church about fifteen years before erected a stone fort about three hundred feet on each side, with walls twenty feet high and four feet thick at the base, with a large gate on its east front facing the highway. Within this fort there were living quarters for fourteen families, who grazed several large herds of cattle, horses, and sheep in the mountains to the east and in the valley to the west. East of the fort some few miles there are extensive sulphur mines, but at the time of our visit they had been worked only to a very limited extent. We also passed through a small valley called Prairie Dog Valley where there is a settlement of prairie dogs. It seems very strange to find this one solitary dogtown in this region, as it is the only spot west of the Rocky Mountains where any of them are found.[17] The overseer of this fort was a man named Hinckley, who was related in some way, by blood or marriage, to Brigham Young.[18] He was very nicely fixed in a domestic way. He had five wives there, with a very liberal production of children.

South of Cove Creek Ranch Fort we came to a junction where a road led east to Fort Cameron, a military post where an infantry company was stationed. We did not visit the fort on that occasion, but continued to a crossing of the Beaver River and on into the town of Beaver, where we camped for the night. Beaver was then a thrifty Mormon settlement about two hundred miles south of Salt Lake City in a fairly good farming region irrigated by the Beaver River. Between twenty-five and thirty miles to the west lies the great Horn Silver Mine and the little mining camp of Frisco, where a Mr. Cullen, Mr. Ryan, and a few of their associates had produced more than twenty million dollars at the time of my trip. I did not visit the Horn Silver Mine, as I was very anxious to reach Arizona as soon as possible, nor did I halt at any point to trade with the Mormon people. I was heading for a region where prices were much more remunerative than those in Utah.

Beyond Beaver we came to an old prehistoric fortress called Paragonah.[19] It was one large structure measuring 150 feet each way, oriented exactly to the cardinal directions, with an adjunct structure seventy-five feet from its southwest corner. This old ruin had been four stories in height at one time. It was built of very gravelly clay with walls about four feet thick at the base. The inhabitants seemed to have entered by means of ladders carried from one story to another. There were around it altogether nearly a hundred mounds, each of which had been at one time a fairly well-constructed house of the same material as the main structure.

We spent a few hours examining these ancient ruins, then continued onward for another five miles to the city of Parowan. We spent the night there at the hotel and trading post of a Mr. Daniel Page, an apostate Mormon who acted as storekeeper, tavernkeeper, and postmaster.[20] He was well posted in all things appertaining to Mormon history, and his social position in Parowan was much like that held by Mr. Bourne at Fillmore. He was a very agreeable man with a very interesting family and, though no longer a Mormon, seemed to be on very good terms with his Mormon neighbors.

Parowan is a beautiful little place. The Paragonah Mountains to the east are wholly in a red sandstone formation, and their erosion has created a reddish soil over the entire region, giving it rather a warm expression. The city itself has a wonderful lot of shade trees, chiefly cottonwood, with a great many orchards and well-built homes. We found it a pleasant place to spend one night and part of two days.

The road from Paragonah to Cedar City was rocky in most places and very rough. When we reached Cedar City, we camped at a travel station owned by a Mormon bishop named Lunt, an Englishman.[21] He told me that the mail carrier or stage driver had told him of my coming and that I was a mountain trader on my way into Arizona, a most unusual sort of man in that country. He said that he had lived there for many years, and that I was the first man to bring a stock of merchandise from Utah to Arizona to trade with white men and Indians. Looking at me in a curious sort of way, he asked, "My dear young man, do you not think that you are running great risks in doing this? You are very likely to have the top of your head shot off before you reach Arizona."

I asked him in reply who he thought would shoot off the top of my head. He indicated that the roads were infested with highwaymen and horse thieves like Idaho Bill, Bill McManus, Dutch Charley, and Ben Tasker, who would cut my throat for one hundred dollars and take my merchandise and mules into Nevada and sell them. "I know I am taking chances," I told him, "but there is now no turning back, and should I have to encounter any of the men whom you mention, I will strive to make it as interesting as possible for them. I have traveled over many wild regions of this earth, and up to date I have fortunately held my own. Two of the gentlemen you mention, Ben Tasker and Dutch Charley, I parted from this morning at Parowan. Last night they had supper and bed and this morning had breakfast at Dan Page's tavern in Parowan. They certainly know that I am going through to Arizona and should they desire to follow me, I shall surely take my chances as to holding my own."

"Well," said the bishop, "I can assure you of one thing, that as long as you are traveling between the settlements of the Latter-day Saints in Utah, you are quite safe. We will do everything to help you should you need assistance, but on your way into Arizona we can assure you that outside of your own strength you will have no protection save that extended to you by the Almighty." I told him that I personally trusted that the protection of the Almighty would be sufficient.

As during the first expedition, our merchandise was guarded by one of us during six-hour watches every night. We only relaxed our guard on those occasions when the entire stock was locked in a warehouse.

The next day we left Cedar City at an early hour against a cold, raw wind, traveling over a road that was in very poor condition. It was well into the afternoon when we reached Kanarrah, where I thought it best to remain for the night because of the continued cold wind. We camped beside the home of a Mr. Shirtz, an Indian interpreter.[22] The natural scenery around Kanarrah is very interesting. Great peaks of red sandstone rise in the mountains to the east, and give the soil, as at Parowan and Paragonah, a pinkish hue. The country is very rugged and very much of it is yet unknown to white men. A few straggling Paiute Indians inhabit that country and eke out a miserable existence from the very limited animal and vegetable life of that barren region.

During the night, the wind continued to blow fiercely until about one o'clock in the morning, when it grew calm and I enjoyed three hours of invigorating sleep after the previous tormenting storm. We were up at five o'clock and at six o'clock left Kanarrah. We reached the Rim of the Basin two hours later.

Now by the Rim of the Basin we mean the south line or shore of the Great Salt Lake of ancient times. The present Great Salt Lake at a very remote period covered about sixteen thousand square miles, eight times greater than the present area of the lake. At that time, the waters of the lake were fresh, for it had an outlet to the Pacific Ocean by way of the Snake and Portneuf Rivers. Its length was over four hundred miles and its width about 150. The south rim of this great central basin extends to within about six miles beyond Kanarrah, from which point the road rises for about two and one-half miles. There the region descends very rapidly to the south, and at this latter elevation the traveler perceives a wonderful change in temperature. The warmth rises rapidly until one reaches the little town of Belleview, where the climate is almost semitropical and the plant life is very much like that of southeastern California and northern Arizona. The warm winds coming up from the Gulf of California create a mild temperature.

From Belleview, our road continued on to Leeds, and thence to Silver Reef, a mining camp of much importance and the first point where I laid over to transact business. The camp was then in successful operation, with three quartz mills reducing the silver-bearing sandstones of the region (the silver occurs in sandstone here, which is rare). About seven hundred men were employed there at that time, most of whom were from Nevada, and many had brought their families. About half the people were Gentiles, or non-Mormons, and the others were Mormons drawn there from the nearby towns of Toquerville, Leeds, and Washington by the high wages. So neat, so clean, so thrifty was the little town of Silver Reef that I was reluctant to leave it. I knew that its thoroughly civilized and American-like expression would contrast favorably with the Mormon towns of southern Utah, and that it would be like passing through a foreign land until we reached the Colorado River.[23]

From Silver Reef, we drove on to trade in Toquerville, a Mormon town about eight miles to the east. The road was through sand almost hub deep, over undulating hills and abrupt hillocks of pure sand until we got within a few hundred yards of the town, where there is a hard volcanic formation upon which the town is built. There one might fancy himself in one of the little old towns of southeastern France or Italy, both on account of the stillness which pervades the place and the numerous vineyards that meet the eye in every direction. The houses were of adobe, of blocks of lava, and also of sandstone. The inhabitants of Toquerville were all Mormons of the most pronounced type, but after obtaining the good will of the bishop we began to trade with them. My goal was to secure some of the produce of that area, for my friend James Haas, of Mineral Park, Arizona, had informed me I could make a large profit by selling it in the Arizona mining camps. I therefore rented three wagons with four mules apiece from the bishop with this purpose in mind.

I rented a house for a few days and moved into it a quantity of muslin, cottonades, cutlery, jewelry, condemned United States muskets, and other kinds of merchandise. I then sent a crier around the town informing the people of my mission. It was not long before customers came forward, but I soon found that I would have to take more cash than the produce I wanted, such as cheese, smoked ham, dried beef, cornmeal, sorghum molasses, and a large quantity of Dixie wine, for they had already disposed of those articles at Silver Reef. I did not want to sell for cash, because my merchandise would not bring half the price in southern Utah that I expected for it in Arizona.

For this reason we reloaded our goods and left the next day, with my wagons and the ones I had hired from the bishop of Toquerville, to the east over a very rough road to Virgin City and Rockville, two little towns nestling under mighty red cliffs that overhang the Virgin River. At Rockville I found a pretty little quiet town. The Mormons often explain that all they wish from the American people is to be left alone in peace and quiet to live their religion, and certainly the wild canyons along the Virgin River afford as much seclusion as anyone would wish. No one, Jew or Gentile, but rarely sets foot along its banks save in passing through the country, and but rarely stays there more than overnight. The inhabitants of these little towns are firm believers in all that Mormonism teaches. They read only Mormon books, hear of only Mormon subjects, live by Mormon rules, and for this reason many of the younger members of the community, knowing nothing of the world save by hearsay, believe that the Mormon Church is all-powerful with the Almighty and that from Rockville in the south to Logan in the north there dwells a people that could successfully oppose the whole world.

After three days of trading at Rockville, I had swapped for all the dried grapes, peaches, apples, bacon, and cheese I wanted to pull through the sand. I will here remark that having with me Sam Roberts of Provo, who was a Mormon, was a great advantage to me in these little strongholds, for his parents were known to some of them, and we moved around with the greatest freedom.

We returned through Toquerville and continued on to Washington, a little town of about fifteen hundred souls, exclusively Mormon, closely built. There are also vineyards there, from which they make raisins. They also make wine, which is a villainous stuff, containing about as much of the juice of the yellowjacket and wasps as it does of the grape. So rascally is the nature of this drink that people of Arizona and Nevada claim that a man who drinks a quart of it will get up in the night and steal his own clothes. Southern Utah for some reason is called Dixie, and its celebrated wine is called Dixie wine.[24]

The population of Washington is made up of Danes, Swedes, Italians, English, Scotch, and native Americans intermarried and mixed in breed until the children rarely know to what blood they belong. South of Washington the Virgin River flows through a flat, sandy, alkali region. Although grapes, peaches, apples, figs, strawberries, pomegranates, and almonds are plentiful in this region, grain does poorly. For this reason the people trade their wine, raisins, almonds, figs, and cotton to the people of more northerly settlements in exchange for flour, cornmeal, potatoes, and other products of those regions.

Three hours' drive from Washington brought my caravan to St. George, the capital of southern Utah and the county seat of Washington County. From the high mesa northeast of town I first beheld the little city at its base and first saw the great white Mormon temple built of basalt and whitewashed with lime inside and out. This temple stands about one-half mile southeast of St. George proper. It is a handsome building, and all the more singular for having been erected out in the sterile deserts of southwestern Utah. It cost about one million dollars to build it.

St. George is an attractive little city of from twelve to fifteen hundred persons, chiefly American and English. In this far-off southern capital, to which even yet no railroad runs, dwell in a secure place many of the high dignitaries of the Mormon Church. Apostle Erastus Snow, his sister Eliza R. Snow, and many of the extremely well-married polygamists live there, with harems containing as many as ten wives each, and the surnames of the children who fill the streets are a marvel to behold.

Fields of cotton and sugar cane occupy the bottomlands below town. There is a mill at Washington where much of this cotton is manufactured into cloth, and this cotton is worn largely by the people of southern Utah. Molasses is made from the cane grown here. Herds of cattle and horses run in a mountainous district to the northwest, and the people of Washington and St. George produce a fairly good quality of leather from their hides. Perhaps because they carry more gentle blood in their veins than the people in neighboring towns, the women of St. George are tidy in their dress and more handsome in appearance than those of other towns of southern Utah. Here, as everywhere else in Zion, dancing is a divine institution and a fine art.

After St. George there was one little town to pass through before we left the Mormon dominion, and that was Santa Clara, about five miles west of St. George. On the way, the traveler crosses a chilled river of lava that rolled in ancient days from a volcano about nine miles to the northwest. This cold, silent mass of lava presents a strange appearance. It is about seven hundred feet across, and about forty feet higher than the surrounding surface. The lava itself is rifted, torn, and upturned. Here and there a wave rises like that seen on the ocean during a high wind. What an indescribable scene was here one day when this tide poured down in a red molten state. It flowed for twelve or fourteen miles and is as plain and fresh today as it was when it cooled ages ago. The entire region round about is volcanic and shows in all directions the results of awful convulsions and earthquakes. Over the lava field and in the washed gravel of the country I found thousands of small balls about the size of grapeshot. They are of an igneous nature and are simply lava which was shot upward to an immense height, formed into globules like rain, and cooled into a solid state while falling.

Santa Clara is a sort of string town with Piedmontese and American families and a total population of about two hundred. It is a quiet little unknown southern Utah town, but, like every other town on earth, it had its prominent man, a downeast Yankee named Pulsipher,[25] who in stocking feet would stand considerably higher than six feet. We camped near his place. He came out and shook hands with me and said he thought from the looks of the mules and horses that if I were to buy a ton of lucerne hay from him I would not be buying it too soon and there would not be much more than ten pounds left by the following morning. Our animals were indeed hungry and in need of a rest for the next ten or twelve hours, if not longer.

Even though this town was inhabited by industrious, unassuming people, they appeared to find life to be a tight fit, for the land about was sterile, very little grain was produced, and the produce of their many two-acre orchards sold at a poor price. Those orchards and a few cattle were all they had to support themselves.

We found Brother Pulsipher, his three wives, and nineteen children to be very pleasant people. He told me that about four hours' ride to the southwest there was a wild, low, desolate volcanic waste where roamed a number of cattle, perfectly wild renegade calves and old cows along with a few bulls. They had escaped either from the Mormons or from California immigrants years ago and penetrated into this awful wilderness. As no one claimed them and there is no way of approaching them but by foot through the lava beds, anyone who wished might hunt them. It would take the entire United States Army, he thought, to get ten head of them out of there alive. He said that it was not difficult to get within shooting distance of them, but driving them out was impossible because the nature of the country prevented a horse from traveling safely faster than at a walk. I asked if there were anyone who would go with me to hunt, and he replied that I could easily get any of the young men of Santa Clara to accompany me there if I wished to go.

In his house there was a man named Carter from a small stream to the west called the Magotsee who said that he had his dogs and guns with him and that he would join me for a two-day hunt. Three other boys were found before bedtime who volunteered to accompany me. The next morning bright and early I borrowed a horse from Bishop Pulsipher, took my man Sam Roberts, and left with a man named Samuel Jamesburg. We took some U.S. government needle guns, caliber 50, a weapon used for larger game, very reliable, and easily handled in a rough country, and 150 cartridges. One of my men had a large sheath knife. We took some grain for the horses, and for us a frying pan, some salt, some bacon, some sugar and coffee, forty pounds of flour, two cans of yeast powders, vegetables, potatoes, a few turnips, and some onions. The four Mormons with us had an old smoothbore musket, a Kentucky rifle, and an old Tower musket, while Mr. Carter had an old flintlock U.S. government musket stamped with the date 1805. They also had fifty pounds of flour, blankets, and other camping gear.

Our destination was Bull Valley. Two o'clock brought us to the rim of a dreary volcanic basin in which green cactus, Spanish bayonet, and gietta grass grew rather sparsely. The lava lay in vast broken fields impossible for swift riding, so we soon saw that we would have to leave our horses and proceed on foot. We found a little spring where we made our camp and put the horses out on fair feed.

We wandered about for almost three hours before we found any cattle tracks. There was no road, few paths, and a broken wilderness in all directions surrounded by a high volcanic rim so elevated that few animals could ever get out of the valley. There was grass and shrubbery growing everywhere, but no cattle in sight. I began to despair of seeing any when one of the Mormons a short distance away on top of some gravel shouted that he saw some cattle about a mile away. There were about eleven head. They were gazing at us, but in a moment they scampered away into the oak brush near them. It was plain to me that we would find it difficult to get within range of them unless we divided and stopped them from different directions.

They were very wary and accustomed to running through the lava. As we pursued them, we soon noticed that the herd had become larger. There were now twenty-one head, and as I watched them through my field glasses I saw there were three old Texas bulls that stood as sentinels in the rear, with outspread horns and heads raised in a magnificent style.

The other men scattered, and I, after clambering over drifts of basaltic rock, jumping fissures, and running in one direction after another, saw that my boots were giving way and I was becoming tired. I found an inviting spot to rest near a bunch of chokecherry bushes with some dried fruit still on them. I was about to go over and gather a handful of them when I heard a rustling noise a few yards to my right where there was another clump of the bushes, and what should I behold but a brown bear sitting on his haunches eating dry cherries. I was not more than forty feet from him. I raised my gun and sent a Minie ball through his head. He fell, rolled over, and groaned twice, then stretched out dead.

The report of my gun startled a number of wild cattle from their hiding places. I saw them bounding away from me at a distance of about one thousand yards; and a moment later two of my comrades rose out of the lava and shot one. I cut the bear's throat and started toward them. They had gotten a fine black heifer. So now we had bear meat and beef. The day was far spent, and I began to think of returning, when we saw Sam and the other two Mormons at a distance of about two miles chasing about twenty head of cattle. As they were coming toward us, I began to prepare for another shot. The three hunters were firing as quickly as they could load, but evidently doing no harm. We lay down and waited until the cattle were not more than sixty yards away and passing us. We fired into the group as fast as we could load, and killed three.

We were now satisfied, with four head of cattle and a bear. We skinned them until nine o'clock that night. We left the dressed meat and returned to camp almost dead with thirst. It was midnight when supper was over and we prepared for bed. When we returned for the meat the next morning, we found that the coyotes had eaten an entire quarter; but it was no matter, for we found we could carry no more than one-third of what was left on our horses.

It was the night of the second day when we reached Santa Clara. All were satisfied with our hunt and thoroughly worn out with the fatigues of the lava beds in Bull Valley. We cut up the meat, both the beef and the bear, salted it, and hung it up to dry in strips. We told others where we had left the remainder of the meat and the hides, and they went out to get it.

From Santa Clara we were to start out into the wilderness, so it was necessary to have everything in shipshape. Harness was to be cleaned and oiled, horses to be reshod, guns cleaned, and the load of merchandise overhauled and put into solid position in the wagons to avoid friction and rubbing which would have caused injury. All this took three days.

The following morning we settled with Mr. Pulsipher, then pulled out of Santa Clara up the steep ridge which lies southwest of town. From the summit of the ridge the road runs over hard gravel for forty miles to

Beaver Dams. We made it all the way to Beaver Dams the first day, over a lonely and desert region in every particular, meeting no one on the way.

Beaver Dams is a mountain stream rising from some springs a considerable distance to the west and northwest. Along the stream, elder, cottonwood, and maple trees grow in considerable numbers. There were quite a number of beaver dwelling along the stream, from which it had taken its name. It was but a short distance from the crossing of Beaver Dams to the Virgin River. On the top of a cliff over the Virgin River there are the remains of a family of cliff dwellers who occupied this entire region ages ago. They also exist near Santa Clara on Santa Clara Creek. At both places there are considerable quantities of broken pottery, flints, and crumbling stone walls. To the east of Beaver Dams lay a broken, wild country on which earthquake, volcano, and flood had each done its work. Strata piled up in divers colors rested upon each other, through which the Virgin River had torn its way. The falls of the Virgin River a few miles away are among the most beautiful to be found in any stream of that region.

We camped at Beaver Dams. After we had hobbled our animals and erected our tents, our roaring fires soon gave forth the smell of jerked beef and bear meat frying in hog's fat. Bannocks of bread were baking before the fire, dried peaches were being stewed on the poles in a large pot, coffee was boiling in another large pot, and sliced potatoes were stewing. Our Chinese cook spread a tarpaulin on the ground and soon cried out that all things were ready to eat. The men we had employed at Toquerville prepared their own meals at a separate camp adjacent to ours.

I had long since learned to love the dry, barren deserts of the Southwest, the hazy atmosphere, the hard, dry roads, the stillness and quiet of everything around, which leaves one's mind when not traveling in the most undisturbed meditation. The atmosphere is salubrious and bracing, but little life is seen on these dry wastes except the occasional badger, sometimes a small fox, and now and then some jackrabbits. Occasionally a crow flies along in his dreamy flight and a gray coyote is seen on the plain watching every action with his anxious gaze. This coyote, one must note, is not the well-clothed, well-fed, sleek-looking individual that his brethren of Idaho, Dakota, and Montana are. In those northern regions water is in abundance. There is a plentiful supply of jackrabbits, moles, skunks, hedgehogs, and other rodents; but in the deserts of the Southwest a poor living is furnished to the coyote. His coat is ragged and patchy. He is always lean, he appears to be undecided in his gait, and his whole life is made up of brooded journeys and long fasts. His daily life is but crickets, lizards, and occasional jackrabbits, while it is a small consideration to travel forty miles to get a drink.

From Beaver Dams our course continued down the Virgin River, and soon we were again in heavy, deep brown sand so uncompromising to man or beast that the axles almost dragged the surface, our poor mules tugging slowly with their heavy loads, sweat dripping from their sides like brine. We stopped for an hour at noon on a sandy bend between river crossings, and when we reached Bunkersville it was dark night. It was a little settlement on the east bank of the Virgin River recently settled by ten families from Utah. They had already raised one crop of cotton, sorghum, squashes, yams, and Indian corn. The little town was situated on a bluff over the Virgin River. The fields stretched out below it on the river bottom. The houses were built of palisades, or adobe bricks, and covered with mesquite branches, Spanish bayonet, and gravel. The town was presided over by Bishop Bunker, who had three wives, and was assisted by his First Counselor, Brother Abbot.[26] Certainly they could not have found a more lonely spot for their settlement even on these deserts, but here they were to toil until the waters of the river were brought out over all the bottomland. Doubtless forty years hence the traveler will find here a quiet little town planted with trees, with better buildings than the ones we found, and with a contented group of Mormon devotees living and reproducing themselves as in other parts of Zion.

From Bunkerville it was yet eighty miles to St. Thomas, the Paiute Indian reservation on the Muddy, a small stream tributary to the Virgin from the northwest. The road was in miserable condition, through sand and across marshes, crossing and recrossing the Virgin River twenty-nine times. So difficult was the road that it required six days to cover that distance, and a more accursed road no man ever compelled a patient mule to travel. At times the sand was so deep that our mules would have to rest every fifty feet, and at other points the pitches over cliffs were so steep that we had to hitch four spans of mules to one wagon in order to negotiate them. Again, the road would be so marshy that we would have to corduroy with branches of mesquite or young cottonwoods for a hundred yards or more at a time. Frequently we would have to drive for life to keep the wagons from sinking in the quicksand. At other points, boulders would have to be removed.

We had to take this river road, as there was no other to take. The hills on either side were abrupt to a height of some hundreds of feet. At night one of us had to watch the horses, for there were Indian horse thieves who attempted to take anything that might fall into their clutches. Not only were the Paiutes from the Muddy Reservation constantly skulking along the Virgin River, but Navajos also occasionally passed over into southeastern California and stole any animal they could find.

The second morning after leaving Bunkerville, I saw ahead of us a man walking slowly and alone. He was going even slower than our loaded teams. When we overtook him, he appeared to be about thirty years of age, naturally handsome, cultivated in speech, but oh, how neglected in appearance! How ragged! How tramplike he was! He had no money, no clothes but those he was wearing, and no blankets, traveling alone and unknown in a weary land. In this lonely, desolate region one is not overly anxious to become shelterer and comforter to men who may be foolish enough to attempt passage of such a place without blankets or provisions. But when he asked to accompany us, I said yes, but, while he could eat with us, he would have to take the ground for a bed and the sky for a blanket.

He thanked me kindly, saying that was all he could desire. Since I was tired myself from riding, I got down from the wagon and told my driver to let this man drive the team, for he said he could do it, and the change seemed to please him very much. That day when we stopped at noon, he gathered wood for the fires, carried water, and made himself useful.

He was in such a ragged state and so supremely dirty that I became interested in his history. His name was Charles Hendricks. He was the son of a Boston lawyer, and had once been a druggist in Kansas City, Missouri. He married into a highly respectable family, but being a member of several fashionable clubs, he took to drinking and gambling. Eventually he neglected his business, abandoned his wife, and became a sot. He became a vagrant, tramping from town to town, finding his meals behind hotels, and his lodgings in back alleys. The prodigal of old had no worse misery than he. I felt sorry for him, as he was a ripe Latin and Greek scholar, a good mathematician, and had an extensive knowledge of medicine. He told me he was going down into Arizona and Mexico. I asked him why he did not overcome his habit of drunkenness and try to be a useful member of society. He said, "I have fallen about as low as I can fall. There is only one pleasure left for me, and that is to get blind drunk whenever an opportunity presents itself, which I am sorry to say of late has been very seldom. In this part of the world no one knows who I am, and I can enter into any town without being cared for or noticed."[27]

It was the twenty-seventh day of January when we reached St. Thomas, and we were so worn out that I resolved upon a three-days rest. We put up our two tents near the residence of Colonel William Jennings, the Indian agent.[28] This reservation is in the southeastern part of Lincoln County, Nevada.[29] The country for miles around is rich, black loam on which a good deal of mesquite and mescrew bushes grow. The pods that grow upon these are used by the Indians for food. It is refreshing to the soul, after traveling through such a dreary region, to arrive at such a spot. The soft, mild wind of the south blows through the cottonwoods and the birds sing where the green grass grows and the clear blue water gurgles in the irrigation canals. It is an oasis to which many a road and desert trail leads from either direction. To the west a wagon road runs to Las Vegas, another oasis similar to this, and on to San Bernardino, California. To the southwest a wagon road leads to El Dorado Canyon on the Colorado River, where a number of silver mines are being worked.

I found the Indian agent, Colonel Jennings, to be a fine, whole-souled, western-mannered man. His wife was a lady of no ordinary kind, either in size or intellect. They had two daughters, one named Fanny, about twenty years old, and the other named Lydia, about twelve.[30] Their home was a large adobe house surrounded by verandas in the midst of a grove of cottonwoods. Muddy Creek ran past the south side of the house, and every comfort awaited the traveler.

About 375 Paiute Indians, here known as the Muddy Indians, dwell here at St. Thomas. They are really a group of renegades, even though credited with being Paiutes, from the Digger Indians of California, the Hualapais and Mojaves of Arizona, Utes and Paiutes from Utah, and a few of the Shoshone from southern Idaho and Wyoming, all of which make up these Muddy River rascals. They are a poor, degenerate lot of people who are rapidly becoming extinct. They take no pride in farming or tilling the earth in any way.

Old Shinbone, one of their wise men, told me that it was a very foolish thing for the Indians to work and try to raise wheat or corn while there was plenty of mesquite and mescrew and rabbits everywhere. I told him that if he raised grain and built houses, owned stock, and worked for the white man, they would all have clothing and better health than living in the half-naked, half-starved state to which they had been subject before going on the reservation. But he said that when the Indians went where they pleased, wore little or no clothing, and had but wild game, worms, lizards, and frogs to eat they were a free and happy people; but now that they were under government care, eating flour bread, wearing clothes, and striving to do like white men, they were dying out and in a few years would be extinct. "When that time comes," he said, "there will be no one living on this reservation but Colonel Jennings and his family."

It is a strange fact that the Indian is a failure in civilization. I have seen them in every situation both in the United States and Mexico, but the savage nature is there and you can never bring him up to the high intellectual plane of the white race short of fifteen to twenty generations. These Muddy Indians had among them but few arts. At one time they made a rude pottery in which to cook. They made bows of mesquite and willow and arrows from the arrowweed, tipping them with obsidian points. These were their sole means of hunting and defense. For clothing they made mantles from rabbit skin twisted into ropes and sewed together. They are a happy-go-lucky sort of fellows with few cares and few wants. I will take back part of the latter statement, for they want everything they see, but make little complaint when they get nothing.

Colonel Jennings learned that I had trade goods, and he allowed me to open up business with the Indians after I had finished trading with his family and dependents. To my surprise, he told me that the Indians had considerable money, as fifty to seventy-five of them had been working around the mines at Ivanpa and El Dorado Canyon sorting silver ores, for which they received two dollars in silver per day plus their meals. They also make considerable money selling grain to travelers. They came up to the tents in parties of from ten to twenty at a time buying knives, jewelry, a few pistols, skinning knives, and a considerable quantity of colored cotton goods. When they learned that I also had a number of government muskets, they wanted to buy those also, and Colonel Jennings gave me permission to sell them after I told him that they were muzzle-loaders and unrifled. I was not permitted to sell either pistols or breechloading guns. To my surprise, I sold them thirty of the condemned Springfield smoothbore muskets for ten dollars apiece. The Indians paid for all of this in silver currency, part of which was Mexican dollars which I accepted at seventy-five cents.

We left St. Thomas after three days. We were joined there by an old gentleman from Chicago named Colonel Pierson, who had come west to prospect, packing all he had on the back of a little mare called Dolly.

The drive from St. Thomas to Stone's Ferry on the Colorado River is an awful one. The sand lies in such drifts as to be almost impassable. I had learned of this uncompromising wilderness from Colonel Jennings and was thus reluctant to leave him and his family, but business required that I press on. We had to carry hay and grain with us over that miserable road, for there is no feed for animals at the ferry.

When we reached Stone's Ferry, we found Mr. Pony Thompson keeping the Hencoop Hotel and running the ferry.[31] The hotel was built of mud, cottonwood poles, and willows, roofed with gravel and canvas, and chained to the ground to keep it from being borne away by the high winds that constantly blow there. It is a desolate place, on the high bank of that lone river. His only male companion was an Indian. To grace the solitary household he had, as a sort of ornament, a young Indian squaw who looked to be about nineteen years old. Mr. Thompson said that she was taking her vacation at his place, that she had been there about a week, and in another week would return to her people out in the desert. He said his business consisted of no more than one party of from one to ten persons with their teams per week. He was a good-natured, well-cultivated young man of about twenty-five years from Boston. His sister, Miss Nellie Thompson, was a teacher at the Muddy Agency for Colonel Jennings's family.[32] The lack of business at this desolate spot gave him plenty of time to read, and he had a fine lot of books. For a time he gave his attention to fishing. He had collected a large number of natural history curiosities of the region, such as a handsome Apache scalping knife which he gave me. He also showed me a loaf of mescrew bread. It was a strange mass for food, and if the reader would like a duplicate, take two gallons of sawdust, pour over it three quarts of sweetened glycerine, and let it harden.

We paid Mr. Thompson fifty-six dollars for ferrying my twelve mules and four wagons and the two wagons and eight horses of my Mormon friends from Toquerville. We crossed at daybreak and headed toward Cerbat, fifty miles to the south. For the previous four days we had been in the Territory of Arizona, but as the country north of the Colorado River was then looked upon as a No Man's Land, it was only when we touched the south bank of the river that we felt we were in Arizona proper.

The first day after crossing the river we made the lone tree that stands halfway between Stone's Ferry and Mineral Park. There was no water save the barrels which we had braced to the sides of each wagon.

At the ferry, we had learned that a war party of Hualapai Indians had recently killed a couple of prospectors, so we saw the necessity of using all caution to avoid falling into the hands of these marauders. When we set up camp, we put our animals on some good grama grass about a mile away, then I had the men throw up a slight breastwork around the wagons and tents against a possible Indian attack. Beside my bed, I laid out two extra muzzle-loading horse pistols loaded with buckshot, two revolvers, two double-barreled shotguns, and two needle guns with plenty of ammunition.

After a general wash, we all sat down to supper. Each man sat cross-legged around our portable table with a cup of well-sugared coffee by his side. Each plate held a fair share of bacon and beans, and a half-dozen loaves of warm bread were piled up on the table. The cast-iron pot held more bacon and beans, there was a tin dish filled with stewed grapes and dried peaches, another filled with butter, and some jerked beef was in yet another pan. On these things a hungry person could make a capital supper in such a dry climate.

After eating, we dug rifle pits under the wagons for an additional margin of safety. The pits were four feet deep, and the dirt thrown up around them formed a kind of face from which to shoot. Night fell, everything was quiet, and we sat about our bright fires. Colonel Pierson, who claimed the honor of having led an Illinois regiment in the great rebellion, was relating his war experiences. Hendricks, the monumental tramp to whom I had given a cheap suit of clothes after he had taken a bath in the Colorado River, and whom we all looked upon as a sort of lucky mascot, was relating how many men he had killed with his drugs in Kansas City. Occasionally in the talk, Sam Roberts would relate how affairs were conducted in Utah.

Suddenly, we heard gravel rolling down a bank some thirty feet away. We listened. It continued. "Indians!" we all whispered. I seized the shovel and threw gravel into the fire and told the Mormon boys to do likewise to theirs. The next minute we were all down in the pits under the wagons shaking with buck ague waiting for the enemy to fire.

Strange to relate, within ten minutes after diving into the rifle pits, Colonel Pierson was weeping like a child, and saying that if he could only see his daughter in Chicago, he was ready to sell his life as dearly as possible. He was armed with a pair of large-sized Smith and Wesson revolvers. I had been in close quarters, but had never had such strange feelings moving up and down my backbone. Sam Roberts complained of the same sensation. Doc Hendricks said, "Oh, heavens! If I had only a quart of whiskey, I would not fear all the Indians in Arizona." Although that night was not cold, our teeth chattered like bird rattles.

We waited with anxiety. We listened for any sound, while our own hearts were beating loudly enough to be heard, but no more noises came. Presently, far up the gulch, we saw a light, and then a fire. This astonished us all. There had been no wagons up there when we came in the evening, nor did we see signs of light when we pitched camp. The flames of the fires grew higher, and we could see Indians and white men around it. I told Sam to hand me my field glasses, and I could see three Moqui Indians and four white men who appeared to be prospectors, for there were packs near the fire, and against them were shovels, picks, gold pans, and three carbines. Sam found three mules feeding along the bank of the gulch, and we realized they were the cause of the noise that had thrown us into such fear.

I took a double-barreled shotgun and told my men to hold the fort until I returned. After checking our animals, I made a detour and came down on this strange fire. The party proved to be four prospectors from Bill Williams Mountain, and three Moqui or Zuni Indians who were going to California to work on railroad construction.

After a while I went back to our tents, but as I came up, Colonel Pierson jumped out of the rifle pit crying to me to stop or he would shoot me. I knew quite well that he was aware of who it was, and began laughing at his false bravery. With a terrible oath he swore that he thought it was Indians about to charge the rifle pits.

Our scare was over, and we came out of our fortifications, except for

Doc Hendricks, who said that he could not wish a better bed. The night watchman took his place, and we slept until the rosy dawn.

The next day we reached Knobman Springs at Cerbat, where my first trading on this second expedition took place.[33] In addition to Mr. Knobman and his wife, there were about a dozen men in that little camp. Everyone was in dire need of just such merchandise as we had with us, so we remained there all day and sold a little over four hundred dollars worth of goods. On the following day we reached Mineral Park, and the next morning our worthy friends Colonel Pierson and Doc Hendricks left us, ostensibly to go to Prescott or Phoenix. We did not see them again.

At Mineral Park I rented a large vacant store building from Messrs. Brean and Spear, and established my trading post for a week, carrying on an exceedingly good business. We unloaded the wagons hired at Toquerville and paid the Mormon boys for their services. When I paid them, the oldest one, whose name was Martin Harris, said, "Well, by hell, it's all right to come into Arizona once over that hell of a road down the Virgin and up the Hualapai Wash, but never again." I gave them three hundred dollars for their services, and they thanked me kindly for all the favors we had shown them. Before they left, they paid me thirty dollars for three of the smoothbore U.S. muskets and fifty cartridges so they could defend themselves on the way home. I never saw any of these Mormon boys again, but as we did not hear of any of them having been killed on the highway, I have no doubt that they reached home safely.

I found that I had arrived in Mineral Park at a very good time, for there was a good deal of money in town, and for eight days I drove a most profitable trade.[34] While there, I learned that on the Colorado River about twenty miles north of Hardyville there were encamped a large lot of Hualapai and Mojave Indians who had come together to trade, and that they had considerable money with them. I also learned that they were short of anything to eat, for it had been a long time since any steamers had come up the Colorado. I at once realized that there was a good field of trade among them, but I would have to take all or part of my men with me, for one man would have to watch the mules constantly, the Chinaman would cook, and the other three men would have to assist me in handling the merchandise. I found at Mineral Park an old acquaintance named Stone Sawyer, whom I had met during my previous expedition. He volunteered to go with me, so I could leave two of my men behind to look after our merchandise at Mineral Park.

We took two wagons loaded with five hundred pounds of flour, three sacks of sugar, fifty pounds of coffee, one hundred pounds of tobacco, a large number of knives, scissors, looking glasses, beads, calico, blue overalls for men, combs, playing cards, dried fruit, lead, powder, gun caps, a large lot of prize boxes, fifty smoothbore U.S. muskets, a considerable quantity of jewelry, fifty pounds of gunpowder, fifty pounds of buckshot, twenty-five pounds of musket balls, and one hundred boxes of musket caps. Two days later we were camped in a bed of the Colorado River fifty miles west of Mineral Park, our tents set up with a kind of counter erected across the tent front from which to deal out goods to the Indians.

I had taken with me my Chinese cook, who was prepared to do my bidding on this celebrated occasion. I had with me a large brass kettle holding ten gallons, which was washed out clean. We drew three or four loads of wood into camp, formed a hearth, and Stone Sawyer constructed a Mexican oven from stone and mortar of yellow clay. Our bake shop was soon under way. Fong Kee began baking bread, cooking the large brass kettle full of beans, and preparing a three-gallon coffee boiler. By ten o'clock the next morning I had on hand one hundred loaves of bread, almost twenty gallons of pork and beans, and twenty-five gallons of coffee. When everything was ready, I sent notice to the Indians by Mr. Sawyer that the next day we would be ready to trade with them. For the rest of the day we baked bread, stewed peaches, baked pies, and converted the camp into a bake shop.

The other goods were removed from the one wagon and placed on the rude counter and underneath it. The remaining wagon was wheeled around so that its rear would be facing the rear end of the tent. The rear end of the tent and the rear end of the wagon were open to each other. Now I stated that in front of the tent stood a counter, and the passage between one end of the counter and the tent was closed with canvas to prevent anyone passing through. The other passage was open to go to and from the fire, which was about ten feet from the tent. Toward the evening of the second day, when everything was ready, the Indians who were camped about two miles farther down the river began to come in.

I will here interrupt the reader to state that usually the government issues more or less from Fort Mojave to all the tribes in the vicinity; but a large part of the Hualapais, having left the reservation to wander at will over northeastern Arizona seldom receive very much from the government, and during the winter and spring of 1877–78 provisions were very scarce at the trading posts of this region. Few boats had come up the Colorado, and although the Indians had a good deal of money, they could obtain but little to eat. It was at such a time that I risked my life and property as well as the lives of others to make a little money amongst these ladies and gentlemen of copper hue.

The Indians came, as usual, in groups of ten to twenty. Never have I seen such hungry human beings. Our bread sold at fifty cents per loaf, or a loaf of bread, a cup of coffee, a plate of beans, and a small plug of tobacco for two dollars. We were kept busy all of three days selling and cooking. Below I give the price of goods sold on this occasion:

Blue cotton overalls, per pair	$3.00
Jumpers to match overalls	3.50
Tobacco, in pound or half-pound boxes	1.50–3.00
Matches, per box	1.00
Playing cards, per deck	2.00
Gun caps, per box of 100	1.00
Lead, per pound	1.00
Gunpowder, per pound	3.00
Needles, per paper	1.00
Pocket knives, each	2.00–5.00
Butcher or scalping knives, each	2.00
Sugar, per pound	1.00
Coffee, per pound	3.00
Flour, per pound	.50
Cheese, per pound	1.00
Calico, per yard	.50
Firecrackers, per box	1.00
Jew's harps, each	1.00
Tin whistles, each	.50
Red, white, and green paints, per pound	2.00
Buttons, beads, and thread were sold accordingly	

Almost all the money taken in was in American silver half dollars and Mexican dollars. Occasionally a greenback came to hand, but they were few. There were about three hundred Indians. They bought and feasted *ad gusto*. Money was plentiful among them, and they stinted neither appetite nor dress. I never saw people that seemed to value money less. One of them would come up with a lot of silver coin tied in a handkerchief. He would begin by spending two dollars for all he could eat, then the remainder for tobacco, cards, jewelry, and colored calico, going away without a cent, but happy as a king.

The smoothbore muskets we had were sold within two hours at ten dollars each. As I had paid seventy-five cents apiece for them in New York City, plus freight of about $1.75, this left me a neat margin of profit.

In trading with Indians the great difficulty is to start trade, for after one buys, the rest will follow. Their ways and manners were still savage. They would buy a hat and at once fill it with holes by way of ornament. A young man would come up to the counter, see a knife to his liking, then a piece of calico he liked. He would buy five or six yards of this red stuff, then pull off the light blue or white pants he was wearing and stand there naked before all while seeing how to arrange his new possessions. At last he would tie the calico like a scarf around his waist, draw the ends down the front, between his legs, and up the back, fastening it to the band in the back. Then he would insert the knife into the cloth on his side, and his happiness would be complete.

A squaw would come up, throw down five dollars, get six yards of bright calico. She would take this, go sit down, and within an hour come back with it made into a dress. In other cases, some of the squaws would wrap the calico or cloth around them like a blanket. They would buy sugar and eat it in masses, and dried fruit the same way; but the flour they would use to make into pretty good bread, as they used yeast. However, they preferred to buy the bread in loaves as it saved them the trouble of making it. I sold some jackets or jumpers to some old Indian men, and to my surprise one of them came up to the tent with the jumper drawn over his legs like trousers. Others would buy a shirt and tie the arms around the waist like a belt, leaving the shirt to hang down in front like an apron.

Except for the very old people, they could all speak a little Spanish and English, and some of them spoke English quite well. Hualapai Charley, who was among them, spoke English quite well, as did a short, squint-eyed man of about twenty-five who was a sort of second chief. I found them quite intelligent, but the feelings of the Hualapais toward the whites were vindictive and bitter, and even at that time a number of them were thought to be out on the warpath. The Mojaves were much more docile and of a more kindly feeling to all white men. The Mojave chief was Aritabe.[35]

During the three days we were with them, everything passed off satisfactorily. As will be seen by the quoted figures, I sold everything at a comfortable profit, and in fact I sold everything I had brought. It might be called a lucky stroke of fortune that they were in want of what I had brought.

The surplus of money the Indians had came from several sources. For one thing, they sell horses to miners, freighters, and prospectors. They are great gamblers, and get much money in that way from the Moquis and Zunis to the east. They also trade and gamble with the Navajos, and with the Paiutes. They sell grain and gietta hay to traders and travelers for twenty-five cents to one dollar a bundle. The Mojaves trade with the soldiers at Fort Mojave, and they are also good judges of silver and copper ores, and earn two dollars a day plus food sorting ore at different mines at Mineral Park, Cerbat, Ivanpa, El Dorado Canyon, and at Hiko, Nevada. At the time I traded with them, they had much more money on hand than usual because they had no place to spend it.

After selling everything we had, we were finished with these gentlemen of nature, and I realized that the best thing to do was to get out of the district as quickly as possible, for with Indians like the Hualapais or Apaches, no one knows when trouble may arise. I told Sam to tie the mules to the wagon. We cut dry grass and fed them, but did not intimate to the Indians standing around that we were to leave soon. I did not even tell Stone Sawyer, whom I had hired at Mineral Park, what I was going to do. The Indians gradually withdrew to their camp some distance away when night came, and when it was dark we had our supper. At nine o'clock we went to bed, leaving Sam Roberts and another man on watch with instructions to wake me at midnight.

When I was awakened, I sent the other guards to bed. When all was quiet, I put the money, which was mostly silver, into bags, sewed them up, and hid them in the bottom of one of the wagons. I moved everything into the wagons but the tent. I fed and watered the mules, harnessed them, and even prepared breakfast. I then woke the others. It was two o'clock in the morning. None of us had much appetite for breakfast, but we each drank two cups of strong coffee. We took down the tent, put it into the wagon, and were off in the cold-gray gloom of three o'clock in the morning.

The rest and high feeding which the mules had enjoyed the past three days gave them mettle. We pulled through the sands noiselessly, for our loads were light, and for ten miles we used buckskin freely. At that point we were on the Hardyville and Mineral Park road, and as daybreak came, we felt quite safely out of the Indian bands of the Colorado. The main road was good, and we kept up a trot until we reached Union Pass at one o'clock in the afternoon.

The excitement of the previous night left me drowsy, so we camped for the day. We set up our tents, put the animals out to graze, ate dinner, and I crept into one of the wagons to sleep. When I awoke at four, I aroused the Chinaman and helped him fix dinner for the others. After sleeping, the men looked a great deal better than when we had arrived. We sat by our fire and chatted until ten o'clock. It was a beautiful night, with the moon pouring down a flood of light over the huge red cliffs. This spot was a bloody memory, however, for it was here that a little more than a year previously I had known a man to kill himself, as I related in the history of my first expedition. Moonlight in any country has some indescribable charm, but in the south, the earth is changed into a great voiceless, dreamy paradise, and such was the night we spent at Union Pass.

Stone Sawyer was a man of more than ordinary intelligence, about forty-five years of age, and quite a gentleman in his manners. He had some good mining property at Mineral Park and over at Babylon Hill, and had accumulated some money since he had arrived in Arizona in 1870. He had traveled much since his boyhood, and, for one who had been in such active life, he was well learned. In studying his ways and manners, it was evident that there was something in the man's soul which constantly recalled his past, and conversing with him about his experiences was one of the memorable experiences of that night at Union Pass.

We were up at an early hour the next morning, crossed Sacramento Valley at a lively gait, and reached Mineral Park late in the evening. I paid off the men I had employed there and began to trade with the local residents in the store I had rented. After two days of trade with them and with residents of Cerbat who rode over for that purpose, I traded for a time with some Hualapai Indians who were sorting ores at the mines. Among other things, I sold them forty smoothbore muskets, which they wanted to use as shotguns. When I finished this trade, I sold two spans of mules and one wagon which I no longer needed to a Mr. Dixon.

We left Mineral Park early one morning and took the eastern road to the town of Hackberry. This was one of the camps I had visited the previous year, but it had grown into a camp of considerable importance, as there was a smelter and mill to reduce the ores from the Hackberry mine. It was a wild, rough camp in which about three hundred men and about ten women fought the battle of life around one mine. There were quite a number of Hualapai Indians with squaws and children around the place, begging, gambling, and busily engaged in every way to make a dollar from the white miners.

Sam Crosier and Bud Grounds had some years before discovered the Hackberry mine. Sam had come from Texas with about five hundred head of cattle. After discovering the mine, he had very soon grown to be a man of vast fortune. He owned the mill and furnace as well as the mine and the only store in the place, so that, all in all, he was the only power in the town. We did a good business for four days in Hackberry, with Sam Crosier himself as our best customer. At the end of that time, we reloaded and prepared to start for the Big Sandy Fork of Bill Williams River, where extensive work was then being done in the Signal and McCracken mines.

The Hackberry mine is situated in the Peacock Range of mountains, to the east of which rises Stein's Mountain. At the west of this mountain there is some pine and juniper timber, some grass, and a small spring. I decided to camp there for one or two days in a grove of timber and secrete the money I had. I told no one of this plan.

Our tents were in place down in a little gulch by the town of Hackberry. Two of my men were out looking for mules, my Chinese cook was attending to our kitchen, Sam Roberts was making a whiplash, and I was reading Victor Hugo's *Les Miserables* by the light of the fire. Three Hualapai women warmed themselves by our fire for about a half hour, then started toward Crosier's store. There was an old mine shaft about twenty-five feet deep and ten feet from our fire. There was still a platform and windlass, but the mouth of the shaft was open. One of the women, having just turned from our fire, could not see clearly, and tumbled into the shaft. The women's screams quickly brought a crowd, and the victim was drawn up, wet and muddy, by means of the rope which was still attached to the windlass.

We went back to our previous activities. After a time, a man with a heavy beard and a large old-fashioned Colt's cap-and-ball revolver strapped to his waist appeared. He had been drinking and was very abusive, saying that he was king of the Rocky Mountains, a fire-eater, bloodsucker, a raw-liver-devouring wildcat, a screaming tiger, and so forth. I saw that he was a dangerous fool, and, as he had his pistol drawn, there was no telling what might happen. While he was turning his head in another direction, I seized a shotgun that was near me, leveled it on him, and ordered him to depart or I would shoot him on the spot. When he saw I had the drop on him, he wheeled and went into a large saloon a short distance away. Perhaps a half hour later, I heard a pistol shot in the saloon, the doors were thrown open, and out rushed a party of men, swearing, shouting, and dragging with them the man who had a few moments before been at my fire asking for blood. The men brought him to the mineshaft the Indian woman had recently fallen into, hanged him by the rope on the windlass, then dropped his body into the mineshaft, which they then proceeded to fill with dirt. Thus was the terror of the Rocky Mountains placed into a ready-made grave. The reason for this execution was that he had shot without provocation a young man tending bar in the saloon.

I did not wish to sojourn in such an atmosphere for long, so early the next morning we went to the campsite at Stein's Mountain as previously mentioned. I planned to stay there for three or four days, so I could write and secrete my money. As there was a long waste of sand to cross before reaching the Big Sandy River, a rest was necessary for the mules as well.

It was a secluded spot. I told my men that they could go out and hunt in the mountains, as deer, turkeys, and quail were said to be plentiful there. I told Sam Roberts to scout about for better grass if there were any and sent my Chinese cook to do some family washing below the spring. I was left alone in camp. The first work was to hide the money, as I was hourly in fear of attack from highwaymen. I took a spade and found a secluded spot which I measured as being 342 yards, nineteen feet southwest from a certain juniper tree. I took a blanket and placed upon it the sod I removed, so as to leave no indication the ground had been stirred. I dug a hole about three and one-half feet deep, and placed the money in it in a large earthen jar we had used for holding preserved fruit on the way. There was a total of $5,854 in the jar. I covered up the hole and marked it with a short stake that protruded two inches from the surface, but which was not visible ten feet away because of the grass on the sod. I then nailed a small piece of wood into a notch I made in a tree twenty-two steps away. By sighting along the piece of wood, I could find the place where the money was buried. I now felt relieved that no one in all the world knew about this except myself, and unless I should die or get killed on my journey, I would return to dig it up.

I then made a map of the area, and proceeded to my other work until Fong Kee called me to dinner. After eating, I took my shotgun and went up into the mountains to hunt until nightfall. Game is quite scarce in that area, both because the Indians hunt it a good deal and because there is so little water upon which animals can subsist. But in the mountains where I now was, snow fell at times and there were several small springs, and there had been no Indians there for some time, so I felt assured that I would find deer. No doubt my men who had gone out early would bring in something.

Quail there were quite numerous in places, and there were also a few rabbits. I had my Sharp's rifle in camp, but, as the timber was quite dense, I preferred a shotgun, one barrel of which I loaded with twelve navy balls, and the other with goose shot. This gun was a muzzle-loader, but a good weapon.

I went rambling cautiously through the woods, peering into every little clump of chaparral and group of pines. I reached a patch of manzanita, and up rose a covey of Arizona quail. I fired, and since I was at a good distance, a single shot brought down nine. I hung the birds in a tree, then headed for the top of the mountain. It was a quiet place, not a breath of wind stirring, which would cause a deer or bear to hear the least noise. I went hither and thither until I reached the top, but saw nothing to shoot at.

I looked around for some time, then started down the north side. When I was about halfway down, I paused to rest in a place where the timber was heavy. I was there perhaps ten minutes when I saw directly ahead of me two deer, slyly eyeing me from about two hundred feet away. I raised my gun and fired directly into the face of the doe. She raised on her hind feet and fell to her side, giving the death kick immediately. The buck ran away through the timber and I saw no more of him. The doe was quite fat. I cut her throat, disemboweled her, and covered her over with some boughs. I took the quail and continued back to camp to get a mule to carry the deer back. When I arrived there, I found Sam Roberts at the fire awaiting me. He had killed a wildcat and twenty-one quail. We took two mules and brought my deer in. Plucking the quail and skinning the deer took all evening. The other two men returned, but had not been fortunate in obtaining any game.

We were all tired that evening and enjoyed a good supper. It consisted of part of the quail and a few slices from the doe along with some fried potatoes, bread, roasted cheese, stewed grapes, butter, and fine coffee. After eating and getting camp prepared for the night, we sat around the fire exchanging stories. I was reading Washington Irving's *Tales of a Traveler* while Sam Roberts lay full length by the fire, and the others listened, with loaded guns close at hand. I was reading Irving's tale of the devil and Tom Walker. I had reached the part where Mr. Walker and his neighbor, looking for Mrs. Walker in the swamp island where she had been doing business with the devil, saw her checkered apron containing her heart and liver hanging to the tree.

At this juncture we heard a low, long whine. Looking up, we saw near our tent a large wildcat eyeing us. In the gloom, his eyes seemed as two balls of fire. The Chinese cook picked up a shotgun and fired it at him. He sprang into the darkness mortally wounded. Taking a lantern, we found him dead about fifty yards away. We went back to our fire and I finished the story. Sam marveled at the strange stories in the books, and I wondered at the variety of life's situations.

We arose early and resumed our journey. At Free's Wash some miles away lived a family, the head of which, Mr. Stillwell, was a United States mail carrier who had just drawn a full year's pay from the government. We had met him at Mineral Park and agreed to visit his home, which was near our route to the Big Sandy. He proved to be a fine man. It was late in the day when we arrived, but we traded with the Stillwells for a few hours, and during that time he spent about ninety percent of his year's pay, besides paying me a mammoth gold ring and a large specimen of gold quartz, literally full of free gold. I strove to treat them royally in return.

The next day, we continued our travel to the Big Sandy River. The road leads over a rather beautiful country covered at that time of year with a coarse sort of grass and occasional clumps of cedar and juniper. We eventually arrived at the ranch of Sam Gordon, a pioneer who had traveled there from eastern Oregon and Nevada and was originally from Soap Creek, a few miles east of Ottumwa, Iowa. He was a natural pioneer. His family consisted of his wife and five children, three girls and two boys. His oldest daughter was named Elizabeth, locally better known as Lizzie. She was indeed a beautifully featured girl, and because she weighed about two hundred pounds, she was locally known as the Big Bonanza. Many who desired to use a more amusing expression called her the Big Kasock.

Her two sisters were attractive and her brothers amiable and well-behaved young frontiersmen.

Mrs. Gordon loved tobacco, smoked a very handsome pipe, was an exceedingly good storyteller, and had seen much of pioneer life. She prided herself on being the best soapmaker who had ever crossed the plains. As might be expected from an artist in manufacturing soap, everything around that home was as neat and tidy and clean as in a New England cottage. Mr. Gordon, or Colonel Gordon as he was locally called, was a gold prospector, rancher, and hunter. When opportunity presented itself, he was very fond of imbibing freely of beer, whiskey, or wine, at which time he would make it very interesting for all who were in his vicinity. That evening we did a lively business with the Gordon family.

The following day we arrived in Greenwood, where I found everything very lively. There were then three mining camps close to each other—Greenwood, Signal City, and Virginia City—all lively, for the silver mines to the west were being vigorously worked. Mills in those towns were reducing ore from the McCracken, Signal, and other mines. There was a great deal of money in circulation, for about five hundred men altogether were working that district. The money was in the form of checks issued on San Francisco banks. Things were especially jubilant when we arrived, for the previous day had been payday. The inhabitants of these towns included all classes of people, from the very best down to the cutthroats and renegades, stage robbers, murderers, and other men of desperate fortunes escaping justice in other states and territories.

I distinctly remember that upon taking the census of the town there were in the three camps fifty-seven white women, twenty-two Mexican women, nine Chinese women, and thirty-two Mojave and Hualapai squaws. Amongst this female population, I do not think there was one over fifty years of age. Of the gentlemen, I do not think I would be overreaching the truth to state that about forty percent had killed his man, and amongst them were several who had killed from two to seven or eight men. I found men working there as miners, millmen, bartenders, and waiters who had elsewhere been doctors, lawyers, preachers, bankers, college professors, and conspicuous figures in other lines of civilized life. Having fallen from grace or been overtaken by disaster, they were compelled upon reaching Arizona to take advantage of the first opportunity of earning bread.

During the six days I traded among those mining camps, I disposed of seventeen hundred dollars worth of goods. Among the goods I sold were fifty-seven U.S. smoothbore muskets, which Hualapai and Mojave Indians and Mexicans purchased for $570.

As before stated, all the money I received was in mining company checks or in Mexican silver coins. I had heard in a confidential way that because of poor management one or two of these mining companies were in a shaky financial condition, and judging from what I had seen in Virginia and Signal, I felt it best for me to get rid of this commercial mining paper as soon as I could.

I visited the three principal mines. Most of the ore was silver, but a small percentage was gold. The rock formation of the country was unusual, as it was in a spongy granitic form. The ores were in veins of a dark oxidized expression. Very frequently the miners ran across geodes that contained clusters of beautiful amethysts.

On the twenty-eighth day of February, 1878, I put the final touches on my traveling outfit, and it was eleven o'clock at night when we started on our way.[36] I took this late hour to avoid the attention of the many desperate characters who infested the locality. The night was cloudy and quite dark. The day before we let it be understood that we were going to start northward, possibly returning to Mineral Park, which was the truth, but I first intended to go farther south and return to Mineral Park some months later.

As it had been impossible to obtain grain for our mules at any of these mining camps, they had been obliged to graze on the poor hills nearby, and consequently were very thin. I had been feeding them as well on Hungarian grass raised by Mr. Tom Despain a few miles north of Greenwood, but it gave them a dysentery and left them very weak for the long journey from Virginia City to Phoenix.

The route for some miles was along the Sandy and wound around along the base of a bluff and through arrowwood and mesquite brush until we left Signal five miles behind. The night was dark and stormy, and rain was falling while flashes and loud peals of thunder echoed from hill to hill. I let my men drive, and I walked ahead to examine the road. I carried a lantern in one hand and a short-barreled shotgun in the other, loaded with twelve navy balls in each barrel. As the rain fell, the road grew so much worse that it was difficult for the mules to pull the heavy load, but we continued until we reached a cave east of the road and about at its level. It was now four o'clock in the morning and we were fifteen to eighteen miles from Signal.

We wheeled out of the road and up to the mouth of this cave, where there was a dry space under a wide protecting shelf of rock, and which was certainly a boon at this time. We hobbled the mules in an out-of-the-way place in the hills, took our blankets from the wagons, and placed them on the ground. We set a watch, then the rest of us went to sleep for three hours. When we awoke at seven o'clock it was storming heavily, with fierce lightning and terrific thunder. I knew the best plan was to remain in the cave for that day, as it would be likely to rain most of the time, and the food we had found for our mules was pretty good. We procured a quantity of dry mesquite wood along the river, and kept up a good fire, for the day was quite cold. The country around the cave on that wet day exhibited a wild and desolate appearance. The hills and bluff overhanging the narrow river bottom were naturally broken and ragged. There were a few cedars, then straggling giant cactus, and here and there clumps of thorny palo verde and manzanita. The giant cactus in spots stood like columns in the ruins of an ancient city. The cave itself was a huge cavity in red sandstone, with a sandy floor and a ceiling perhaps thirty feet high. It was from twenty-five to thirty feet in width, and extended back about sixty feet. Here and there on its interior walls there showed veins of brown iron ore, or limonite, and one could see where bats had been dwelling for ages along its rough arch.

We put our merchandise bales into better order, placing into more snug positions our boxes of muskets, of which I yet had more than 250. We did some little repairing to our harness and carefully examined and greased the wagon spindles. The Chinaman washed our extra linen. That morning after breakfast, Fong Kee had put a large pot of beans on the fire, with a square of excellent bacon in the center. All that day those beans continued to boil. We renewed the water from time to time, and when night came they were cooked to suit the tastes of a French epicure. With other food supplies on hand to accompany the beans, our evening meal was monumentally satisfactory.

The next morning a clear sky greeted us, and after breakfast we packed up and pulled out. The mules looked bad, for the grasses nearby did not seem to their taste, and there was no grain. The winter feed at that time in western Arizona was poor. By the time we reached Date Creek our mules were completely broken down, so that we were compelled to go into camp. I saw at once what was to be done. We would turn out our mules and let them rest until they could pick up in strength. I would leave my three men to take care of camp, and I would go on foot to Prescott, where there was a bank where I could cash the checks issued by the McCracken, Greenwood, and Signal mines. I knew one of these companies was in a doubtful condition, but did not know which one. There was a little station, or wayside saloon and eating place, kept by a man named Pierson at the point where we camped, so this spot would not be so solitary for my men; and possibly Mexicans or other parties coming up from Salt River with produce for Signal, Greenwood, and Virginia might have oats or barley that could be purchased for our mules. I gave my men instructions and left them fifty dollars in silver.

I put a big lunch into a knapsack with a large roll of checks wrapped in strong paper and a canteen. Taking a double-barreled shotgun, I started alone, taking a beeline over hill and plain for Prescott. The evening after leaving Date Creek, I reached the ranch of a Texan named Morehouse, where I stayed all night, then continued in the morning and reached Prescott as the sun was going down.

As I was in a sort of rough dress and did not want to be conspicuous, instead of going to the Hotel Montezuma, I took a room at Dan Hatz's boarding house. The next morning, as soon as the Moses Goldwater bank opened, I presented my checks and gave three and one-half cents on the dollar to have them cashed. I received in turn three five-hundred-dollar bills, fourteen one-hundred-dollar bills, five fifty-dollar bills, and one hundred dollars in five-dollar bills.

I returned to the hotel, where I sewed up this money in a secret pocket inside my vest. Then I bought some bacon and other little wants, put a lunch in my knapsack, and mailed some letters at the post office. I obtained a few copies of the *San Francisco Chronicle* in which were several of my recent letters. After a late dinner I took my knapsack and shotgun and started back to Date Creek. That night I camped by a lonely fire in the Bradshaw Mountains, and by the close of the next day I reached my camp.

I found my outfit well cared for. Fong Kee asked me if I had brought back any bacon for the beans. When I told him I had fifteen pounds of excellent fat and medium-lean bacon, he seemed to be very happy. During my absence the mules had materially improved on the grass that was turning green rapidly from the late rain. The roads were drying rapidly.

The young man named Pierson who was trying to do a little business at Date Crossing was a fugitive from justice. During that evening's conversation he confidentially informed me that he came from Oregon, and had left there by the light of the moon after having killed a man who objected to him courting his daughter. "Now they call me Pierson," he told me, "but to tell you the truth that is not my right name, and I do not intend that anyone will soon find out what my true name is."

Date Creek is a small stream that rises in the foothills of the Bradshaw Mountains southwest of Prescott and sinks into the sand some miles below Date Creek Crossing. It was on this little stream that General Crook destroyed a considerable body of Apaches some years before. There were large arrowwood thickets along its banks, some manzanita, and occasionally some mesquite. The general appearance of the country is wild and desolate.

The morning after my return, we started for Phoenix by way of Wickenburg and Smith's Mill. I did a considerable volume of business in those places and brought away a considerable quantity of gold bullion. When we reached Phoenix, I sent the bullion and the greenbacks I had gotten by cashing the checks in Prescott by express to New York City.

The climate of Phoenix at that time we found extremely pleasant, and produce there was cheap compared with what we had to pay in the mining camps. We remained for several days to allow the mules to recruit. Money was scarce, so trade there was not even up to average; so I took a journey down the river to examine a number of prehistoric monuments and old ruins and to purchase prehistoric pottery or stone implements plowed up by farmers. Strange to say, all I could get was three stone axes and one small pot cut from lava.

We visited the Maricopa villages about twenty miles west of Phoenix and found the inhabitants an interesting lot of savages who make a fair type of pottery and a good quality of wicker work from willows. They own a considerable number of horses and raise wheat, corn, melons, squash, carrots, and a good deal of lucerne, somewhat like alfalfa except that it has a larger stalk. These Indians eat great quantities of lucerne, of which they are very fond. The Maricopas number about four hundred; but they are an immoral band, and a few years will behold their extinction.

There was a Mormon settlement called Mesa, less than two years old, on the Salt River about thirty miles above Phoenix to the east.[37] They were doing quite well, as they were working on land that had been cultivated in ancient times by the extinct race. I expected to find these Mormon farmers in possession of a number of ancient artifacts, but they had not preserved many of the few they did find. I obtained from a young man a bird cut from jade which he had found in a field, and a few beautifully carved seashells. From Mr. Jones I obtained the tooth of a rhinoceros found at a depth of forty feet while digging a well.

Mesa consisted of forty or fifty families of English and native Americans from the Utah towns of Provo and Farmington. Their leader was Daniel Jones, a Mormon pioneer who had been a missionary among the Paiutes and other Arizona tribes for many years.[38] He could speak many Indian languages and Spanish. He was very interesting and very hospitable to travelers. We enjoyed our visit in this settlement and regretted that we could not remain longer.

Strange as it may appear, of the stock we had at that time, the chief articles purchased were the U.S. muzzle-loading muskets. The men and boys also bought pocket cutlery, prize boxes, and cheap musical instruments, while the women invested almost entirely in laces and fancy articles which one would not have thought would be the first articles of requirement by pioneer women, but such is human nature in all lands.

Brother Daniel Jones requested me and my men to remain one day more in their midst, as they had planned a dance that coming evening in our honor. To be agreeable, and admitting that we were inclined to enjoy such entertainments even when far from home, I acceded to his request, and the evening that followed was a very pleasant one indeed. The dance took place in a hall that was used for a ward meetinghouse on Sundays and a schoolhouse during the week. Returning a thousand thanks to Mr. Jones and all his happy associates, we departed for the regions farther south.

My stock of merchandise consisted of a rather fine and high-priced assortment of goods such as silk, laces, and broadcloth which we thought we might be better able to sell in the region south of Phoenix where there was more wealth and ready money. The previous year, while at Hermosillo, I had made acquaintance with a merchant whom I shall call Jose Reverado (though that was not his real name) and had sold him some goods.[39] When I returned to Arizona on my second expedition, I wrote to him, describing the goods I had with me, especially mentioning the two hundred smoothbore muskets, which were excellent as shotguns as well as for revolutionary and other social purposes. I also mentioned a line of cutlery, men's and women's requirements, field glasses, spectacles, and especially a plentiful supply of bowie knives and daggers. I stated that if he desired to trade, we could meet at a prominent cave in the Santa Cruz Mountains with which we were both acquainted. It was an exchange place for highwaymen, mountain traders, and professional freebooters. After trading there, he might well return into his own country without giving the Mexican revenue officers any annoyance, and in that way make the smugglers' percentage.

Mr. Reverado wrote to accept my offer; so on the twenty-third day of March we began our lonely march from Phoenix across the regions to the south. The country at that season was beautiful, with grass growing in low places, the cactus in bloom, and birds twitting from every limb. Three days' easy driving brought us to Florence, where we did a very profitable trade for a time.

At Florence, I determined that my best course of action was to leave the wagons behind and proceed by pack train. I took my eight mules and hired eight more, renting packsaddles for all, and four saddle horses. I decided to do this because of the roughness of the country into which I was going and the great difficulty of using wagons in the vicinity of the cave. This way, I could make great shortcuts across that country and save a great deal of time.

We left at three o'clock one morning and traveled along over plain and through mountain passes until the lower end of the Santa Cruz Mountains lay before us and we struck the trail that was sketched on my map. After we had pursued this course over this tortuous Indian and Mexican trail, I at length began to fear that we had taken the wrong route. But, after passing over a low country and reaching the base of a mountain or terrace, I beheld a solitary horseman on a point about a mile away. He was waving his hand to us, so I knew we were right and near the cavern. The horseman rode up, shook hands with us all around, called down a thousand blessings on our heads, and told us he had been awaiting our arrival for two days. It was Reverado.

Their camp was in a small basin or alcove in the mountains beautifully shut out from the world. The cave was of considerable size. It showed signs of having been long the rendezvous of the wild Apaches, who had lately been replaced by prospectors, hunters, highwaymen, or bands of smugglers like those with whom I had come to trade. There was a small spring about one hundred yards from the cave, very good grass abounded, and we had plenty of provisions, so I was in no hurry to leave. There were three other Mexicans besides Reverado, one of whom was a nephew, another was a brother-in-law, and the other a *creado*, or servant, part packer and part cook. They had killed two deer before our arrival, and with what we had with us there was no end of good cheer. Spanish beans, venison, Mexican bread or tortillas, loaf bread, honey, sweet potatoes roasted in the ashes, excellent coffee with good sugar, and a mountain appetite with which to relish these things left us happy.

We piled our goods in packs and bales in the large open cave which was well lighted during the greater part of the day by the southern sun, and spread our blankets alongside the merchandise. Although the cave was well lighted, it was black as jet on its walls from the smoke of centuries of barbarians' fires. Quantities of bat guano that filled the fissures of the cavern walls gave off a not overly pleasant odor. This ammonia odor came from pitchlike guano in every remote crevice, but was soon overcome.[40]

As usual, my own party was well armed, each one with a Sharp's carbine or short shotgun and a Colt's caliber-45 six-shooter. We guarded our mules day and night against plundering visits from Indians, Mexicans, or white horse thieves.

While eating supper, I noticed something burning among the ashes, and Antone, the servant, told me it was mezcal which they had put to roast, and that by morning it would be excellent. After supper we sat by the fire smoking Mexican cigars and telling old and new stories until almost midnight. Señor Reverado had served his country as a lieutenant in the wars of Maximilian and had been engaged in many petty revolutions, sometimes on the side of the government, sometimes the reverse. He had been a miner, but was now engaged in business at Hermosillo and sometimes doing a little smuggling. "It would be impossible," he told me while sitting there by the fire, "for me to pay duty to the government and make anything myself, so I never lose a chance of this kind, as it enables me to sell at a fair profit and give my customers goods at a very reasonable value." He told me that he had smuggled goods for twenty years and had never been taken in the act, while others had been taken in their first attempt.

His nephew had a concertina or accordion and the servant a mouth organ. They played far into the night, and it was after midnight when we fell asleep.

I awoke before the others to the breath of a balmy morning. I went outside and saw the mules on the side of the mountain to the west quietly feeding on the sweet green grass and the watchman reclining against a juniper tree. Fong Kee soon prepared our breakfast. The mezcal was taken from the ashes in a prime state for eating. It was better than anything of its kind that I had ever had before. When breakfast was over, the cooking utensils were moved to one side, our blankets rolled carefully, tarpaulins spread on the floor of the cave, and the goods were opened one bale at a time.

I had but little difficulty in trading with Señor Reverado. All the goods were placed at a reasonable price which gave me about 150 percent profit on a large part of my merchandise, 200 percent on others. The muskets were still priced at ten dollars, and Señor Reverado stated that he would at once close the deal on them. I still had 160 of the five hundred with which I had started. As they were smoothbore, Señor Reverado saw that they could be used either as shotguns for hunting or, if necessary, for political or revolutionary purposes. They had been the most inconvenient feature of our mule packing and had taken up the service of a little more than half of my packtrain from Florence, so I was glad to get rid of them.

The muskets disposed of, our trade began on bolts of dress goods, such as silk, poplins, and cotton fabrics, then rolls of blue and black broadcloth, underwear and shirts for men, two bales of laces and varieties of women's goods, four cases of pocket knives, razors, and bowie knives, then thirty-six caliber-45 Colt's revolvers. I received a variety of exchange in payment, including American greenbacks and trade dollars, Mexican silver dollars, about fifty pounds of silver bullion, and a few Mexican gold doubloons. The sun was setting when we finished our business, and each was left to start on his respective way the next morning.

Señor Reverado piled his goods in his own corner of the cave, and in the greatest good fellowship we remained another night in the smoky quarters. While breakfast was being prepared the next morning, we separated our mules from those of the Mexicans. After we had eaten, we saddled the ones that were best spirited and easiest in gait, packed up our money and specie, and took a sorrowful farewell of Señor Reverado and his party.

We returned the extra mules and pack saddles to their owners in Florence. The next day I sold two wagons and four mules to a mining company for one thousand dollars. With what remained, four mules and one wagon, we continued our northward journey.

We passed through Phoenix and on past the Vulture Mine. While crossing the Hassayampa Plains we beheld a barbarous-looking outfit coming toward us, consisting of three spans of horses hitched to an old wagon on which there were high bows and a loosely fastened old cover, dirty and flopping in the wind like the torn sail of a ship during a storm. They proved to be a pioneer family named Drew from near Bozeman, Montana. He was a millwright by trade but was now seeking a new location in which to settle, and was headed for the valley of the Santa Cruz in southeastern Arizona. I found he had money and was in a trading humor. We concluded to trade wagons, I receiving two hundred dollars to boot. The one we obtained was an old miserable ruin, narrow-tracked and long-coupled, but we hitched our remaining two spans of mules to it and bade Mr. Drew and his family good-bye.

In Wickenburg we shortened the old wagon by about one-half by putting in a short coupling pole and cutting away half the bed. In this way it was a much lighter draft and, as we had but little load, we spun along beautifully. We passed through Signal and Greenwood and returned to Free's Wash, near where I had buried the money earlier. I went there and dug up the treasure, which had not been molested.

We continued back through Mineral Park and on to the Colorado River, then up to the rascally miserable sand-drifted region of the Virgin River with its many crossings of quicksand, and on to St. George and Silver Reef. We remained there for one day to meet some old mining friends, then pushed northward. In time we reached Provo, where I paid off Sam Roberts. We continued to Salt Lake City and Ogden, where I paid off and discharged my remaining two men and the Chinaman. I sold my narrow-tracked wagon for a song and disposed of my four mules and harness to a Montana freighter. The net proceeds totaled $6,954, and so ended the expedition on June 29, 1878.

(September 9, 1883—San Francisco)

Map of Don Maguire's third expedition to Arizona; found with manuscript and believed to be drawn by Maguire. USHS

3.

Third Arizona Expedition

WHILE PREPARING IN NEW YORK CITY for my third venture into Arizona and Mexico, I again intended to procure a quantity of goods for the Indian trade in southern Nevada and Arizona. But upon returning to Utah I was informed through my correspondents in Arizona and at Eldorado Canyon, Nevada, that conditions were not at all encouraging for trade with those Indians; so I was compelled to thus reconsider my course in relation to the goods then in transit to York station in Utah.[1] In carefully weighing the situation, I decided to trade instead with the Paiute Indians of eastern Nevada.

In the counties of White Pine, Lincoln, and Nye there was an extensive wandering population of Paiute Indians outside the reservation who sometimes worked around the mining camps, the men cutting wood and sorting ore, and the women doing drudge work for white families. Many of them also worked for cattle- and horsemen and on ranches scattered over a wide area. These Indians thus lived their own life, and worked when they felt like doing so. Others would live temporarily at unappropriated springs in the wilderness, while grass was abundant for their horses and there was an abundant supply of rabbit meat, crickets, grasshoppers, pine nuts, and grass seeds for themselves. Such Indian gathering places as these were called rancherias. There were very few white men then in these thinly settled areas, and many of them were living with Paiute squaws on cattle and horse ranches, some of them raising families, and occasionally employing Indian men and women.

On my first expedition, I had pretty well studied the Indian situation in Utah and Nevada, had done business at many of the Paiute rancherias, and knew that in parts of those areas, the semi-industrial Paiute Indians had considerable volumes of ready money, and that there was also much trade to be obtained from the limited white population. I saw that my best plan of disposing of my stock of Indian goods shipped to York was to make a side expedition into Nevada for a term of from thirty to forty-five days. My mind was made up quickly.

As soon as I returned to Ogden after my journey to New York City I proceeded to Corinne, Utah, where I supposed I could obtain good mules at lower prices than I had hitherto paid to Bishop Layton at his stock farm southwest of Ogden. I would have to have, as on my previous expedition, twelve head of mules to haul three wagons.

I was only successful in securing four head of mules at Corinne of such class animals as I required. These four head, however, were well matched, young, and of high merit, and I paid for them five hundred dollars. I obtained them from Mr. Adam Cuhn, a wholesale merchant at Corinne, who had them in trust and for sale from a mountain freighter. The remaining eight mules required I was compelled to obtain from Bishop Layton near Kaysville, Utah, for nine hundred dollars. At Ogden I again purchased three Peter Schettler wagons from Burton, Herrick, and White. Mule harnesses for this coming Arizona expedition I obtained in Salt Lake City.

While at Corinne, I hired a teamster of considerable reputation in his line, Isadore Mooncraft, a native of Ohio, thirty-four years old. I also obtained a Chinaman named Quong Hing as cook. He was recommended to me by John Guthrie, a Corinne banker, and proved to be a very good man. Because of his reported ability, I was compelled to pay him sixty-five dollars a month with board, and I paid Mooncraft seventy-five dollars a month with board. A third man, Mandel Cole, a Virginian, I hired also for seventy-five dollars per month. Cole would not hire out for longer than sixty days, as he had plans after that date to go to California.

With the above men, mules, horses, wagons, and tents and camping outfits, I drove at once overland from Ogden to York, Utah, which as previously stated was the terminus of the Utah Southern Railroad, at which point I found the merchandise shipped from New York City awaiting me.

The first and initial point for trade was at Frisco, in Beaver County, Utah, where the famous Horn Silver Mine was then being worked. I opened trade there for ten days, doing extremely well with the population of that mining camp. Finishing my business there, I wheeled my caravan down to Horseshoe Bend, a half-day's drive east from Frisco, where at Bingham's ranch I left two wagons loaded with merchandise for the Arizona trade. I also left eight mules and one of my men to look after the property. I took with me Mandel Cole, Quong Hing, and one wagon loaded to its utter capacity with goods for white and Indian trade.

It was yet the month of July, 1878. Leaving Horseshoe Bend, I again passed through Frisco and went westward forty miles to Wah Wah Springs, where at the end of the first day's long drive we rested at Squire's Station, or spring. A father, mother, two sons, and four old-maid daughters dwelt there. His name, if I remember correctly, was Samuel Squires. They were most interesting people, living there in amity, worldly prosperity, and perfect contentment.

The next day we went on to Thousand Springs Valley, to the well-known ranch of Colonel Cleveland, with whom I traded extensively and sojourned on my first expedition to Arizona in October, 1876. From there we went on to Oceola, Nevada, at the northwest base of Jeff Davis Mountain, where there were placer gold mines. I opened trade there for three days and purchased gold dust to the value of fifteen hundred dollars, on which I cleared at the San Francisco mint one dollar and twenty cents per ounce.

My next objective was Kern Creek, southern White Pine County, and northeastern Nye County, Nevada, where then dwelt a Mr. Alexander McCulloch, a ranchman and Indian trader. I had thirty days previously written to Mr. McCulloch of my desire of visiting his locality with a stock of Indian goods, and would trade at his place; and, as on my first visit, I was to pay him fifteen percent of all sales. When I wrote, I requested that he send out Indian couriers to Duck Creek, Hot Creek, Duck Water, and upper Steptoe Valley informing rancherias of Paiute Indians that a trader of Indian goods would reach his place by the next full moon, and for all who had money to come forward.

When we arrived at McCulloch's place, we unloaded the entire stock of goods into his storehouse, which was now empty and prepared for me. I had remained there but two days after putting all things into readiness when the Indians began coming in, all of them having more or less money, most of which was in silver coin. I had legal protection, as I had secured a county trader's license, and, the Indians not being on a government reservation, I was thus entitled to trade with them the same as with anyone else.

The men and women sent as messengers stated that I had with me paints, calico, Indian beads, knives, sugar, prize boxes, combs, looking glasses, needles, thread, fish hooks, tobacco, cards, colored cloth and other articles. The Indians would also be given a chance to gamble, run horse races, and carry on Indian dances and courtships, so that such a coming together would constitute what in mountain parlance would be called a "general blow-out."

Mrs. McCulloch hired three or four of the neighbor ranch women to assist her in baking from six to eight hundred loaves of bread, two hundred pies, and twice as many doughnuts in a large outdoor Italian oven. Ten head of sheep, two steers, and three hogs were prepared for slaughter.

On the third day, the trade with these Indians was on full blast, and for four days, or as long as money lasted, business was good. Mr. and Mrs. McCulloch were called upon for all the food supplies they had provided for anxious Indian stomachs. Dancing, horse racing, and gambling went on day and night, as I kept up the sale of goods. As no whiskey was permitted, there was fairly good order. Of course, when the horse racing was on, wild excitement was rife, and during the nights medicine men carried on the chants and drum beating usual at Indian ceremonials. On the evening of the fifth day, I had sold out completely, and Mr. and Mrs. McCulloch had disposed at good profit of all the food supplies. The affair began in friendship and ended without bloodshed.

On the morning of the seventh day, the Indians scattered without ceremony, seemingly to the four winds, going back to their rancherias. The McCulloch family and myself were left to count the returns. Mrs. McCulloch gathered in a little over seven hundred dollars, and I made $4,143.50, from which I paid $619.55 to Mr. and Mrs. McCulloch for their fifteen percent commission, leaving me a net profit after deducting all costs of help and other daily expenses of $2,270.75. Even this is much less than I would have made had I been enabled to sell this lot of merchandise to Arizona Indians.

After the Indian trading was completed and the Paiute customers departed, the closing event was a dance given by Mr. and Mrs. McCulloch at their home. All the white inhabitants of Kern Creek were invited, including the Lemons; the Saburnes; Dick Barnes and his wife, Szrar; Moses Landers and his Indian wife; Peter Rascob; and Eusebius Seiboldt and his sister Catherine, the local schoolteacher. A dozen couples from Cherry Creek were invited, including Mattie and Blanche Bates and their admirers James S. Carlton and Winfield Porter. The Cherry Creek people arrived on the Elko and Pioche stagecoach that ran past McCulloch's ranch. Two violinists came down from Hamilton. The dancing began at one o'clock in the afternoon and continued until seven o'clock the next morning, when guests, fiddlers, and entertainers were completely done for and when musicians and dancers gave over all efforts and retired for rest. At six o'clock the next evening, by the light of the summer moon, most of the guests departed.

At Kern Creek Eusebius Sieboldt, who had been an overseer for Mr. McCulloch and whom I found to be an excellent man, desired to join my command when he learned that Mandel Cole was then ready to leave for California. I hired Eusebius Sieboldt on the same terms as Mr. Cole, who took a stage for California. I saw him no more.

I here repeat that Eusebius proved to be an excellent man. Sieboldt and his sister were natives of a little Maryland town, evidently of very good family. His sister Catherine was engaged to teach school at Kern Creek for two years. Eusebius took temporary leave of his little sister, then my party returned to Horseshoe Bend in Beaver County, Utah.

Prior to my starting for my Indian trade adventure in Nevada, I had ordered by telegraph from New York City to be forwarded to me by express to York station a large consignment of gentlemen's silk handkerchiefs, twenty-five double-barreled shotguns, twenty-five pairs of field glasses, and a quantity of goods for my Indian friends at St. Thomas Indian reservation on the Muddy River in Nevada. When these arrived, I continued on my southward journey, going first to St. George by way of Mountain Meadows. I wanted to camp one night on that accursed spot where one hundred and thirty persons had been inhumanly massacred in September, 1857, after having surrendered themselves into the hands of white men under the promise of mercy, which they were not shown, but atrociously murdered under circumstances the most revolting in American history.

It was late one afternoon when I reached the scene of the massacre. It is a narrow valley between low mountains. There had been there formerly a flowing spring near to which the immigrants on their way to California were camped when attacked by John D. Lee's Utah militia and a small party of Paiute Indians. At the time of our visit to this spot the spring was totally dried up. A deep gully or wash had been cut through the locality, supposed to have been done by a cloudburst some time during the sixties. The grass once so abundant had disappeared. The scene around was bleak, gray, and desolate. On the spot where the massacre had taken place there was a cairn or pile of boulders adjacent to the banks of the deep wash. There was no other monument. About 1859, federal officers from Camp Floyd erected here a large cross, but that had been destroyed. Less than two miles to the northeastward, but out of sight because of low hills, was the small ranch of Jacob Hamblin, who for years had been a Mormon missionary and interpreter to the local Paiutes.

It was late in the evening. Since we had some barrels of water and bales of hay with us, we camped there for the night. We set up our tents, prepared our evening meals on a fire made from wood we had taken with us from where we camped the previous noon. It was a time of the waning moon. After our supper had been eaten and our camp put into order I walked out alone over the field round about the spot where our camp stood. It had grown quite dark. There were some clouds in the sky. A few score stars gave a faint light. Coyotes from the hills to the westward sent forth their long, mournful howls. I thought of how their ancestors twenty-one years before on just such a similar night howled and feasted on the unburied slain that were left to rot and fester on this desolate spot.

From Mountain Meadows, the next morning we went through Gunlock Valley, midway between Mountain Meadows and St. George. Before the close of that day we reached the neat and tidy little Mormon city, St. George, situated in the southwest corner of Utah. I prepared to go to Silver Reef, a mining camp twenty miles to the northeast, where there were several parties whom I wished to see. I left my caravan in care of my men at Crosby's hotels and stables, where the men put up our tents for camping, and I took the mail stage up to Silver Reef.

I transacted my business with Colonel John Wall, a prominent mining man of that camp, and some other matters, then found an old friend, Con Dawson, whom I had known some years previous. I employed him to accompany me on this third expedition, as he was an excellent salesman. He had come to California during the early fifties, had been with General Walker in Nicaragua, and later went into the Frazer River excitement in British Columbia. He mined on the Comstock and carried on mercantile work in California and Nevada. Now down to the first principles of his fortune, he was anxious to take service with me. The next day we returned by stage to St. George.

At St. George, Utah, through a commercial firm of Woolley, Lund and Judd, I made purchases of bacon, hams, wine, honey, Utah raisins, and other Dixie products at sacrificial prices, as well as certain other lines of merchandise at figures beyond where I could have obtained them elsewhere. I employed three more wagons with four horses to each wagon and six teamsters to take the purchases made at St. George into Mojave County, Arizona.

As it took four or five days to gather the local produce, I and my four men were compelled to be patient. We passed our time either in visiting amongst the Mormon families in St. George or attending to our own caravan that was now being well rested for a long journey through the sands of the Virgin River to St. Thomas and the Colorado River.

St. George is the metropolis, the Paris, the Athens, the Mecca of southern Utah. Owing to its semitropical climate, the Mormons call Washington County, Utah, "Dixie," inasmuch as they had for some years been growing cotton, pomegranates, figs, almonds, English walnuts, sugar cane, yams, sweet potatoes, very fine cantaloupes, gourds, and watermelons. At St. George, Silver Reef, Leeds, Washington, and Toquerville here in southern Utah from October 1st to May 15th the climate is delightful, springlike, and dreamy, the scenery weirdly beautiful and impressive. These southern Mormons are becoming like the country round about, taking to a dreamy, easy, pleasure-loving life, fond of dancing and making the most of privileges granted by the orthodox branch of the Mormon religion.

The temple here at St. George does a thriving business. From other parts of Utah come hundreds of the faithful Mormons, men and women, some to be sealed for eternity to their wives, and others to be sealed to women who are not yet their wives. Other men and women come to be baptized for themselves for the first time; others, men and women who have been exposed out in the Gentile world and who there might have committed sin, come here and in the temple are again baptized a second, third, or fourth time, as are also those who fall from grace at home either by horse- or cattle stealing, false swearing, or by being too sociable with brothers, sisters, wives, or daughters. Then again, men and women go through the temple to be baptized for the dead—such nice people as he or she may have known or read about, who did not know of the truths of Mormonism but, had they known of this true and everlasting gospel, would most certainly have become Mormons. For these and such, a member of the true faith has only to act as proxy, go through the temple, take the name of such or such a brother or sister, be baptized in the great laver, or bronze tank, and the departed of good heart is saved unto eternity. For this reason I have been told that George and Martha Washington, General Lafayette, Paul Revere, Andrew Jackson, Millard Fillmore, Abraham Lincoln, Julius Caesar, the poets Virgil, Homer, Dante, Petrarch, Robert Burns, Lord Byron, Tom Moore, along with their wives and sweethearts have thus been saved through baptism for the dead according to the formula taught by the true and everlasting gospel of Mormonism.

Owing to the fact of our good behavior, gentlemanly ways, and also because I was doing business with the people, my men and I were quite welcome in the homes of the church dignitaries. Whilst in St. George we attended two or three dances, and the local bishop doing the services at the ward meetinghouse prayed for us conjointly with the young Mormons who were going to drive the teams hired to haul our purchases into Arizona.

All things being ready in due time, my wagon train pulled away from St. George by way of Santa Clara, thence down to Beaver Dam and on to Bunkersville. After making the fifty-seven quicksand crossings of the Virgin River, we reached St. Thomas, where I found myself once more at the Paiute Indian reservation of the Muddy River Indians. I found welcome from Colonel Jennings and his worthy wife, whom I had seen the year before.

Upon reaching St. Thomas we had the satisfaction of having a mystery solved. The day after leaving Santa Clara, the town near St. George, Utah, our route veered over into the state of Nevada and, leading southward, the road was going down a gradual slope. The country was wide open as a broad plain. While seated next to the driver on the front wagon, I saw two objects far ahead on the right-hand side of the road. At first I took these objects to be two animals lying down, but drawing my field glasses upon them, I found them to be two men outstretched by the roadside. We first saw them at a point perhaps half a mile away. When we reached the spot, we found them to be two dead men, one of them shot through the head and lying on his face, the other lying on his back, his arms outstretched. He had been shot through the neck, through the right hand, and through the right leg at the knee. A good deal of coagulated blood was upon the ground near them, and on their faces and necks. One of the men appeared to be about forty years of age with rather long brown hair. He had a short beard and mustache. The other man I would take to be about thirty years of age. Both were of medium build. They were dressed in fairly good clothing and wore dark woolen shirts. Two hats lay near them, and both men wore spurs.

A Colt's six-shooter lay near to one of them, and alongside of the man shot through the side of the head there lay a United States Army carbine, caliber forty-five, Model 1873. Around the spot were the boot tracks of three or four persons and the tracks of horses showing the imprints of the toe corks of the horses' shoes. Brass cartridges for revolvers and for the carbine that lay near the dead man and shells for a forty-four Winchester rifle were there. It was evident that there had been a gunfight and that two of the victims were left where they had fallen. But who were they, and by whom were they killed?

We did not touch the bodies. I made note of the time of day in which we saw them, and the appearance and dress of each. When we reached Bunkerville, we reported our gruesome discovery; but no one could or would give us any information. At St. Thomas we learned from the mail carrier that the two dead men were named Sloan and Graham. They were two of four horse thieves and stage robbers; the other two were named Bill McMannus and Texas Charlie. They had been overtaken by the sheriff of Lincoln County, Nevada, and his deputies for a stage holdup near Desert Springs, Nevada. In the fight, Sloan and Graham were killed and McMannus was shot through the left arm. He and Texas Charlie escaped by riding at a furious gait down into the chapparal along the Virgin River to the east. Later in the day on which we saw the dead men, a sheriff's posse from Pioche, Nevada, and another posse from St. George, Utah, with two wagons and a half-dozen mounted men came for the bodies. They were taken to Pioche and buried.

We pitched our tents at St. Thomas and a fine campfire was soon blazing. I went over to Colonel Jennings's house, which constituted the Indian agency of St. Thomas. There I purchased some fresh beef, and as I was cutting up some of it to fry for supper a young man of about twenty-five years rode up to our camp. He was well dressed in a suit of gray tweed with a white shirt and wore considerable jewelry. He was mounted on a spirited sorrel horse. He spoke quite pleasantly and inquired if he could have supper with us.

While eating supper he asked many questions about the town of Silver Reef and about Salt Lake City. I supposed from his dress that he was a gambler going from some of the mining camps of northern Arizona up into Utah. When supper was over, he wanted to pay me for it, but I would not accept and told him to tie his horses to the hay from which my mules were eating. "I see you have clothing for men on board your outfit," he said. "I will do some trading with you by and by, or perhaps in the morning." He went over to the house of Colonel Jennings, where he secured a bed for the night, then returned to our fire to talk until bedtime.

He seated himself on his saddle, and removed from his waist a large money belt which he deliberately opened, saying that he feared it might have been dampened by sweat during the day's hard riding. He began taking out bills in packages of twenties, fifties, and one-hundred-dollar bills. I was almost petrified from surprise at seeing a man showing so much money to strangers in a far wilderness. He ran through his hands about ten thousand dollars in greenbacks. Looking them over, he put them back into the belt and again buckled it around his waist.

I said to him, "Young man, you must have been selling a mine or robbing a stagecoach. Which was it?"

He laughed and said, "Neither. I have been contracting over at Tip Top Mining District south of Prescott, Arizona, and this little swag constitutes my summer's earnings, and I do not intend that it shall get mouldy, so I take it out to air it occasionally. But now that we have time, throw some of your clothing in sight. I want a heavier suit of clothes than these to wear as I am going north."

I requested Con Dawson to take two bales of clothing from one of the wagons, and the dandylike cavalier chose a suit of clothes at forty-five dollars, with shirts and underwear to the value of ten dollars more, handing to me a fifty-dollar U.S. Treasury note and a five-dollar bill for payment of the purchase. I was going to wrap up the suit for him, but he said, "No, leave them in the wagon where I can have them in the morning," and with this remark he bade us goodnight and went to his lodging at Colonel Jennings's.

After breakfast at the Colonel's, he returned. We had taken care of his horse during the night, and, after talking for a few moments, he took the suit of clothes he had purchased the previous evening and changed clothes behind a clump of willows, throwing the suit he had taken off on the ground. I said to him that we would wrap them up in a parcel and tie them to his saddle bow.

"No," he answered, "They do not amount to anything." And, after shaking hands with us, he rode away. The fine suit of clothes which could not have been worn more than a week or ten days, and which he threw on the ground, Con Dawson very wisely picked up and appropriated, saying that he had been desiring such a suit of clothes for a long time.

At Colonel Jennings's we learned still more about the extreme liberality of this young man. He had arisen quite early and went into the barnyard where he killed two chickens and told Mrs. Jennings he wanted them for breakfast, and that she might charge accordingly for them. After breakfast, he gave her a ten-dollar note, saying that she might keep it all for his breakfast and lodging. She said that it was too much, and returned eight dollars, whereupon he threw the eight dollars to her little girl Liddie, telling her to buy candy with it when she would next go up to St. George.

He had told me that his name was Harold Sinclair, but I knew that was a lie, as such a name was too high-toned and far-fetched to travel with in a sand-reefed, sagebrush desert; and I felt that he was nearer to the truth when he told Colonel Jennings that his name was George Howell.

We moved our wagons over to the agency buildings, where we remained for one or two days to rest and trade before attempting the heavy sands between there and the Colorado River. My old friends the Muddy Indians came to see me about noon, and a number of their old men, amongst them the gray-haired Chief Shinbone, told me that they were very glad to see me back again, although they had not much money this time. However, I told them to sit down under one of the large cottonwoods near the Colonel's house. The Colonel coming up and hearing what was being said, winked at me and said, "Go on and smoke the pipe of peace, and when you are through come into the house."

We sat there in a circle. A large Indian pipe that I had with me was filled with tobacco, lighted, and passed around four times, each one taking four whiffs in silence. After this, one of the old men wanted to know what I had for sale. I said I had some Indian goods, and that on the morrow I would be very glad to open trade with them after having talked with the agent, Colonel Jennings, to get his permit.

"Oh," said Shinbone, "Colonel Jennings. Let him go to the devil. Maybe so he not want us to trade, but he no let us trade; I go up to St. George and buy from the Mormons." I then told him and the others that Colonel Jennings was my friend and he was perfectly willing that I should carry on trade with them, and for them to be ready on the next day and I would have a wagon unloaded in the storehouse to trade with them. So the circle was broken up until evening when we were to meet for another big talk and another smoke.

On that evening they gathered at the same place. I went out there, bringing with me about ten pounds of cubed sugar on a dish, and the pipe of peace, which we smoked for about an hour, after which I passed around the cubed sugar four times, which they appreciated very much; and then in a very thankful way they left me for the night.

The next morning I sold them between three- and four hundred dollars in goods, receiving my pay almost entirely in silver coin, some of which was Mexican dollars. By noon the next day I began my trade with Colonel Jennings, to whom I sold the remainder of my stock of Indian goods for the sum of eight hundred and seventy-four dollars, almost one-half of which was profit. Such was the inducement of trading with Indians in those early dangerous days. Had I sold those same goods on the lower Colorado I would have made a profit of almost three hundred percent, but to Colonel Jennings naturally enough, and according to the rules of justice, I must allow a fair margin for profit.

When I finished trading, I concluded to remain for one more day, to visit with himself and family, and talk with the Indians. Chief Shinbone was lamenting that the Muddy River Indians were not so many in number as when I was there the previous year. They were growing fewer and fewer, and poorer and poorer. He told me all his woes, those of his own and of all of the Paiute tribe at that point. It was with a feeling of relief that our big talk ended, for I hate to see humanity anywhere on the decline as it was amongst those poor vagabond Muddy River Indians.

The drive from St. Thomas to the river was heavy with deep sand as usual. On my previous expedition, we crossed at Stone's Ferry on the Colorado, but on this occasion I changed my course, going lower down to Bonelli's Ferry.

Mr. Bonelli was a Swiss Italian who, having become a member of the Mormon Church, immigrated to Utah and settled at Santa Clara, west of St. George, where he owned a very profitable vineyard and manufactured a large quantity of wine each year. To add to his revenue, he came down to the Colorado and established a second ferry, dividing the profits of that industry with young Mr. Thompson at Stone's Ferry.[2] As he kept a small stock of trade goods in his store at the ferry and desired to trade with us, I remained at his place one day, selling him several hundred dollars worth of goods, chiefly men's clothing, gloves, a number of double-barreled shotguns, and a number of Colt's improved six-shooters.

The next day we crossed the Colorado and continued toward Mineral Park, the county seat of Mojave County. We found the road very heavy going from the Colorado until reaching Nobman's Station near Chloride

Camp, some miles north of Mineral Park. Mr. Nobman was a down-east Yankee of German descent, married to an Irish woman of the second generation. They also handled a small quantity of merchandise, and we spent one day selling them several hundred dollars worth of such merchandise as they could handle.

At Mineral Park the usual welcome awaited me and my men, and I sold at a very reasonable profit all the Utah produce I had purchased at St. George. I then paid off the six men I had hired to bring the produce down from Utah. For the next six days I was very busily engaged in trade, selling a similar line of goods to what I had sold the previous year.

After my trade was completed, a number of people insisted that my men and I should remain in town for a dance they were going to have in our honor the following evening.

As on my former expedition, the entertainment was a most interesting one. The beauty and chivalry of the camp was present that night in the town's one large hall. At midnight there were refreshments consisting of roast beef, bread, canned fruit, and a very agreeable brand of Mexican wine. The affair lasted until seven the next morning, and my entire force and I were so jaded by our night's dancing that we were compelled to lay over until the following day. We started away from their hospitable little town at five o'clock in the morning, fearing that if we remained until a later hour they might attempt inducing us to remain for another dance the following night.

I did not on this occasion attempt to go down to Signal or Greenwood or Virginia mining camps on the Big Sandy, as we learned that the mills down in that region were shut down and the mines employing but very few men. So, upon our leaving Mineral Park, my next point of interest was at Hackberry, where we ran up our colors and for four days carried on an exceedingly profitable trade, as we had done on my previous trip.

To the northeast of Hackberry there was a large cattle camp or ranch owned by some men from Texas, to which we went next. It was situated near a spring around which grew scrubby pines and juniper. The chief owner was a Texan named Bud Grounds. As well as being largely interested in this ranch, he was a large part-owner in the Silver Lead mines at Hackberry. He had a wife and two daughters who gave the camp home a comfortable air. They lived in a log house roofed with cactus and pine bows, covered over with a stratum of clay about six inches in depth. Saddles and long-hair ropes, or riattas, were hanging on the outside of the house. There was a shed or veranda on the south side of the house, and there were three more saddles lying nearby on the ground east of the house. Three large hounds were there also. From the rafters of this veranda hung two quarters of beef and two deer.

The interior of the house was warm and pleasant. Mr. Grounds came home a short time after our arrival. I had known him from my previous expedition. He was a whole-souled, good-natured fellow. Some years before, he had brought a band of cattle into these hills and fortunately had discovered a very profitable silver mine near Mineral Park, known as the Morning Star. Later he also became part-owner, as I have stated, in the mines of Hackberry. We pitched our tents at his place and spent the next day trading with him and his family and from ten to fifteen cowboys in his employ.

The country around Hackberry and Mineral Park abounds in good grass, and from Hackberry to the northeast lies a magnificent country for grazing livestock. This country extends to Bill Williams Mountain about sixty miles away. Over these plains and rolling hills here and there are large clumps of pine and juniper, and in the hollow lands there exist groves of walnut, ash, and hackberry; but these, however, are of slender growth owing to the extremely dry climate of Arizona. Deer and antelope are plentiful in these wooded localities, and through the chaparral there are quail, pheasants, and in places considerable numbers of wild turkeys.

Over this part of Arizona are rich gold and silver veins in every mountain, but only few of them were worked at the time of my travels there. The red soil of the region proves the presence of iron ore in abundance. There exists plenty of good building material of stone and wood, and although water is scarce at present, it will be but a few years until artesian wells will pipe forth living streams to irrigate the stockmen's herds that will increase tenfold in this well-grassed region. The great Hualapai Valley, which runs north and northwest of this region east of Hackberry, has excellent soil with abundance of grass. Let water be brought upon this vast area and it would produce more than all of New England.

The Hualapai Indians wander from their reservation along the south side of the Colorado River into these hills and plains to hunt. They are at the present time peaceful toward whites, although during my two first expeditions into Arizona they had been rather warlike for some months, during which time they were suspected of killing four or five prospectors.

From Mr. Bud Grounds's ranch we went south to the old overland road running west from Prescott to Hardyville on the Colorado River. At this point I thought it wise to continue to the south and visit a small mining camp where deposits of rich silver ore had been discovered during the previous summer, and at which point there were then supposedly forty to seventy-five miners. Much of my stock of merchandise was suited to the requirements of such people. In a day and a half we reached this new mining locality, then known as Cedar District. I found there were some very rich silver ores which also contained considerable values in gold. I found there several men whom I had previously known at Mineral Park, and about a dozen from Greenwood, Signal, and Virginia, where they had been mining the year before. The locality was a very interesting one, and for three days we remained there doing a fairly good business. My Chinaman, Quong Hing, was kept very busy feeding the many visitors who came to trade.

From the Cedar District, we again turned northward to the old overland road from Prescott to Hardyville; and on this road we traveled eastward until we reached a point about fifty miles west of Prescott, where we turned to the right down into Walnut Grove, or Walnut Grove Valley. This is a long, narrow valley, cultivated in spots, and in the hills on both sides there exist gold, silver, and copper veins that were then but little worked. The gravel along the bed of this valley's main stream carries considerable placer gold and in past years a good deal of gold has been taken out. Walnut Grove was, between the years 1860 and 1875, the scene of very many bloody murders by the Chiricahua Apaches, who then roamed over all this western part of Arizona. Many prospectors and miners in this region fell victim to these savages.

For three weeks my caravan traded in the region of Walnut Grove Valley, Williamson's Valley, Skull Valley, Peeble's Valley, and Kirkland Valley. The settlers in these valleys at that time were not many in number, but all were well-to-do, having considerable herds of cattle, bands of horses, and many flocks of sheep. Inasmuch as each ranchman produced considerable grain and vegetables that sold at astoundingly high prices, money was plentiful amongst them, so my trade with them was exceedingly profitable.

But my chief interest at that time was to study the prehistoric remains that lie scattered over each of these valleys and which form a part of the vast field for the archaeologist in Arizona. All of these valleys lie to the northwest and southwest of Prescott along the west base of the Bradshaw Mountains and beyond to the west. Each valley is surrounded by moderately high volcanic mountains, and on the high peaks of these little ranges stand old fortifications and watchtowers built by the extinct race, who seemed to have inhabited this entire central region of Arizona in remote centuries. In every mountain pass we find breastworks of stone erected to dispute passage by the enemy, and throughout each valley are large quantities of broken pottery, spearheads, flint arrowheads, broken hand mills, stone axes, and now and then a stone cup or bowl hewn from limestone, lava, or pumice. The foundations of houses are to be seen, the stone walls partly standing or scattered around. Now and then we find the walls of buildings erected of adobe brick. Stone axes so found are usually partly broken, no doubt having been abandoned or thrown down by the victors who did not think them worth carrying away.

In the plow furrows ranchmen frequently bring to light stone hatchets, chisels, hammers, pipes, and other ancient articles. Graves are found, in some of which the dead lie as mummies. In others, the ashes and incinerations would cause us to believe that those prehistoric people were cremationists. In digging down to the floors of the old ruins, we usually find them of hardened clay, and usually there is a hearth in one corner on which yet lie charred coals and the remains of corn cobs, bones of animals, and many little objects of their handicraft.

These ruins tend to prove that a very numerous population was banished from their homes by war. On the floors of some of the old buildings we found the skeletons of men, women, and children who had been killed when these habitations had been attacked and destroyed. Round about such skeletons we frequently found the charred remains of garments of woven cotton or other fibre. Beads; bone needles; bone, stone, and shell jewelry; and pipes frequently were found. We obtained several beautiful jewels of turquoise, as well as abalone and other sea shells. Sometimes we found beads of malachite and travertine of different colors.

After some days, I came to the ranch of Mr., or Colonel, Genung.[3] He was a ranchman or freighter, at that time away from home hauling freight from Ehrenburg on the Colorado River to the Tiger Mine up in the Bradshaw Mountains about one-and-a-half-days' journey from his home. As he had several men employed at his ranch and also three families who were his assistants, I remained there two days and carried on a very profitable trade. I spent the third day with part of my force examining and making drawings of the ancient ruins in the vicinity.

From there, we traded in the adjacent valleys and also collected prehistoric relics by purchase or personal discovery. I secured several very fine stone axes, six earthen pots, two stone pitchers, a number of pipes, and much jewelry, the greater part of these in Peebles Valley. From the wife of a Mr. Dixon I obtained two exceedingly handsome stone hatchets which showed superior skill in finish and design.

Through all of these valleys may also be seen the graves of white men and Mexicans killed by Apaches. In Bell Canyon to the west, through which I passed and repassed with my caravan, we found the graves of twenty-seven persons, five of which were for United States mail carriers killed while galloping through this narrow defile, which is almost nine miles in its entire length. The passage through the canyon is so narrow in places that the Indian warriors would shoot from the rocky cliffs on either side, and sometimes so close to their victims were they that the fire from their rifles or muskets would set on fire the clothing of their victims.

Many a poor victim from Ireland, England, Germany, France, or Spain, as well as Mexicans and Americans laid down their bones there, and many more will become victims to the same warfare before the Apache is thoroughly conquered.

We saw in Bell Canyon three large, black crosses over the graves of Mexicans murdered there some years previous, one of them being a native of Chihuahua, another from Magdalena, and a third from some other town of the Gulf of California. Many graves had no markers, and from time to time on either side of the road the bones of unburied victims lie hidden in the chaparral. The love of gold and silver brought these men into these hills; but they did not die in vain. Arizona will redeem itself in the years to come, and around the hearths of hundreds of Arizona homes the children of pioneers with deep interest will listen to the tales of the bloody old days that were passed when Arizona was being brought into civilization and pioneers laid down their lives in subduing the bloodthirsty Apache.

We spent seventeen days in the group of valleys west of the Bradshaw Range. Afterwards we journeyed down to Antelope Peak and camped at its base, where we spent eight days prospecting for gold quartz and hunting for quail, wild turkeys, and deer. We killed two deer, three turkeys, and about four dozen quails. We found a number of exceedingly rich specimens of gold quartz, but located no veins of sufficient width to justify making locations; and, there being no water at that time in any of the tanks either on the summit or farther down, we could not pan the gravels. In the chaparral on the north and west sides of the mountains I encountered three very prominent veins in which the gold was free, but from the tests I made by crushing and panning, I did not estimate the value per ton to be more than five dollars, so I did not think it worth locating them. Antelope Peak, however, is destined without question to produce immense values of gold in the years to come.

We then passed around Antelope Peak's south base, to Yaqui Wilson's old station, only to find that this famous old adventurer with whom I had done business in my previous expeditions had been killed in a gunfight some two months previous. We found that his lifeblood yet marked the doorposts against which he had fallen when shot.

Yaqui Wilson's station, or little camp, was situated at a conspicuous point, two roads running to the northward. The right-hand road passes over into the Bradshaws to Prescott, the other into the chain of valleys from which we had just traveled. Another road passes to the south, crossing the Hassayampa to Wickenburg and there forking, the right fork going to Ehrenburg on the Colorado, and the left fork heading for Phoenix and Tucson.

Yaqui Wilson had in his day been a man of some prominence. He had lived for a time in North Africa, chiefly in Morocco as a trader; but some men in Arizona claimed that while in Africa he was a bandit and robber amongst the Moors. He spent many years in South America, was with Walker in Nicaragua, and, after that adventure failed, returned to Mexico. Here he took sides with the Liberals against the Emperor Maximilian, and when that man was subdued, Yaqui cast his lot among the Indians of the Yaqui River in Sonora, whence arose his name Yaqui.

He was said to have been a native of Pennsylvania and led a wild life. Lastly he came from Sonora and settled south of the foot of Antelope Peak and kept a station for travelers. He owned some placer-mining ground on which he used annually to employ quite a number of Yaqui Indians, working with them during the rainy season. He sold liquors and other supplies to travelers. He was always ready for a game of poker. Poor fellow, he found a bloody grave at the end of a stormy career. He was about fifty-five or sixty years of age at the time of his death. He was somewhat auburn in complexion, wore a heavy mustache and chin whiskers. His mortal remains were laid to rest about one hundred and fifty yards southeast of his trading post.

A good-natured Swede whom he had in his service when killed was managing the station on the day of our arrival. I much regretted the death of Yaqui Wilson for the reason that he was one of the conspicuous old-timers of that region and should have survived according to the laws of nature for another fifteen or twenty years. Some weeks later I was much pleased to learn that the man who killed him was given twenty years in the penitentiary at Fort Yuma. He died there three years later.

That evening when sitting in my tent at Yaqui Wilson's station I somewhat changed my plans for the following few weeks. Instead of swinging over to Prescott by way of the Bradshaw Range as first intended, I saw that I would yet have sufficient time for a side expedition to the southeast to a mining camp recently opened up, known as Tombstone. The rich silver mines at this point were discovered some eighteen months before by a man from Oregon named Ed Schefflin,[4] and at the time of our arrival at Antelope Peak Tombstone was a roaring district. It was said that money was very plentiful, and although life was said to be quite desperate there, I felt like risking an immediate expedition there.

We reached Wickenburg the first day, where we supplied ourselves with sufficient grain and baled hay for our mules, and passed the night on the banks of the Hassayampa. That evening I visited my old friend Mr. John Peebles, the man to whose wife I sold the monkey and other odds and ends on my journey the year before. Owing to the shortness of my time in that romantic old camp, I did not visit any of my Mexican friends, not even the Reverados.

The following morning my caravan pushed forward over the Wickenburg and Phoenix road. I did not deem it wise to stop for trade in Phoenix, as my objective was Tombstone. However, as we arived there early in the afternoon, I paid my respects to Miss Mattie Hughes and my merchant friend Señor Peralta.

From Phoenix I was five days in reaching Tombstone, and found it a truly wild and wooly aggregation of humanity.[5] There were a dozen mining properties, most of which were producing very rich silver ore. There were between seven or eight hundred persons, men and women, in the camp, besides a number of Yaqui Indians that were employed in wood cutting and charcoal burning. Quite a number of the population were Mexicans. The camp at that date had four supply stores, seven or eight saloons, three restaurants, four lodging houses, four gambling houses, two livery stables, four hay corrals, three lawyers' offices, four deputy sheriffs, perhaps fifty gamblers, and some fifteen to fifty women of easy ways.

I remained in Tombstone just five days, during which time I sold merchandise to the value of $1,879. A considerable part of my pay for the same came in the form of Mexican dollars worth at that time sixty cents each. I was fortunate in meeting a number of men whom I formerly knew in Nevada, a dozen or more from Los Angeles, California, and also from Panamint, California, several I had met in Prescott, and, most interesting of all, more than a dozen whom I had known in Helena and Virginia City, Montana.

I was very pleased to have visited this new and important silver-producing district, which seemed destined to survive for many years. I deemed it somewhat strange to have passed so many digs in a new roaring mining camp of the old times and not to learn of the death of from one to half a dozen persons by gunfire or knife thrusts during my stay there; but such were the facts, and a few persons made excuse that for a number of days things had been very quiet in that way.

From Tombstone I wheeled back to the north. The country in central Arizona around Prescott and at two or three military camps was sufficient in the trade possibilities for that season to take over all of the merchandise I yet had with me. Now somewhat lightened by the sales of the previous six weeks, my four men, three wagons, and twelve mules were able to go forward at a much livelier gait.

At Florence I spent three days doing some business and renewing my acquaintance with my friend Albert McDonald and a few others with whom I did business the previous year. From Florence I traveled the Salt River road toward Phoenix and remained for one day at Hayden's Mill, trading with Mr. Hayden and his attendants. At that point I turned to the east, and less than a day's travel brought us again into the settlement of our Mormon friends at Mesa City near the south bank of the Salt River.

I was surprised at the improvements made during the previous year. The place had grown to be a thrifty town. I found my friend Daniel Jones to be even more sanguine than before about the future of Mesa. During the year just passed he had been down into the state of Chihuahua in Old Mexico, visiting the governor there and making arrangements for opening up another Mormon settlement, or stake, in that state, which was done and became quite prosperous. I had expected to do considerable business at Mesa and in collecting more antiquities gathered by the people there. In business I did very well during four days, but as to antiquities, other parties from New England had visited the place some two months before and gathered up everything in sight, paying exceedingly good prices, so on that occasion I did practically nothing.

From Mesa we crossed Salt River to the north and eventually reached the military post of Fort McDowell, a camp that I had visited two years before. I found a hearty welcome there, the commanding officer now being Lieutenant Colonel Brown.

Two companies of cavalry and one of infantry were stationed there, with a force of fifty Apache scouts. These Apache scouts were young men of from eighteen to thirty years of age, employed by the government to hunt down members of their own tribe who might be on the warpath. They were furnished daily rations, and most of them had their squaws with them. Each of these Apache scouts was dressed in blue infantry trousers, army infantry shoes, and gray shirts, and each carried a canteen and a three-banded fifty-caliber breechloading United States musket. They were paid thirteen dollars per month, and they were quartered three to a dog tent.

This force of fifty Apache scouts was commanded by the renowned Al Siebers, well known as a man of unlimited nerve and of great experience with the different Apache bands. He had served as captain of Indian scouts for more than ten years before I met him at Camp McDowell. I was much impressed with the man and took great interest in the record of his early life, about which he told me all I desired.[6]

We stayed four days at Camp McDowell, doing very good business. From there we continued northward, going as far as Black Canyon, the point at which I had been wounded in an Apache ambuscade two years previous. At Black Canyon we turned westward until we reached the road we had left some three weeks before. This region on the northern Hassayampa contains thousands of acres of gold-bearing gravel sufficiently rich to pay very well, but insufficient water with which to work them. It has been time and again proven that there are hundreds of places in that region where miners having sufficient water to work a sluice might make forty dollars per day.

We continued over into the western park of Black Canyon, which is a volcanic region, but the decomposed quartz of the mountains to the northward through past ages has been ground into a very fine sand. There is much of it; but, owing to the small amount of water to be obtained at any season, only little work is done in attempting to recover it. A few men, however, made small fortunes in Black Canyon in the years between 1860 and 1875.

In the little camps scattered over the Hassayampa and Black Canyon and on Bumblebee and Big Bug creeks I purchased a considerable quantity of gold dust; and in the United States assay office at New York City it brought from eighteen to nineteen dollars per ounce. It was quite coarse, from small chips up to nuggets of twenty dollars in value.

Throughout this placer-mining region of Arizona are little camps of eight or ten men, Americans and Mexicans, some of them doing well and some of them in a desperate fight to make enough to buy whiskey, tobacco, flour, and bacon. The climate is dry and pleasant throughout the year, so that a shed covered with Spanish bayonet or rawhide is their only shelter, and the dream of golden treasures that may come to hand is their only consoling thought.

As there was but little money to be made in that level country, we turned north up to the Bumblebee, another gulch of less importance than Black Canyon. A few families from Kansas strove to make a poor living by ranching, mining, and station keeping.

We remained at a station kept by one Mr. Sessions[7] over Sunday, and on Saturday night we had a dance. Mr. Sessions had five daughters, and three more women came from neighbor houses. A few miners and prospectors along with Dawson, my other men, and myself made, with the young ladies, the party of the evening. It was through good fortune that a wandering musician had arrived that afternoon with his violin and other earthly effects on the back of a little seventy-five-cent donkey. We employed his services forthwith, and that night's memory long will live in the bosom of everyone who was present.

There was quite a large room in which the dancing took place. A large fireplace in the south end of the room threw out warmth on that rather chilly night. There were jigs and reels, round dances, easy gliding and bounding leaps as the hours sped, and a pot on the fire containing a rather strong quality of punch to cheer the soul that would lag in the evening's merry movements. At midnight there was a good supper of venison, beef, bread, mescal, sweet potatoes, jerked beef, doughnuts, coffee, etc. It was eight o'clock on Sunday morning before the fiddler's rosin gave out and the dancing ceased.

During the remainder of Sunday I wandered out to examine the prehistoric remains that lie scattered along Bumblebee Creek and the adjoining fields. These consist of the foundations of stone or sun-dried-brick buildings, and prove that this stream, like all others of central Arizona, was once densely populated.

From Bumblebee we took our course by way of Turkey Creek to Prescott, where we arrived on the twenty-fourth of December, 1878. I rented a vacant storehouse next to the post office, which had been secured for me some two weeks before by my friend the postmaster, Mr. Otis, to whom I had written. After unloading our merchandise in the storehouse, I then had my wagons driven over to a dwelling house I had rented in the western part of town, and once more my Chinese cook Quong Hing began serving us much better meals than I had been getting at Arizona hotels. As the day of our starting housekeeping in Prescott was Christmas, we kept it as a sacred holiday. At about seven o'clock that evening a quickly improvised table was graced with a roast turkey and all other queenly luxuries that I could secure in the Prescott market, added to the fairly good things that we had with us.

The day following Christmas my men and I put our storeroom into order, advertised my coming in the *Prescott Miner*, the chief paper of that day, and trade once more began. In the early morning and the evening, I sent two bell boys or callers to the different streets calling at the homes of the inhabitants, informing them that I was once more back in Prescott and inviting them to come over and inspect my goods.

I continued to trade until the day before New Year's. During that time the little city of Prescott was very lively. The sidewalks were crowded with soldiers from Fort Whipple and gold- and silver miners from Bumblebee, Turkey Creek, and the General Custer, Peck, and Tip Top mines to the south of Prescott from five to fifteen miles. In the town there were white men, Mexicans, and Hualapai Indians—everyone in their holiday dresses. Music and dancing were carried on in the homes and in the hall of the high school, and in one or two dance houses where German girls tripped the light fantastic.

It was evident for two days before New Year's that it was useless to attempt further trade until the second or third day of January, so we fell into the enjoyment of the New Year's holidays with the rest of our countrymen, and I gave Quong Hing a four-day holiday. My men and I during that time ate our meals at the aristocratic Montezuma Hotel. In our own little rented residence we fitted ourselves up in as becoming a manner and dress as the holiday season demanded.

On the previous visit to Prescott I had become acquainted with the principal people of that town, including His Excellency, Governor Safford,[8] and the honorable Thomas Fitch and wife, whom I had formerly known at Virginia City, Nevada, and also at Salt Lake City, Utah. Again I was pleased to meet Mr. and Mrs. Alexander; my friend C. P. Head, a merchant; my merchant friend E. L. Bashford; and Captain Burns from Fort Whipple. There was also Mr. Moses Goldwater, the local banker; Daniel Hatz and family; Mr. and Mrs. Ales, with their daughter Margaret; and two score of young ladies and gentlemen prominent in Prescott society. There were also the teachers of the local high school. But the crowning social feature of those pleasant holidays was my opportunity of meeting Governor John Charles Fremont, formerly general in the United States Army, and perhaps better known as a great explorer of the Rocky Mountain region and the California Pacific coast from 1842 to 1846, when he took part in the conquest of California during the Mexican War, and his wife, who was a daughter of Senator Thomas H. Benton of Missouri.

Governor Fremont gave a levee or function on the eve of Christmas at which men and I were present, and two days later I was very fortunate in spending two hours and a half with the Fremonts. At that time I quizzed the good man, who was now almost eighty years of age, relative to his expeditions across the Rocky Mountains, his experience during the Mexican and Civil wars, and his present prospects as governor of Arizona. I found the governor and his good wife amongst the most interesting and amiable people with whom I have ever become acquainted in any part of the world; and on three different occasions during my subsequent days in Prescott I visited them, finding a welcome and learning from them much which was of great value to me in a historic way. Little had I thought in my boyhood days when reading of the achievements of John Charles Fremont in his explorations that I would in later days be permitted to spend three evenings conversing with him.[9]

On New Year's Eve we had all the festivities the town afforded at a levee or reception given by the governor at the gubernatorial mansion, and of course the guests that evening were as numerous as the territorial capital of Arizona could muster. I remained for a short time and at ten o'clock returned to our quarters.

I found my men all there save Dawson, whom I had left at the post office on my way to the governor's mansion. He had said he would meet me in a short time, but I sat at our house writing until almost one o'clock in the morning. The other men had gone to bed. As it was the morning of the new year, I took my pistols and fired thirty-five or forty rounds to honor the departing year and welcome the new one, but yet my brave Dawson did not appear.

Just as I was preparing to go in quest of him, I heard a footstep and the door opened, and Dawson appeared with something under his coat.

It proved to be a black-and-tan pup about three weeks old. I asked where on earth he had been and where he had obtained the pup.

"Oh," he said, "I was making numerous calls and this dog I brought to you as a present." It turns out he had found him on the edge of the bulrushes some three blocks to the south, where he was yelping and crying. As the pup seemed to have no known relations and was in a forlorn situation, I adopted him. As he was found in the bulrushes, I told Con we would call him "Moses."

When I resumed trade, I found business exceedingly good, both in Prescott and at Fort Whipple, where I was permitted by the commander and post trader to carry on business with the officers' and soldiers' families. From over plains and mountains I had brought into that little city a stock of goods worthy of being handled in any part of the world, and the trade with which I had been favored was very satisfactory to me.

After ten days, I planned to go to the military post of Fort Verde, about sixty miles to the east, where I would trade for a few days with a number of cattle- and horse raisers in Verde Valley. I also wished to explore the very extensive ruins along the Verde River and in the Mogollon Range east of Verde Valley. Our twelve mules had been placed in the care of Dan Hatz, who ran a feed yard and stable in the western part of Prescott. My men daily went over there to look after our mules and began preparing our wagons for departure.

On the fifth of January, 1879, we started for a journey of trade, hunting, and prospecting into the high-timbered Bradshaw Mountains south of Prescott. They are well wooded with fir, pine, cedar, and juniper, and contain a good deal of game, such as deer, wildcats, mountain lions, turkeys, and flocks of quail. Springs of good water are found throughout the region, with abundance of excellent grass.

From Prescott we reached the Peck silver mine, which was then working and where we stayed one day for trade. From this mine I obtained a rare lot of very rich silver specimens that would run as high as eight to twelve dollars per pound. The silver vein of the Peck mine is very narrow; in no place is the rich ore body wider than six inches, and it is sometimes only two inches, but universally very rich. The ore is what is known as horn silver. The mine from its date of discovery to the time of our visit paid immense dividends to its owners.

A few miles beyond the Peck Mine we reached the General Cook, which for some years had been worked at great profit; but at the time of my visit it was closed down for mill repairs. I found Mr. Charles Hunt in charge of the property, a very competent man in all lines of mining and milling. He was somewhat of an adventurer, having been some years before a filibuster with General Ryan on an invasion of Cuba. He was taken prisoner with General Ryan and his associates, barely escaping execution by the Spaniards. Fortunately, through the efforts of our American minister to Spain, his life was spared. He was now striving to make his living in a more agreeable manner.

From there, our road led us next to the Tiger silver mine, for I had a letter to the manager. He had forty men employed at the mine. We remained there one day trading with his workers. The night following, I descended into the mine and spent several hours examining its workings and the mineral veins. Like the Peck Mine, the ores were very rich, although the veins were narrow. The mine was not for sale, so I had no opportunity of securing a lease or bond on it or I would have done so for my New York associates, for I liked the property very much.

A short distance to the south, but still in the Bradshaws, I found the Tip Top silver-mining property, where I remained one day and a half, doing several hundred dollars in business with the fifty men employed there. The manager, Rufus Palmer, had his family living at the mine, as well as the family of his assistant, Oliver Wilson.

We then doubled back to a point some nine miles from the Tip Top Mine, then turned perhaps two miles to the left on a fairly well-beaten wagon road. This took us to a copper mine known as the General Robert E. Lee. I found there quite a number of narrow veins of marvelously rich red-oxide copper ore, or cuprite, running as high as eighty percent copper. There were also in the surface veins considerable quantities of rather fragile malachite, very little of which was of gem quality. Up to that point copper mining in Arizona would not pay, because of the high cost of shipping the ore to the Colorado River, thence to Panama, and by steamship to Cardiff or Swansea in Wales; so no copper was then being worked in Arizona or California.

After finishing our business at the different mines in the Bradshaw Mountains, we went into camp by the side of a beautiful spring and prepared to hunt and prospect for a few days. We discovered several veins of silver-bearing ore, but upon having the ores assayed at Prescott, they proved to be too low a grade at that time for working, so I gave no further attention to them. We killed two deer and some scores of quail, on which we feasted. In this easy way of life the week glided away rapidly, and we then returned to Prescott, where we passed two days in preparing for our departure.

As might have been expected, I had accumulated a little over ten thousand dollars in greenbacks, a good deal of it in large denominations. I was in constant dread of robbery, and not having utter faith in the banking conditions of Arizona, I was left between two fires as to purchasing exchange on New York City or risking carrying it myself.

I had traded a freighter one of my Schettler wagons which was comparatively new for one that was pretty well worn, plus boot of about two hundred dollars. The other Schettler wagon, with four mules and harness, I had agreed to sell to Mr. Joseph Melvin of Camp Verde for two hundred and fifty dollars. I had settled upon the old wagon as the vehicle we would drive out of the country. When we returned to Prescott after our short expedition into the Bradshaws, I had the old wagon driven to the rear of the storehouse, where there was an enclosed backyard with a gate and high fence. I set my men to work baling merchandise and doing some work at our quarters. I began work on the wagon. On the bed of the wagon there were brace boards on each side consisting of one vertical piece eight inches wide and two oblique pieces eight inches wide, one on each side of the vertical brace board. I carefully removed one of these oblique brace boards and cut a channel on its inner side ten inches long and five inches wide. This brace was an inch and a half in thickness. I cut the channel an inch in depth and dressed it out very carefully. The ten thousand five hundred dollars in currency I got into bills of the denomination of one-hundreds, fifties, and five-hundreds from the post trader at Fort Whipple. I put these bills into one package, wrapped them in a canvas covering, and forced them into the mortise in the brace board. I then carefully replaced this board, returned the nails, and left no indication that it had been tampered with. I thus felt that I was acting in the safest manner, as no one would expect to find a treasure hidden in such a place. I was thankful that a group of hunters and desperados in the log cabin of the Hatz corral had all left during our absence in the Bradshaw Mountains, for I did not desire their presence while we were yet in Prescott.

My plans for the remaining part of this expedition were to start eastward from Prescott through Copper Canyon, going down into the Verde Valley, where I would deliver to Mr. Joe Melvin the four mules, harness, and wagon for which he had bargained with me. We would do business there for two or three days, then with ranchers in the Verde Valley, and examine the prehistoric ruins of that region. Then we would go eastward across the Mogollon Mountains and on to St. Johns, from which I would continue either to Santa Fe and the terminal of the Kansas Pacific Railroad and thence to New York City, or down the Little Colorado to Lee's Ferry on the big Colorado, then across the Buckskin Mountain to Kanab, on to Silver Reef, and back home.

We left Prescott on the 16th of January, 1879, reached the Verde River two days later, and drove over to the ranch of Joe Melvin one and a half miles south of Camp Verde. From him I learned that the soldiers, officers, and other government dependents at Camp Verde would not be paid for about ten days, so I decided I would devote that time to trade with local ranchmen and to exploring the Verde Valley ruins.

In the valley there were a number of white families, ranchers, well-to-do people—most of them from Missouri and Arkansas, with not a few from Texas. Their farms and cattle ranges reached in many cases a considerable distance east and west on the highlands beyond the Verde River and for about thirty miles north of Fort Verde. The small farms produced potatoes, corn, sweet potatoes, vegetables, butter, beef, pork, and mutton, all of which found a ready market at Fort Verde and at Prescott. I found money plentiful, and did very well commercially among them.

The country along there is beautiful at any season of the year. The old prehistoric ruins give it an air of mystery and antiquity, while far to the north arises the vast bulk of San Francisco Mountain that in most years shows a cap of perpetual snow resting above a dense timber belt. To the east rises the vast dark ridge of the lonely Mogollons.

After making our headquarters at the Melvin ranch, I began investigation four miles south on a number of spots near the river where broken pottery lies scattered and the ruins of old stone walls mark the site of a settlement.

It would be yet six days until the troops would be paid off at Fort Verde. In that time we would not be able to explore the entire building, so we saw that our best course would be to leave this neighborhood and go over onto the Beaver River and explore an old castle or palace situated in the side of the mountain cliff.

I had seen enough of the ruins in the Verde Valley to prove that there must have been fully forty thousand people in that valley and its tributaries alone. We had already examined enough to show the manner or way in which they lived, and from the buildings on the Beaver River, which were said to be well preserved, I hoped to learn more about these extinct people.

The commander of the fort described the exact location of the ruins on the Beaver Park so minutely that it was quite easy to find the spot. It was about two o'clock on a Sunday afternoon when we started for the ancient castle, and, after driving about two hours over a steep ridge, we looked down into an amphitheater containing about one hundred acres of land, level as a table and covered with a dense body of dry grass. The mountains all around it were steep. It was a spur at the foot of the Mogollon Range, and on the east side of this space of level land ran Beaver River. Rising from the river on the north side was a massive precipice about two hundred feet in height. This mass of limestone was about half a mile in length, and about midway in its length and two-thirds of the way to the top we beheld an immense building.

I was filled with astonishment at the magnitude of this vast pile of masonry at such an awful height and in such an airy situation. Descending into this amphitheater by means of a road built by the soldiers at Fort Verde, we drove to within about forty yards of the structure. We unhitched and unharnessed our mules, gave them each a liberal portion of barley, put hobbles on each, and turned them out to feed on the plentiful grass.

It was growing late in the evening, but a full moon lit up the whole region, and by the light of the last streaks of dying day and of the moon we gathered wood for our fire. The scene around was a wild and lonely one, shut in by high mountains, and it was with curiosity that we awaited the morrow when we might climb into the old palace that towered far above us.

The Beaver River is about ten yards wide, and although at that time of the year it was low water, we had to bridge it with cottonwood logs from the south bank to a high rock midway in the stream which was level with the south bank, then with timbers of the same length to shoulders of limestone extending out from the mighty cliff. We found two of the three ladders which had been used by a party of U.S. Army officers who had visited the cave some years previous. We constructed another ladder, repaired the two old ones, and after much dangerous work got those three ladders firmly fixed. By means of these and the old steps cut into the cliffs, we four reached the building.

The scene from the front wall is one I will never forget: the river below us, the vast amphitheater in front of the cliff extending above and below. The happy thought struck me that we could bring our entire camp outfit up into the ruin, with my books and papers and all our baggage, and occupy this castle until we were ready to return to Fort Verde. There was good grass for the mules, the wagon was perfectly safe, and in the castle we could command a view in either direction and need have no fear of an attack. Wood we could carry to the foot of the precipice, and by means of a long rope and pulley which we had in the wagon we could bring everything up to the tower, and by letting down a bucket we could draw up water.

We descended and began collecting a large pile of firewood. I ascended with a rope and fixed our pulley block in the window of the east tower, and two hours later we had wood enough for the entire time we would remain. The next things to come up were our provision boxes, bedding, guns, goods, and baggage. It was something like freighting a vessel; but it had a wild idea about it, so that pleased me. The wagon was securely fastened to keep out rain. The mules were fed again, rehobbled, and left to themselves where we could have a friendly eye on them.

We ascended again to the palace and for the first time in our lives prided ourselves on owning and occupying a castle. Our fireplace was arranged in the southwest tower, and there our kitchen furniture was carried, including provisions and messbox. Into the upper hall we carried our clothing and bedding. Our merchandise was piled up in one of the lower rooms. About three o'clock in the afternoon we kindled a fire in the watchtower and began preparing supper. A half-hour later ham was frying in one pan, California raisins were stewing in another. Bread was baking in a skillet. The odor of old government Java coffee wafted through the old palace. Potatoes were being sliced to fry in the long-handled frying pan, and when the ham was removed from the fire these potatoes were put into it with part of the grease which was tried out of the ham. Water was put in also until the pan was filled. A large tin plate covered them and they were put on the fire to stew. While they were being prepared, slices of baker's bread from Camp Verde were being toasted at the fire and buttered with Verde Valley butter purchased for one dollar and fifty cents per pound. With the ham we fried ten Arizona quail killed that day, and in this way we had as varied a supper as doubtless was ever prepared for any of the ancient governors of this castle. From a few boards a table was prepared, and covered with a cloth, and our supper was ready.

I determined to sleep in the great hall, and when our kitchen was put in order we spread our blankets in a cozy corner. The night was warm, the sky was clear, and a bright moon poured down her mellow light on the valley below. The old palace took on new lustre as the gentle beams of night's queen came stealing through window and porthole. It fell upon the great corridor and penetrated far into the cave. Looking down upon the towers below, the space around, and the cliff beneath, it seemed as though we should hear the voices and see the forms of the ancient people who on nights like this in the dreamy long ago walked this corridor and looked down on their fields beneath, green with blooming corn, listened to the rippling of the waters of their own glad mountain river, and in their aerial castle thought themselves the happiest people of all the world.

But 'tis past. They are gone, while voiceless loneliness enwraps the traveler who contemplates the works they left behind. It was far in the night when our talk of the dead races came to an end, and in a still wondering mind I wrapped myself in my blankets and was soon asleep.

The work of the next day was to take notes about the old ruins, make drawings of the castle, and attend to the general requirements of camp. We called our great roost "The Ancient Palace of the Lost Kings," and I am free to confess that I never enjoyed a few days in any old ruin more than I did in this.

On the second day, I took my gun and went up into the mountains to the southeast, where I killed a deer and a dozen quail and pulled them up into the castle. Our pup, Moses, in the meantime, was thriving. The mules were enjoying a blissful rest, and I was proud in the thought that I was the undisputed owner of a castle in the air.

All went well until the evening of the fourth day, when the sky became overcast and deep peals of thunder began to roll through the hills. Flashes of lightning were followed by rattling claps of thunder. In a little time big drops of rain began falling, which were followed by more and more until a frightful storm was raging over hill and valley. This was an additional novelty to our midair residence, and I enjoyed the wild disturbance of the elements.

We were safe and dry where we were and we kept watching the storm until quite late in the night. When bedtime came, we changed our bedroom, carrying our robes and blankets, guns, money, and the dog down into a room where there were four bedsteads of masonry. There were two candles burning, and after chatting and smoking a while we went to bed. The pup, Moses, was left to sleep on a little buffalo robe. Our guns and pistols were at hand, for in those days, though a man might live between heaven and earth as we were then living, yet he was in Arizona and must be prepared.

We must have been sleeping for several hours when we were awakened by the most unearthly noises in the back part of the great cave. It was a sharp long screech, so damnable as to arouse every nerve in one's body. The men were aroused and sitting up in their beds wanting to know what in Heaven's name we were going to do, especially Con Dawson, who told me he thought Indians had come up the ladders.

Well, I had the buck ague for a moment and was soon out of bed, as were the other men, and had my Sharps carbine at hand ready to receive the first callers. Quong Hing grew excited, saying that it was the devil, and he wanted to get out of the building. Eusebius shouted to him to keep quiet or he would shoot him. Strange to say, Quong Hing immediately became quiet.

The noise died away after perhaps a half-hour, and we grew brave. Together we ascended into the other rooms, reached the great hall, and with cocked pistols crept to where we could take a view of the space in front; but we saw nothing. I could hear my heart beat as I listened for a sound and looked for a way to see a form move; but all was silent, so we stole back to bed and lay there for an hour waiting for more noises like those already heard, but they did not come. While so listening, I fell asleep. When I awoke it was broad daylight and Quong Hing was preparing breakfast.

We remained there another night, but no voices or sounds were heard. I made light of it to the men, saying that it was an owl; but Quong and Eusebius said it was not, and they were anxious to leave the old air castle, especially Quong Hing, who was anxious and excited. He claimed that either an evil spirit or the devil dwelt there. I have now no doubt but that those sounds might have come from a mountain lion who had some means of entrance into the castle. It may have been heard by the savages of this vicinity and done much to preserve the old palace from their attacks and its ruin.

After eating our last dinner in sight of our lately occupied palace, we packed everything, including our pup, Moses, and departed from Beaver Park, taking a regretful last look at the old palace of the lost kings. Let it be here stated that this wonderful old structure, the most interesting of the ancient remains in all of Arizona, was the next year cruelly plundered and accidentally set on fire by some Texas cowboys who almost completely destroyed it.

We reached Melvin's ranch before sundown. After supper, Mr. and Mrs. Melvin had our entire party over to their house. Even Quong Hing put himself into his gala Chinese dress that he carried with him, and we others did likewise from our own wardrobes. That evening we were honored in meeting at Colonel Melvin's home First Lieutenant Edward Green; his sister Viola; Lieutenant Stanford and wife; Eula Crowninshield from Providence, Rhode Island, now a schoolteacher at Fort Verde, escorted by Lieutenant Green. Also there were the post trader, Major Hull, and Louise Claymore, a lady cousin from Detroit, Michigan.

They were interesting people. The men, all of them, had seen severe service fighting Indians in Kansas, Texas, New Mexico, and Arizona. Major Hull had been in the Mexican War of 1846–47, took part in the battle of Buena Vista, and had an excellent memory with wonderful powers of observation. Miss Viola Green was an excellent pianist, and my man Eusebius Sieboldt played very well on the violin, so part of the evening we had dancing to their music. About midnight, Mrs. Melvin announced that she and Quong Hing had prepared an Arizona midnight feast in the dining room. For some hours previous I realized that there was something of the kind going forward, but the midnight dinner so prepared was a surprise, and it was a dinner the likes of which I had found rarely equaled at home or abroad.

There was Arizona turkey and Arizona quail, with accompanying dishes that in variety and preparation would have been a credit to the table of a Russian grand duke. As to quantity and as to its preparation and flavor, it would have recalled the best features of a Thanksgiving dinner in far-off New England homes. Lieutenant Green had taken over from Fort Verde that evening a half-dozen bottles of light wine that gave spirit to the dinner, and fortunately I yet had with me two boxes of cigars that in merit equaled the wine.

We sat and ate at leisure. Every tribe of Indians in Arizona was discussed. Every implacable bloodthirsty chief whom the American infantry or cavalry had to face for the previous thirty years was talked about. Old Mangus, Nana, Cochise, Geronimo, Victorio, and Mickey Free were each and all given credit for their vices and virtues, their atrocious murders of white men, women, and children in the most diabolical manner. Lieutenant Stanwood told about the wonderful fight at the Great Caves when so many Apaches were exterminated at the end of the famous ride. Bell Canyon with its massacres was talked about. He told of the wagon train surrounded on the Hassayampa where every man with the train died fighting to the last, how the mules and horses were captured and the wagons with their tons and tons of valuable merchandise for the forts or mines were plundered and burned. He told of the scores of Indian attacks on wagon trains after long sufferings on the Colorado River, and of those near the great Vulture gold mines. Then we listened to the story of the capture and trials of the two Oatman girls in 1852, Olive and Mary Ann, of the death by starvation of the poor little creature Mary Ann, and the continued suffering, misery, slavery, and final release to freedom and later prominence of Olive Oatman.

Next we talked about famous Arizonans, amongst them Henry Wickenburg, King Woolsey, who planned the famous or infamous Paiute treaty, and Yaqui Wilson, who was credited with having been at one time a slaver and pirate on the coast of Africa but was now lying in his own blood on the Hassayampa. We discussed the merchants Lord & Williams of Tucson, Peralta at Phoenix, A. L. Bashford and C. P. Head at Prescott. In a kindly way we talked about Arizona's governors Goodwin, McCormick, Safford, Hoyt, and the immortal John C. Fremont and his wonderful wife, Jessie Benton Fremont, then happily occupying the gubernatorial mansion.

We gave attention to Arizona's mining men: Joe Genung, John Peebles, Ed Shefflin, Jacob Valentine, Thomas Miller, Lieutenant Mowry, Alexander McCracken, James Haas, Bob Grey, Jack Swelling, Mr. Alexander, and Mr. Peck of Prescott. They talked about these wonderful people and also of Mrs. Ales of Prescott, about her marvelous daughter, Mrs. Joe Genung, and her other wonderful, beautiful, but ill-fated girl of many woes, Margaret, who had recently died of a broken heart; and the Rev. Father Becker and the Rev. Mr. Taylor, conspicuous ecclesiastical lights, were made mention of and praised for their many virtues.

We did not overlook giving praise to army men who in the past and even then were standing up against the ruthless Apache, striving to make

Arizona a pleasant place and a safe place in which to live; for which reason we talked about General Crook, General Miles, General Carlton, Captain Burkey, Captain Burns, Captain Sturges, with scores of others who gave many of their best days to the redemption of Arizona from barbarism. Following the men of military renown, we discussed the women of Arizona as to their merits along the lines of beauty, ugliness, tenderness, toughness, charity, malignity, those who were known to us to be atrociously masculine, and those who were delightfully feminine. We discussed the probabilities of what Arizona would be one hundred and fifty years from that night when every river, every mountain stream, and every living spring would be handled and developed to its utter capacity for irrigation and electricity, when all of Arizona's Indian tribes would be civilized, educated, or utterly exterminated.

Lastly, we talked of Arizona's mineral wealth, its gold, silver, copper, lead, bismuth, antimony, plumbago, zinc, iron, manganese, tungsten, its gem stones such as turquoise, unsurpassed garnets, amethysts, crystals of quartz, amorphous malachites, and diamond-bearing meteors found in Black Canyon.

We observed silence on Gila monsters, red-eyed rattlesnakes, the forty-nine kinds of lizards that inhabit Arizona's deserts, and left to the accomplished botanists a description or even a dissertation on the unsurpassed cacti and thorned plants that grace or disgrace the deserts, plains, and mountainsides of Arizona. Then at three-thirty in the morning we parted, and it was less than one hour until deep sleep held us in tight embrace.

The next day we attempted to trade at the ranch of a stockman named Arnold who lived on a mountain stream near Fort Verde. My mission to his home was a failure, and I will here allow oblivion to rest on his memory and all that was his, including the irrepressible sharer of his joys and woes. We returned to the Melvin ranch; and the next day at eight-thirty a.m. we bade adieu to our worthy friends Mr. and Mrs. Melvin. Alas, it was to be a long farewell.

We then went over to Fort Verde, where I spent three days trading. Camp Verde, or Fort Verde as it is usually called, is situated thirty-four degrees, thirty-three minutes latitude, and thirty-four degrees and fifty-seven minutes west of Washington,[10] 3,500 feet above sea level and eighty feet above the Verde River. It is a handsome post, and at the time of our last visit it garrisoned one company of cavalry and two companies of infantry, and also a company of Apache scouts numbering forty men under a white lieutenant. The garrison was then commanded by Captain Charles J. Porter, whom I found a most excellent man and like most military officers a thorough gentleman.[11]

After trading at Camp Verde, the greater part, or almost all, of my merchandise was disposed of. I purchased from the commander fifty condemned army cap-and-ball pistols, caliber forty-five; twenty-five caliber-fifty Springfield three-banded needle guns and one thousand rounds of ammunition for the latter; twenty-five Spencer carbine seven-shots, caliber fifty-four, with two thousand rounds of ammunition; and twenty-five condemned Sharps carbines, caliber fifty, with twenty-five hundred rounds of ammunition. At the fort we laid in a full stock of provisions for the journey to the Little Colorado or to Santa Fe, or rather enough to last until our return to Silver Reef, Utah. Then with good wishes from all friends we started on our journey from Fort Verde over a rough road through a wilderness.

The road from Camp or Fort Verde turns to the eastward past limestone bluffs that overhang the Verde River Valley, then over a sloping plain covered with cedars until a high volcanic ridge is reached from which one may see a forest running as far as the eye can see to the north and south.

The first day's drive brought us to a point a few miles from an old ruin and famous spot called Montezuma Wells. This is simply a vast reservoir one hundred feet below the surface of the volcanic surface round about. At the depth of one hundred feet there is a beautiful body of bluish water about one hundred feet across. We reached its margin by means of steps cut in the wall rock by the ancient inhabitants of the country; for, like every other place in Arizona where water exists, there were human dwellings. We spent a day at this spot going through the old ruins but finding little in the way of antiquities, as it had been frequently visited by others. We returned to our camp at nightfall.

The next day we started early in the morning. We had barely left when a tremendous snow storm set in. We were in the foothills of the Mogollon Range where the altitude was high, the atmosphere rare and cold. The road after about twenty miles of travel became rocky, and the snow falling upon this volcanic rock rendered it miserable traveling. At times the mules would lose their footing; one would fall and others would follow. At other times the wagon wheels would bounce from rock to rock or sink into the deep fissure of some volcanic ledge.

As we had but limited hay we could not camp until we reached Stoneman's Lake; but to reach that point in such a storm would be impossible. The road was so bad that we were compelled to walk, and at every step one was likely to sink knee-deep into holes between rocks, for we could not see where to place our feet. Our animals were having the same problem, so we did not make much headway. Do as well as we might, we could not make one mile an hour. The mules were falling and stumbling, and were cruelly bleeding from hoof to knee. We ourselves, with wet feet, tired bones, and disgusted feelings, halted and unharnessed the mules and tied them to trees. We gave them a feed of hay and soaked barley.

We built a fire to warm ourselves, then cut down a number of short cedar trees to build a shelter for our mules, as we could not set up our tents because of the storm. We were able to place them in it about three hours later. Then we made a clearing for our tents. We removed the mattresses from the wagon and made a comfortable bed for our dog upon an extra mattress filled with hay before leaving Fort Verde. We had a plentiful supply of grain, about four hundred pounds, which we felt would be sufficient to feed our animals in making the crossing of the Mogollons. At Fort Verde I had obtained a camp stove, and this was set up within one tent, and Quong Hing managed, notwithstanding the storm, to prepare a good supper, leaving us to forget the toils of the day. We had as usual our camp chairs and a folding table with us, and thereby had even in that howling wilderness in a frightful winter storm the comforts of home. It is only in such places as this that I ever obtained much solace from tobacco, and well do I recollect the pleasure I drew that evening while sitting by our fire from smoking a few good Havana cigars, from two boxes obtained from the sutler at Fort Verde.

It was possible we might have to turn back, and even if we went forward we might have to forgo a hunt in the high ridges of the Mogollon which I had promised myself. After the terrible storm of the night, the morning dawned with a clear sky; but a cold wind was blowing, and so very bad was the road that it was far in the afternoon when we reached the vicinity of Stoneman's Lake.

The road we were now traveling was the overland road laid out by government engineers some twenty-five years before, running eastward from Fort Tejon, Inyo County, California, down the Mojave River and across the Mojave Desert to the Colorado River at Hardyville, and eastward to Prescott and Fort Verde. From Fort Verde it went across the Mogollon Mountains and across the desert to the Little Colorado at St. Johns, then eastward to Santa Fe, New Mexico.[12] This stretch crossing the Mogollon in stormy weather was, because of the falling snow, the very worst in twelve hundred miles of wagon road, none of which was any too good.

Stoneman's Lake covers a few acres. Like Montezuma's Well, it is a vast depression in a high mountain, timbered tableland. At the time of our visit a man named Walker lived there with his wife and three children. The Arizona and New Mexican Stage Company carried the mail from Prescott to Santa Fe by horseback riders three times per week each way.[13]

The riders stopped at rude state stations along the route, at which feed and a relay of horses were kept; and at each station rather limited accommodations and food supplies were available for the limited number of travelers who crossed this desolate region. Mr. Walker had a liberal quantity of a very coarse kind of hay that grew along the lake.

We camped on the high ridge in the dense timber adjacent to Stoneman's Lake and led our mules down over the dangerous path to Mr. Walker's stable yard. It was with the greatest difficulty that we were able to put our two tents into place, as a strong wind was yet blowing terribly, and although we were yet in heavy timber with tall trees around us, they seemed to give but little shelter. However, we secured the tents, gathered a large pile of firewood, set up our stove, and with Quong Hing preparing supper we showed defiance to the inconveniences of the stormy wilderness. All that evening and a great part of the night the wind blew wildly; but, as we had almost reached the watershed of the continent, I did not fear but that we could pass through.

This road had never been traveled extensively on account of the rugged nature of the route from the summit of the Mogollon to Fort Verde. I have traveled much and am free to pronounce it the worst road I ever passed over. On the government maps it is shown as the road of the thirty-fifth parallel.

On the third morning after the beginning of our frightful storm the wind settled and we were happy to be confronted by a balmy day. We had much snow on the road ahead and around us, but because of the warm morning it was melting rapidly. When we had settled with Mr. Walker, we pulled out toward Chaves Pass, a mail station about thirty miles to the east.

We were on a difficult road until we reached the summit, then headed down a gradual slope at a fair pace, our wagon lines in good hands and our carbines in our laps, as we were in dangerous Apache country. Two miles beyond the summit we met Al Siebers, chief of Indian scouts from Fort McDowell. He was mounted on horseback, and trotting at his heels were twenty Apache scouts armed with three-banded, fifty-caliber United States muskets. These Indians were as usual on foot and had a scarcity of clothing for the season of the year. Each of them had a blanket strapped on his back containing provisions and such articles as were required for a flying pursuit. The party had been out after renegade Apaches from San Carlos reservation far to the south, and with such success as we will soon see. Siebers informed me that about three to four miles farther we would see a smoldering fire to the right of the road and some Apache Indians, but not to be disturbed, for they would give us no trouble, for he had met them the previous evening and settled accounts with them.

When we reached the point indicated, we found two dead squaws and three bucks lying there around the fire. Three gun barrels with broken stocks of the Remington pattern and some torn clothing were lying near the fire. The dead Indians wore shirts and leggings. The squaws had skirts of calico. They were doubtless a renegade war party who had been overtaken in surprise by their kindred who were out as government scouts and put to death. The sight of these five dead Indians caused us to make all haste to Chaves Pass lest we run into an ambuscade, and as a result we reached Chaves Pass long before night.

Chaves Pass is an old site of ancient civilization. There is an earthwork structure five hundred feet square, twelve feet high and twenty feet across its embankment. The hollow square inside shows small mounds, which were at one time a group of buildings. Around it are numerous small mounds, the remains of adobe or cement buildings. At another spot are the remains of old pottery. This ancient fort was supplied by water from a spring nearby and must have had a garrison of several thousand men. It would indicate that it was situated in this pass as a powerful outpost of the great empire lying to the west.

We found there a stage or mail station occupied by two men. From them we learned that the party of Indians we saw dead by the campfire were renegades from San Carlos. We learned that they had been intercepted and killed by the Indian scouts two days previous, and that the others who escaped were on their way into the desolate wilderness of the San Francisco Mountains, which they would soon reach.

Emboldened by this information, I ventured to take a hunt in the Mogollon Range which lay to the south and west of Chaves Pass. One of the assistants at the mail station was a young man named Steele from the state of Iowa. He had an exceedingly good gun, so I had him come with me. The game we wanted mostly was turkeys, but as here and there quail and bighorn sheep abounded, we took with us a shotgun, rifle, and two carbines. There were also mountain lions in considerable numbers in that part of the range.

We took two saddle horses and two pack horses and left my four men to take care of my outfit. I accompanied Mr. Steele about seven miles to a point where there was a famous turkey roost, and we made our camp about a mile to the right, as we expected later to go and hunt our turkeys by the light of the moon. At the campground we saw signs of several flocks of turkeys having passed there recently. We made our camp in the low open space, picketed our horses, and started on foot with our rifles into the dense timber to the west, where we expected to find deer.

I was somewhat surprised to see, far out in this dense, quiet forest of the Mogollon, ancient remains in the form of broken pottery and occasionally walls of buildings. We found a few springs, and around them lay more broken pottery, rock walls, old canals, and every sign of human occupation at one time.

We ran across several flocks of quail, a species common to Arizona and California. They differ much from the quail found in Missouri, Iowa, and Kentucky in being darker in color and having at the top of their heads a beautiful tuft of clean white-tipped feathers. They are easily hunted and excellent to eat. We allowed them to pass, as we wanted larger game. It was almost night when we started back to camp, and near a hollow in which there was some water I saw three large deer eyeing us from a spot not forty yards away. We fired and killed two of them, a buck and a doe. The third one bounded into the undergrowth and escaped.

We returned to our camp, which was but a short distance away. Taking our two pack horses, we went back and brought in the deer. We disemboweled them and hung them on trees near the fire. After eating, we put things in order for the night by tying our horses to trees near the fire, then spread our blankets about ten yards from the fire in a clump of undergrowth so that should Indians come up we might see them and they not see us.

After talking for a while, we went to sleep. I was soon awakened by the snorting and stamping of the horses. Immediately I was on my knee, gun in hand, and gazing towards the fire; but I could see nothing. The horses were standing cock-eared, gazing into the wooded darkness below. I awakened Steele and told him that there was danger on hand and to make ready.

Our horses became more excited, and presently up came a huge Arizona lion, which with ravenous screams seized hold of one of the deer carcasses hanging on the trees. The horses were rearing wildly, but I knew they could not break loose, and as quickly as we could draw bead upon the lion we fired. He was standing where the light of the fire fell full upon him. Both our shots struck him, one in the head and the other in the breast. He sprang upward and backwards, falling on his back, stretched his legs and paws, and after a few screams he was dead. He was a very large lion, measuring from the tip of the nose to the end of the tail nine feet four inches. We left him at the foot of the tree.

The moon had now arisen, which would enable us to see the turkeys roosting in the branches of the high pine trees. We saddled our horses and took along our pack animals, and when we reached the turkey roost found that it was well stocked with game. Our first volley brought two turkeys tumbling down through the branches and aroused the whole colony into much excitement and cackling. They seemed bewildered and kept flying from one branch to another, and we killed five more. By this time the entire flock took flight into the dense wood to the south. We already had enough, so we gathered up the seven we had killed and returned to camp two miles away. It was now almost daylight, but we went to bed, as we were very tired. The sun had already arisen when we awoke.

The two deer, the mountain lion, and the turkeys were more of a load than our two pack horses could well carry, so we placed part of the game on our saddle horses and we walked back to the mail station. When we reached Chaves Pass I was so tired from the long walk and the excitement of the previous night that I left the dressing of our part of the game to Quong Hing and my other three men. I laid down to sleep and when I awoke it was seven o'clock in the evening and supper was almost ready. That evening we did ample justice to the broiled venison, which was quite fat.

In no part of Arizona are there such good fields for sport or hunting as in the heavy timber and abundant grass of the Mogollon Mountains. It was then but little frequented, as few mines had been found there. The black-tailed deer, the white-tailed deer, the antelope, and a very small species of deer occur here and also in the Santa Cruz Mountains. The antlers of the small deer are not more than eight inches in length, and in weight it does not exceed forty pounds when dressed. They are not numerous even in the Mogollons, and I do not know of any other place on the American continent where they abound, save in the Mogollon and the Santa Cruz mountains.

In this part of Arizona there are mountain lions, brown bears, coyotes, a few gray wolves, gray and red foxes, skunks, porcupines, turkeys, and quail. Wild ducks and snipes may be found at various spots where large springs form in their outflow ponds or marshes. There are quite a number of elk. In the various streams there are abundant fish, chiefly mountain trout. This is a wonderful hunter's paradise, and through these deep forests the archaeologists of the future will find a region rich in antiquities.

The Mogollon is well wooded and watered. The rock formations of this region are lava, limestone, porphyry, volcanic trap, basalt, and slate with much feldspar. The region appears to have undergone tremendous volcanic convulsions, and fissures abound over all its surface. The Mogollon is an extension of the Sierra Blanca, or White Mountains, which are much higher than the Mogollon. In these two ranges and Black Mesa rise the headwaters of the Gila in New Mexico.

The waters of the Little Colorado arise in the Mogollon and the region to the northwest. It is in this well-wooded romantic region that the Apaches have long had their strongholds, and the Camp Apache and San Carlos reservations are located in the lowest part of this same region.

These reservations encompass 2,528,000 acres and in 1879 contained 4,457 Apaches of various branches of the tribe. The tribe is divided into several bands, including 1,512 Coyoteros, 1,050 Pinals including 629 Arivaipas, 207 Chiricahuas, 352 Yumas, and 618 Mojaves. After many wars with the United States government, these bands were finally compelled by conquest to dwell on their separate reservations, but they frequently break their treaties and escape to kill many whites and Mexicans. Generals Crook, Miles, and Howard for years were engaged in conquering these irrepressible rascals, and it was in 1872 that the government first attempted to force them onto reservations. The name San Carlos was given to their reservation at that time, and it is under military control of about 350 white soldiers and fifty Apache scouts at Camp Apache.

The Apaches are by far the most cunning and treacherous of all the American tribes. From the first appearance of the white man, they have shown themselves to be alert and cunning, ever ready to steal and plunder; and bloodshed and property destruction are their greatest pleasures. For two hundred years they have been real terrors of Chihuahua, Sonora, and Durango in Old Mexico, as well as Arizona until 1872. Every year for scores of years they would descend annually into Mexico, striking some unprepared town or settlement, killing the male inhabitants and carrying away women and children, horses and cattle, goats and sheep, murdering every man or boy that might fall into their hands and putting the torch to every dwelling.

During the last generation their great leader was the Chiricahua chief Cochise. For twenty years prior to 1872 he and his band were the most dreaded of any Indians on the continent. He died in 1874 at the San Carlos reservation and left behind him several sons who have shown a spirit of willingness to submit to the laws of peace. His son Taza is chief of the Chiricahuas.

Although the Apaches have been taught agriculture on the reservation, numerous raids against the whites in Arizona and Sonora have taken place. Generations of training in civil pursuits and formal education will be required before the Apaches will become submissive members of the American nation. These Indians have always refused Christianity. In their natural state they are spiritualists. In the early years of Spanish discovery, Franciscan and Jesuit priests unknown and alone entered these regions and preached Christ crucified to every tribe. By the Pimas and Papagos they were accepted as messengers from Heaven, and these Indians today are largely Roman Catholics. Amongst the Apaches and other tribes these missionaries found only ill treatment or the crown of martyrdom. The peaceful gospel of Christ was poorly suited to those Apache men of blood. Father Kino spent almost twenty years amongst them only to find martyrdom at their hands. The place of his final rest after martyrdom is not known. Fathers Sedalman, Font, and Garcia, Spanish Jesuit and Franciscan priests with a few assistants, spent the latter half of the eighteenth century amongst them; and, although some of their work has borne good fruit, most of these wild tribes continue to be a perverse nation.

To control these various Indian tribes, Arizona has nine military camps: Camp Apache, Camp Bowie, Camp Grant, Camp Lowell, Camp McDowell, Camp Mojave, Camp Verde, Camp Thomas, and Camp Whipple, which last is the headquarters of the Department of Arizona. The population of Arizona, whites and Indians, at present is about seventy-five thousand, and it is a country rich in gold, silver, lead, copper, iron, and other minerals. With its grazing and agriculture, these resources will in time make it the jewel of the mountain regions. Arizona has nine months of delightful weather, but the other three months are little short of hell on earth, so great is the heat.

I awoke at an early hour the day after our hunt and found the skies clear and the day most agreeable. Because of the miserable lava-covered road of the previous fifty miles west of Chaves Pass, we found that our mules required reshoeing and that much injury had been done to our wagon tires. For this reason we thought it best to remain one more day at Chaves Pass Station, as there was a blacksmith's forge there. Mr. Dawson was an exceedingly good worker in steel and iron, and we had with us a sufficient number of fresh mule shoes and toe corks. With the other two men acting as his assistants, we reshod the four mules by one o'clock and then put the wagon into good condition.

The reader will recall that at Prescott I placed in a side brace on the outside of this wagon a sum of almost eleven thousand dollars in United States currency. Since that time I had accumulated from the sale of merchandise a sum of about thirty-five hundred dollars, also largely in United States currency, and this I wrapped in tarpaper tightly bound with strong cord and hid within a two-gallon can of axle grease. I had also in one of our provision boxes about five hundred dollars in American and Mexican silver coin, so that in that wagon, which was a somewhat unpretentious vehicle, there was hidden almost fifteen thousand dollars.

I fully realized the chances I was taking, but those chances were necessary because it was very difficult getting treasure out of the country in any other way. I had so far been very fortunate in the character of the men whom I had in my employ on each of my expeditions. They proved to be men in every way faithful and upright. At the same time, I found it at all times advisable to be extremely cautious and watchful, as daily I came in contact with men who would murder a traveler or any helpless victim for five hundred dollars.

Now, in looking back at those days, I marvel not only at the chances I took of being robbed or murdered but also that, although during each expedition I had different men in my employ, there was never an altercation or a quarrel among them. My three Chinese cooks were faithful from the beginning to end. I never lost one horse or mule by accident or theft. I may state that I was extremely fortunate, and in my mature years I certainly would never have attempted the dangerous life I went through during my three Arizona expeditions.

One more station lay between Chaves Station and the Little Colorado. This was known as Haywood's Station. Mr. Harvey Haywood was a stockman who married a Spanish lady of New Mexico, and at his residence took care of the stock belonging to the mail company and gave the usual comforts to the traveler.

About five miles east of Chaves Pass, we met the United States mail carrier riding horseback. He was seemingly in great haste and said but little to us, although I desired to ask him about the condition of the road. We were now completely outside the timber belt of the great Mogollon forest and traveling down an open country. The rock formation was almost entirely of red sandstone, and the vegetation was almost wholly tufted grass or bunch grass with a rather inferior growth of stunted sagebrush. About nine miles after we met the mail carrier, we saw a man lying by the side of the road some distance ahead. Thinking it might be a highwayman waiting to have us throw up our hands, I halted my driver and took out a pair of field glasses. There was blood upon his face, and I saw that he was dead.

We drove forward to where he lay. He was lying on his back, his arms outstretched, his broad-brimmed white hat lying near him. He wore a gray coat, dark blue woolen shirt, and heavy woolen pants thrust into his boot tops. A bullet hole showed where he had been shot in the head. He wore a mustache and was light-haired. He seemed to be thirty to thirty-five years of age. Near him lay a large red cotton handkerchief in which there was some bread and some roast meat. The handkerchief was tied at four corners, forming a sort of small bundle. We did not touch him.

We reached Mr. Haywood's early in the evening. He was absent, but his wife and a hired Mexican man were there. We found the place very comfortable for the night, and obtained both hay and grain for our mules. We put up our tents as usual, and within an hour Quong Hing had our supper prepared. There was quite a large house for the freighters or travelers near Haywood's residence, where they could cook and spread their blankets. It was about thirty-five or forty feet in length, with a floor of one vast flag of red sandstone on which the house had been built.

We told Mrs. Haywood of the dead man on the road, and described his clothes and his features. We also told of having met the mail carrier earlier in the morning. Mrs. Haywood said that the man was from St. Johns on the Little Colorado. He had stopped there at the Haywood Station the previous night, and in the morning he and the mail carrier had high words regarding remarks that the man had made about a young Mexican lady at St. Johns. She said the man had started away toward the western mines of Arizona, where he intended to obtain work, that the mail rider followed, and she believed that the latter had killed him. The man some time before had joined the Mormons at Sunset Crossing, and was baptized into that church. This was on the Little Colorado.

Mrs. Haywood said that his name was John McMullen. He had been paying his addresses to a girl in the Mexican settlement of St. Johns or San Juan, but was rejected by her. It was then that he spread evil reports relative to the girl's chastity, whereupon the mail carrier, who was her successful suitor, swore vengeance upon him.

McMullen went down to the Mormon settlement at Sunset, where he was baptized. According to his own statement, he was a good miner, so the bishop at Sunset thought it wisest for him to go to the mines near Prescott where he could earn money for the common good of the community. What became of his body I know not, as by law we dared not touch it, and to report the finding of it to an officer would involve the loss of a week in a country in which I did not wish to tarry.

The country east and northeast from the Mogollon Range to the Little Colorado River and far beyond is in carboniferous red sandstone. It is generally rather barren on the surface, but along the Little Colorado the soil is quite good. I felt certain that extensive coal deposits exist in that region.

Another day's drive brought us to the Mormon fort on the Little Colorado.[14] It was built of palisades made of split cottonwood timber of about ten to twelve inches in diameter, and was about three hundred feet square. There were two large gates on the north and the south, swinging on heavy iron hinges. There were about seventy families in the fort. A Mormon bishop officiated there, and the place bore an intensely religious and formal air. A man named Lot Smith from Farmington, Utah, twenty miles north of Salt Lake City, Utah, was bishop over this community. His first counsel was a man named Ramsey, by birth a Scotchman.[15]

To describe the main features of this interesting community I will have to go back three or four years into Mormon history.[16] About 1874 Brigham Young called upon the Mormons to join an order he was going to establish, called the Order of Enoch. This was a work about which he claimed to have been inspired by the Almighty, and its nature was that every Saint who could bring himself to enter was to sign over all his earthly possessions to the Order of Enoch, or Church of the Latter Day Saints, his land, money, horses, and cattle—in a word, all he possessed—and it was to become the common property of the church. In return, each man and woman was to receive bread and clothing and house room for himself and family until death, and the same was to extend to his family after his death so long as they were willing to toil in that way. But no man of the rank and file was to handle a dollar of money as his own.

After giving the Order of Enoch all that had not been taken from them as tithing, they were to live unitedly as one family, working according to orders from the bishop or taskmaster of each community. When any man required anything for himself or family he asked the bishop or taskmaster for it, and if the bishop or taskmaster thought that he did not require the favor he must go without it.

Now this plan did not work very well. Brigham Young started it thinking that he would cut off all outside trade in Utah; but, willing as most members of the church had been to live according to rules of the faith, many of the Mormons seemed to be averse to this sort of life and would not accept a bait of this kind. However, many did, and this community far away on the Little Colorado was simply an example of socialism.

I found that all business would have to be transacted through the bishop. I bought from him a thousand pounds of grain for ten cents per pound, which he claimed was a great favor to me. Of course I thanked him for it and made it a point for my men and me to be as agreeable as possible, as I wanted to see as much and learn as much as possible of the institution there as I could.

I told my men to go and prepare their supper in our tents, as I desired to remain and see what kind of table living there was in the community. I managed affairs in such a way as to have the bishop invite Dawson and me to eat with him. A bell soon announced that supper was ready. This first course was for the young married men and wives and for the young unmarried women and men.

Dining took place in a long hall fifty feet in width by one hundred feet in length, where there were three long tables. For each person there was a tin plate, a steel knife and fork, and a tinned iron spoon. By the side of each plate there was a little pot or cup made of clay and burned in a kiln near the fort. To every four persons there was an earthen pitcher, homemade at the local kiln, and filled with molasses. There was a similar pitcher big enough to be its father, which was full of water. In a large tin dishpan there was a quantity of beans and fat pork. There was also a large quantity of corn bread, and this was all there was to eat and drink on either table.

There was a bishop's counselor, deputy, or elder at every table who called on all to arise and offered a long prayer thanking God for all the good things in sight on that table, for the fine quarters they possessed, for health and strength, and for the great jewel of religious faith of which they were in possession. Then all fell to eating, and during the meal not one word was spoken by anyone.

When the meal was finished, the aforesaid elder or bishop's counselor again arose and thanked God for the excellent supper of which they had partaken. He asked Providence to protect them as a body and as a people, to give to the young strength to resist the falsehoods of the Gentile world. He prayed that God would hasten the perfection of the Latter-day Saint kingdom over all the land, and that the enemies of the church might be laid low. He told the Lord that they knew they had the true and everlasting gospel, and that he himself hoped the Almighty would strike him with forked lightning before he would be permitted to apostasize from a church so pure and holy. A general "Amen" went up, and then a hymn was sung, after which we drew out and let the children of both sexes come to supper. Their supper consisted of corn bread, molasses, and water.

There was a dance after supper in which old and young took part, the tables having been removed to the sides of the hall to allow dancing. After the dance had ended, the bishop (or perhaps he was the president), Lot Smith, arose and again thanked the Lord that they had been permitted to take a part in this very pleasurable dance that evening; then everyone separated for the night. Dawson and I returned to our tents where we freely talked until late hours of what peculiar creatures we mortals be.

This band of men and women had been called by the Almighty, as they put it, to come here and build up this establishment. It was to be merely a church plantation where everything belonged to President Taylor,[17] including the men, women, and children who toiled in the fields or in the workshop. Of course, the average intellect of this body of humanity was not extraordinarily high and they reasoned not as to the cause for which they toiled; but, satisfied with the homely fare and the generally peculiar privileges afforded by their faith, they were content to toil and ask no questions.

This place, known as "Lower Sunset," is forty miles from the Moqui villages.[18] I was determined to visit those peculiar Indian towns or villages, as I looked upon them as being a remnant of the ancient race that once peopled Utah with well-built towns as far north as the present town of Willard. I determined to leave my men in quarters and go myself with one member of my party and a guide I would hire at the Mormon fort. Dawson was the man to accompany me, and Bishop Lot Smith furnished me a young man named Isaac Hunter. I also obtained from him four saddle mules, one of them being a sumpter, or pack mule.

We started early in the morning, taking an Indian trail over a broken country to the east of Sunset. We had rations for eight days, six pair of blankets, and two hundred pounds of wheat for the mules. Each had a six-shooter, forty rounds of ammunition, and a sheath knife. Matches and all articles necessary for preparing fuel were taken. I took with me my shoulder bag containing pencils, notebooks, compass, and barometer.

The mules were exceedingly good, and we moved rapidly over the broken and desolate sandstone. At noon we camped for lunch where there was water in a cavity among the rocks, and after feeding our mules a quantity of soaked wheat we started onward. There are knolls and rolling hills of red sandstone, scattering groups of cedar and juniper all the way to the Moqui villages. Here and there along the route one beholds bare, desolate walls of prehistoric villages. These little houses are now doorless and roofless, but they were well built and were no doubt occupied by a thrifty people. This occupation must have continued for several generations, because of the piles of refuse and material that gradually accumulated.

On our second day near sundown we beheld a crazy-looking pile in the distance ahead. Putting spurs to our mules, we soon reached the base of the cliffs on which stands the Moqui village Oraibi. We met four of the men of the community who were returning from their fields from three to five miles from town. Finding that they understood Spanish much better than English, I addressed them in that language, telling them that we desired to visit their village and remain perhaps one or two days.

We reached the town by a peculiarly constructed ancient roadway approaching from the desert. Our coming was soon made known to the chief, who welcomed us and gave us a large room for the night. This was quite neat and clean, the floor being formed of a kind of reddish cement. Our mules were placed in one of the rooms on the ground floor and given corn fodder, of which the Moquis had a good deal in a very well cured state.

We found the inhabitants a simple, quiet people, and I think them the most industrious people I have ever seen in any country. This race is thought to be descendants and of the same blood as the people whose ruins lie all over western and central Arizona.

After taking a bath in a large earthen tank, we sat down and talked for an hour with one of the old men, who continued to look at me and my companions very curiously, possibly because of our dress. He could talk some Spanish, but very little English. I learned that he was eighty-six years of age and a near relative of the high chief Manuello. He said the chief was going to visit me in an hour. He wanted to know if we had plenty of tobacco. Realizing that morning that it would be useful to cut up six very large plugs of tobacco, I had them all in a bag at my saddle bow. I gave him a few pieces of this tobacco and two cigars.

While he was talking to me, a young girl of about eighteen years brought in four earthen bowls, in one of which was stewed mutton and in another a quantity of well-cooked Spanish beans. She returned in a moment with two more little pots, one full of drinking water and the other with a kind of syrup made from the root of the mescal plant. She came back a third time with a pile of yellow and red bread wafers made from thin corn paste baked on heated rocks or plates of red sandstone before a hot fire. She carried this on a square of matting made from the fibre of a species of cactus plant. Although we had provisions, I saw that it would be bad grace for us not to receive this food, which was quite ample and which we found to be palatable.

We found that we had arrived just after their famous snake dance,[19] a weird, devilish-like ceremony in which they take forth from places where they have been secured numbers of rattlesnakes, and each dancer, seizing one between his teeth, goes through a wild dance with the writhing serpents distorting themselves in a mad effort to escape. This snake dance is one of the few repulsive and most barbarous ceremonies still practiced by this otherwise very interesting people. At the time of our visit the year's religious ceremonies and great social entertainments had just ended. Everything was peaceful. Storytelling and the relating of legends and traditions were being given by the wise men of the pueblo, or city.

I found this pueblo to be the chief stronghold and situated on the most westerly of the three mesas on which stand the six pueblos of the Hopi, or Moqui, people. Chief Juan Miguel informed me that on the east [First Mesa] stood Sichomoir, with about 125 people; Hano, with 175; Walpi, with 225; and down in the little pueblo on the plains there were about twenty-five. On the mesa west of the first or east mesa, or the middle mesa [Second Mesa], stand the pueblos of Mishongnovi, Shungopovi, and Shipoloir.[20] Shungopovi has 250 people; Mishongnovi, 225; and Shipoloir, 130. On the third, or west mesa, stands his own pueblo of Oraibi, with a population of 955, the largest and most important of the six pueblos. Thus on the three mesas in the six pueblos there are about 2,500 souls, and this Hopi, or Moqui, semi-civilized nation holds a reservation having an area of 2,270,000 acres, cultivating annually 2,500 acres of corn producing 25,000 to 30,000 bushels of grain.

They are a careful people, always laying away in chambers a quantity of corn to guard against famine should crops fail through drought. From 1,000 to 1,200 acres are under fruit orchards, including peaches and apples. 2,000 acres are put under production of melons, pumpkins, squashes, beans, onions, chile, parsnips, and sunflowers. Tobacco of an excellent quality is produced. Barley, wheat, and cotton are produced in limited quantities. The Hopi people claim to have fifty thousand sheep; ten thousand goats; one thousand cattle; 4,500 mustang horses, burros, and mules; five hundred hogs; and great numbers of chickens and turkeys.

Owing to the scarcity of water, they do not have any, or very few, ducks and geese. Although wild game is not abundant, the Hopi people are inveterate hunters and fond of eating every sort of wild game. Rabbits in some localities are very plentiful, and when they are to be obtained in great numbers the entire male population of a pueblo will go out after them, thus securing sometimes thousands in numbers during a single hunt. Their skins are made into clothing, their flesh dried or made into pemmican. Coyotes are hunted for their skins, and are caught in deadfalls or killed in the chase.

In stature the Hopi people are rather undersized, although well built. Both men and women have docile, pleasing features of face and eyes, with cheekbones of some inclined to be prominent. They usually have even and well-preserved teeth, small and well-shaped hands and feet. The young girls and married women are quite handsome. The girls marry early as a rule, usually from fourteen to seventeen years of age. Unmarried women of twenty to twenty-five are seldom seen. The young men take wives when they are from eighteen to twenty-five years old. They are monogamists, and both men and women lead good moral lives. Women bring forth many children, but not more than forty percent live to the age of ten years. I was not able during my short stay at Oraibi to learn just how marriage affairs were arranged amongst them save that presents are passed to the father and mother of the girl to be married. A short courtship precedes the definite undertaking of married life.

Among this race of people there are many albinos, or white Indians. A very strange domestic custom exists among the Hopi, in which some of the men dress as women, doing women's work in all lines. I do not know of a similar example amongst any other people of any country or any time.[21]

Boys and girls under ten years of age in the summer go almost naked. Young women from twelve years until married wear a peculiar headdress, a sort of shell-like whorl on each side of the head, which is rather attractive. When married, the girl wears her hair in two braids down the back or resting on the breasts, right and left. The dress of the women consists of a sort of woolen or cotton overgarment. Buckskin or leather moccasins are usually worn by all women, and they wear an abundance of beads, necklaces, earrings of silver or brass, and finger rings homemade from silver coins, many of which are enriched by settings of turquoise or garnets.

The married women wear a finely woven ceinture or belt made from native wool with many colors. The men wear a cotton or woolen shirtlike garment, trousers of cottonade or wool, sandals or moccasins, and almost as much native-made jewelry as the women.

These people spin and weave their own cotton or wool into excellent and durable fabrics. They are very skillful in dyeing many colors, and expert in tanning skins or hides. They are skillful in working metals but have never learned to smelt ores. When first visited by the Spaniards in the sixteenth century, these pueblos were living in the stone age; but after becoming acquainted with iron and steel, gold, silver, lead, and copper they have grown to be very skillful in every line of metalwork.

The Hopi people take much interest in native music and are fond of singing. Their musical instruments are the drum, fife, piccolo, tambourine, flute, and whistle.

The Hopi houses have stood many centuries. They are from two to five stories in height and achieve durability and strength with walls sufficiently strong to resist the attacks of savage enemies. The approaches to their towns or pueblos are natural fortifications from which a few armed warriors can render it almost impossible for enemies ever to enter. At each pueblo cisterns are numerous and filled in the wet season and carefully guarded at all times.

The Hopi from past centuries to the present are exceedingly skillful potters, making all sorts of earthen vessels, fashioning them very neatly, and decorating them in many colors. In ancient times they were armed with stone axes, stone lances with flint points, and stone knives. The basic materials of their tools were flint, agate, jasper, quartzite, and obsidian. In changing from the implements of the stone age, the Hopi have modernized only to such a degree as to make living more agreeable; but all weapons are now made of steel, as are those of all their neighbors.

In domestic life and government they are now as they were before the coming of the white men. They never, even under the old Spanish governors, became Christianized, but continued to believe in a sort of polytheism—different powers that control the winds, the waters, the air, the clouds, the soil, the mountains, the deserts, and the valleys. They are all spiritualists and believe in the hereafter. The souls of the dead go to the devil in some region not exactly known; others go into a happy life that is provided if they have been fairly decent or half-decent in life.

During our three days at Oraibi I worked continuously to learn all I could relative to the present and past of this wonderful people, and no doubt Juan Miguel thought me the most inquisitive man he had ever met. We were kindly treated during our stay. I purchased a few of their blankets, belts, women's ceintures, several pieces of silver homemade jewelry, three bows, and about twenty arrows. I gave to a few of the headmen a pocket knife and a skinning knife each.

Juan Miguel questioned me very exhaustively relative to what kinds of guns and pistols I yet had with my caravan at the Mormon fort, and the prices of each. He then wanted to know how long I would remain at the Mormon settlement. He cautioned me to be very careful while passing through the Navajo country, as the Navajos were skillful and cunning thieves and at times murderers as well. To guard us against evil men and evil spirits, he gave to each of us a small bag of prayer meal that had been prepared by the chief medicine man, bidding us when we felt nervous or in danger of enemies, high winds, or high waters, to take a pinch of about a teaspoonful into our mouths and chew it until the danger had passed, assuring us that, if it did not do us any good, it would not do harm.

We returned to Lot Smith's fort near the Little Colorado, spending one night and two days on the road. During my several days' absence, my mind constantly reverted to my party left at the fort, because there was hidden within my wagon almost seventeen thousand dollars. It was hidden in such a way that I had but little fear of its being discovered. Although I had confidence in Sieboldt and Mooncraft, I did not know what might happen; but upon our return I found all things well and our mules much improved by a whole week's rest.

Now I previously stated that this Mormon settlement was presided over by Lot Smith, a man of rather gloomy manners. In Utah he formerly lived at Farmington, between Salt Lake and Ogden, until called to establish this mission of communistic life on the Little Colorado. He had quite a history. When General Albert Sidney Johnston's army of United States troops was marching into Utah in the latter part of 1857, he, with a body of mounted Utah militia, attacked three large but poorly guarded government supply trains and burned all the supply wagons. This crippled the incoming army and compelled almost five thousand men to camp with only a starvation quantity of food for five months in a savage wilderness until fresh supplies were brought from Fort Leavenworth the following spring. Their suffering that winter was terrible. Knowing these things, I was not very much impressed with the man who was the author of their misery, but I compelled my personal feeling to conform to the necessity of business, safety, and the requirements of a student and explorer, and made myself as agreeable as possible.

Lot Smith unfortunately had not ingratiated himself with the Indians. I learned that on several occasions he had had trouble with the Navajos, and a considerable time after our visit a Navajo stole his favorite riding mule. Smith, instead of going to a Navajo camp nearby and informing the headman of his loss and demanding that the mule be returned, took the matter into his own hands, and with three or four of his neighbors started in pursuit of the thief. The Indian, accompanied by two or three others, crossed the Little Colorado River into a broken country to the west.

The Indian and his associates saw Lot Smith and his party approaching at some distance, and secreted themselves behind a group of immense sandstone boulders. Upon the approach of Lot Smith and his partners, the Indians opened fire, instantly killing Smith and wounding one or two of his associates, who beat a retreat. The Navajo and his companions succeeded in making their escape, and as their names were not known to the white people at the fort, they were never apprehended. So ended the life of a prominent early pioneer leader of Utah Territory, Lot Smith.[22]

Upon my return from the Hopi country, I entered into trade with Smith and his counselors, selling them six hundred dollars worth of caliber-fifty breechloading muskets, a number of cap-and-ball cavalry revolvers, and a considerable quantity of ammunition. They purchased these because of the danger they were constantly in because of the Apache and Navajo Indians. The prices were about three times what I had paid for them at Fort Verde, but as Lot Smith charged us outrageously high prices for grain, hay, and shelter for our mules and guide to and from Oraibi, I was only moderate in advance in the sales of arms.

After closing up our business for the day quite late in the afternoon, imagine my surprise to see arriving at my tents Chief Juan Miguel with four other Hopi men of prominence. They wanted to purchase a number of carbines, muskets, and Colt's pistols, and a number of knives. They had three hundred dollars in American coin, for which I sold to them ten fifty-caliber three-banded needle guns, five remodeled fifty-caliber Sharps carbines, five Colt's cap-and-ball cavalry pistols, one thousand rounds of ammunition, and one dozen hunting knives. They were mounted on Mexican ponies with three pack animals. They started back the same day, as they were anxious to reach home as soon as possible lest they be intercepted by a superior number of Navajos and robbed of the firearms just purchased. So closed my experience with the Hopi inhabitants of old Oraibi.

It was a morning in early February, 1879, when we drew away from the Mormon fort. The day was beautiful for the season of the year, and our mules were in fine trim for travel. Isadore Mooncraft, Eusebius Sieboldt, Quong Hing, Dawson, and the pup Moses were all glad to leave, as our stay at the Mormon fort had grown somewhat monotonous and we had a long way to travel before we would reach Silver Reef in southern Utah.

We found the road fairly good for the first day, and night brought us to the famous Petrified Forest. We had not been notified as to the distance or extent of this wonderful phenomenon. It was almost sundown when we reached its edge and proceeded to camp near a small tributary of the Little Colorado.

Unhitching our mules, we put our tents quickly into place, watered the mules, and gave them grain. Isadore Mooncraft and Quong Hing proceeded with their axes to procure firewood. It was growing dark, and thinking we were at the edge of a grove of fallen timber made so by a hurricane, one of them struck a log and discovered that we were simply at the edge of the petrified forest. Although the bit of the axe was broken, a short distance to the east from our camp were two- or three-score trees of desert cedar from which we obtained ample excellent wood.[23]

For several hours in the morning we studied the wonderful features of a once magnificent forest that had been turned into stone during the carboniferous period. The forest then was buried beneath hundreds of feet of blue earth and carboniferous sandstone, lying there for ages and ages. Still later, during subsequent ages, erosion by winds and floods wore away the surface until the old forest was exposed to view, its ancient groves of magnificent trees in a mostly prostrated condition and in great confusion, but all turned or converted into jasper, agate, and cherty petrified matter, and all showing the form and features of the groves of an ancient wooded country. The annular ring marks, the knots, cracks, inner wood and bark are still plain to view, but petrified. It was quite easy to distinguish pine, fir, cedar, walnut, birch, mesquite, and oak amongst the fallen giants.

Many of the trees lying there were more than one hundred fifty feet in length, mostly broken into sections, some of them broken at right angles into sections of from three to eight feet in length. At one place a half-dozen trees broken only into two or three sections lay across a deep dry ravine, forming bridges or footlogs for twenty feet across this streambed. We wandered over a considerable part of this area and estimated that it must cover about four square miles. At the time of our visit the locality was known to few persons. We discovered the petrified but broken skeletons of elk, deer, gigantic tortoises or terrapins, wolf bones, and other unidentifiable animals.

So great was our surprise that we did not leave the locality until one o'clock in the afternoon. We gathered about two hundred pounds of very choice specimens of petrified wood and animal remains and would have taken more except that the roads were now bad, and we knew that our mules would grow thin before reaching Silver Reef. Besides, I expected to purchase or trade for a quantity of Navajo blankets when reaching Moencopi to bring with me to New York City.

When we would reach the Navajo country, which was now but a short distance to the north, I intended remaining there for from two to three days investigating conditions amongst the Navajos and trading with them. For this reason we were cautious to keep a careful night watch on our wagon and mules, and late and early keep our hands on our weapons lest we be taken by surprise.

We were twenty-five miles northward from the Petrified Forest when we encountered the first Navajos, about fifty of them, men, women, and children, driving before them several flocks of sheep, with their camp equipage packed on a dozen pinto Mexican horses and they themselves riding other ponies. A few boys were following the sheep on foot.

They at once wanted to know what we were doing in their country. We told them we were passing through to the north. They next wanted to know where were our hogans, which meant that they desired to know where our homes were and from what point of the world we had come, and if we had anything to sell, swap, or give away. As I knew that it would not be wise to attempt trading or doing business with these fellows until we had reached a point far into their country, we did not tell them that we had anything to sell or trade, nor did I intimate that I desired purchases of either Navajo silverwork or blankets.

They next wanted to know why we were all so well armed, and asked if we were soldier men. We told them that we had been in the Apache country and for that reason provided ourselves with pistols, muskets, and carbines. "Yes," said one of the more talkative ones, "You were certainly very wise in being watchful while in the Apache country," as they were also enemies of the Navajo, but that as we were now in the Navajo country, we would be perfectly safe. For that reason, we should either make presents of our guns, pistols, or knives to the Navajos, our friends, or trade them to them for blankets, ponies, jackasses, or Navajo silverwork.

We told them that as yet we desired holding on to our weapons as we might encounter bands of Ute Indians farther north, but to be agreeable and show them that we were their friends, I distributed amongst them a quantity of plug tobacco cut up into squares of one inch each way. They thanked us kindly for this favor and then asked us to buy two or three sheep that we could kill on the spot and take with us, as the carcasses we could easily carry with us in our wagon. This we also declined and went forward on our journey. I was very interested in this party of Indians. They were bright and intelligent and had good features.

It was only a few hours until we came to three Navajo hogans standing near the road. These hogans are dome-shaped and are constituted of such material as they can obtain in the vicinity. Usually there are four center posts of cedar, willow, or cottonwood. From these, posts or tree branches radiate out to where the circular wood or stone walls reach to the height of from four to seven feet above the ground. Such structures are wind- and waterproof. There is little light within these structures, save where there is an opening at the apex of the roof so that smoke can escape, a fire being always in the space made by the four supporting posts that hold up the hogan roof.

For two days we passed many of those hogans, and on either side of the road there were remains of prehistoric stone houses built on high points where the former builders or occupants could observe the country around for a long distance. Such structures in many places were very neatly and well built, the angles or corners carried up symmetrically, the gaunt walls in many examples having a very fresh look as though built but recently; yet no doubt very many of them must have stood there for centuries. Very many of them were without windows or doors. Doubtless entrance into them was by means of ladders and through openings in the roof. This was proven by there being inside many of such buildings the large sandstone circular slabs about one inch and a half in thickness and about three to three and a half feet in diameter that had been used as entrance space covers similar to those we had seen still in use at Oraibi.

The region through which we were now traveling was what is known as the Painted Desert. It is a rather flat region, the rock formation being of carboniferous age. The red, gray, blue, and green sandstone measures alternate, the red predominating, and a wild, warm, romantic expression rests upon the entire region. At distant points mountain peaks, or as termed in Arizona and Mexico, *pichos*, arise far into the heavens. San Francisco Peak to the west was now almost one hundred miles away, snowcapped and wooded up its sides for a long distance above its volcanic base. A very large part of this country over which we were traveling was practically worthless save for grazing sheep, goats, cattle, burros, or horses. Except for the Little Colorado now lying to our left, there were no large streams. Tanks in the red sandstone measures that retain springs of limited flow constituted all the waters to be found for man or beast. To the Navajos all these tanks were known for generations, and where they are sufficient in volume these Indians had planted peach or apple trees and berry or currant bushes, and patches of sandy soil with corn, pumpkins, squash, melons, tobacco, cotton, red peppers, potatoes, parsnips, and turnips.

Every mile of that wild, unique land was interesting to us. I made copious notes of unusual sights at the Navajo hogans, and at their mule- and sheep camps we studied their work of preparing wool, making blankets, and their wonderful work in making silver finger rings, rings for the ears, brooches for the wrists and arms, and silver discs for belts, as well as silver decorations for bridles, spurs, pistol and knife scabbards, decorations for saddles and bridles, and other leather mountings.

Four days after leaving Sunset Crossing of the Little Colorado and the Mormon fort we reached Moencopi, a sort of trading post or home station in the Painted Desert country. Here we found a man named Ben Hawley with his family, a Mormon from Battle Creek, or Pleasant Grove, ten miles north of Provo, Utah, who appeared to be a sort of missionary and Indian trader, holding a government permit for that purpose.[24] He was purchasing wool from the Navajos at five cents per pound, exchanging with them such articles as tobacco, calico, men's cotton shirts, coarse shoes, cotton trousers, paints, and beads.

As there was a blacksmith shop at Hawley's place on the Moencopi and I wanted to study and trade with the Navajo tribe, we camped for four days a few hundred feet from Hawley's residence and trading post. Hawley had on hand a quantity of charcoal, and as Mooncraft and Sieboldt were good blacksmiths, wagon repairers, and mule-shoers, they set to work reshoeing our four mules, cutting, rewelding, and resetting our wagon tires, and replacing lost nuts, bolts, and screws. From Moencopi to Lee's Ferry on the Big Colorado, the distance is about eighty miles, counting for the curves and angles in the primitive road. For our mules we obtained barley from Mr. Hawley as well as very well-cured alfalfa or lucerne hay, and, as he had a storeroom that we could use in our trade with the Navajo Indians, I felt quite pleased with the situation.

My men soon had everything well fixed for our camp, and we were about to sit down to our evening meal when up walked from the south over the same road we had traveled that day a man, dark-skinned, heavy-set, with long hair and beard. On his shoulder he carried a short gun or rifle of the old muzzle-loading type but of enormous weight and very richly mounted with silver decorations. He came to our tents and at my invitation ate supper with us. At first sight I took him to be a prospector, but soon found that he knew little about mines or minerals or very much in a practical way about anything else. He said that he had been on our trail since we left the Petrified Forest, but, as our gait was too rapid for him and we had twenty miles headstart, we were at Moencopi ere he reached our camp.

I spoke of the Petrified Forest as a great feature of great age, and he said that he was well acquainted with it and the cause of its destruction, as well as of the different petrified animals. He stated that it had all taken place at the time of Noah's flood, and that several nights previous to our meeting he had a revelation to that effect. Since we did not know positively to the contrary, we did not dispute him.

I asked him his business in those parts, and he said he was a Mormon missionary among the Indians of that desolate region. He said his name was Peter Jonathan Edwards. His home was in Salt Lake City. He was on a three-year mission amongst the Navajo, Hopi, and Zuni Indians. Another year would release him from his mission amongst those Indians, after which he expected to do missionary work in the Sandwich Islands. I asked him if he had made many conversions amongst the Navajo or Hopi people. He said as yet he did not know that he had, but he felt he had good reason to believe that the gospel was being considered very seriously by each of these nations. He had sowed the seed of the everlasting gospel amongst them, and the next missionaries amongst them would reap a rich harvest of souls.

Along with his heavy, short rifle, he carried with him a frying pan with a small copper pot, a few spoons, knives, and forks, a tin cup, and a large, tanned black-and-white ox hide that he used for bed and covering at night. This hide was tanned so that it was very flexible. He used a small but sharp axe to cut firewood. With his rifle of large bore, he could use buckshot or bullets. A large part of his living he said was made up of rabbits, mountain rats, chipmunks, and occasionally a pine hen; but also at times for his meals he was forced to accept crickets and grasshoppers. From Indians he obtained at times parched corn and such other kinds of foods as they themselves consumed.

He also said the Petrified Forest was the identical locality where Noah had built his ark, that he had discovered the spot where the timbers had been dressed for that famous vessel, and where the petrified chips and shavings and ends of timbers were yet abundant, but in a petrified state. He was fully convinced because of a dream that he had recently that the ark itself would yet be found in a petrified state on some of the high mesas of that region. He further stated that the petrified bones we saw in the fossilized forest were the bones of animals for which Noah did not have room in the ark and so, as a consequence, they were drowned in the great flood, and that they were there for a proof that the account of Noah and his ship given in the Bible was literally true. He stated that wandering as he now was in that land as a sort of missionary and prophet, he was really a sort of St. John the Baptist, one crying in the wilderness, "Make ready the way of the Lord." He was heralding the coming of one, the latches of whose sandals he was not worthy of untying, and who in that desert land was to come and complete the work of which he had been laying the foundation.

After eating supper with us, he said that he must now go and meet Brother Ben Hawley and deliver a letter he was carrying from Lot Smith, and that he must start at the break of day for Oraibi to deliver a verbal message of a religious nature to the people of the six rock cities, as he called them. Then, raising his hands high above his head, he gave us his patriarchal blessing, took up his heavy rifle, his tanned oxhide bundle with its repacked contents, and passed out of our tents. We never saw him again, but Ben Hawley told us the next day that he was a sort of half-cracked missionary who had been appointed to labor amongst the Navajo, Hopi, and other Indians in Arizona and New Mexico. Up in Utah he had become a sort of harmless nuisance around Salt Lake City, so it was thought best to give him a commission amongst the Indians of the Arizona wilderness and later let him go to the Sandwich Islands. As on this occasion, he frequently carried messages from one Mormon settlement or colony to another.

I had Mr. Hawley send two of his men out to points round about to inform the Navajos that there was a trader at Moencopi and for them to come in with money, blankets, or silver ornaments to trade. On the second day after our arrival fully one hundred Navajo men and women arrived.

Eusebius Sieboldt, Isadore Mooncraft, Con Dawson, and I harnessed our mules and ran our wagon up in front of the empty store building I had rented and unloaded it. The wagon was placed at the side of the warehouse. Our tents were taken down and placed with our camp outfit near where our wagon stood. This was all done shortly after daybreak. Our mules were put back into the nearby corral. At ten o'clock we began trading. This band of Indians was a good representative makeup of the entire tribe. Some of them were exceedingly fine-looking men and women with noble features, wearing a very bold and manly expression; and all of them were quite pleasing.

For trade and sale we yet had about forty guns of different kinds, all of military type, which we had obtained at Fort Verde. There were yet remaining seventeen Colt's cap-and-ball revolvers, about one hundred knives of different kinds and patterns, fifteen hundred rounds of ammunition for different guns and pistols, a considerable quantity of Indian beads and paints, and a small stock of colored cottons, especially large red and yellow bandana handkerchiefs. There were a few magnifying glasses, a few pair of field glasses, about seventy-five pounds of plug tobacco, spectacles, and small mirrors. Save the field glasses, optical instruments, and spectacles, almost all of what we had now on hand was what I had obtained from the sutler at Fort Verde.

The items the Navajos had for trade were Navajo blankets, large and small, silver work of different kinds, some tanned buckskins, some deer, wolf, mountain lion, and fox skins tanned and yet having the fur or hair intact. We inquired the prices of the blankets and of the silver jewelry and other articles of work such as furs, knives, saddles, and bridle ornaments. We had previously known that Navajos asked outrageous prices for anything they might have for sale. Their blankets they placed at from eight to forty dollars each, their silver jewelry and other ornaments at ten times their weight in silver coin.

I at once informed Manuelito,[25] their high chief, who happened to be one of the party visiting us that day, that I very well knew what their blankets, jewelry, and furs were worth. I then went over all of our own stock of goods, gave them my prices, and said that if they wanted to trade on such a basis we would proceed; if not, we would close the store and I would pack up our stock of merchandise and leave their country. I knew well enough that human nature was well developed in them and that although they were shrewd traders, yet like all other classes of people they were anxious to exchange what they possessed and what they could always have for things they wanted but seldom had an opportunity of procuring.

After about two hours of talking amongst themselves in an excited way, off to one side, they presently returned and trade began by their taking all of the three-banded breechloading caliber-fifty Springfield muskets. I had also the Sharps caliber-fifty carbines at twenty-five dollars each. They gave me two well-made, highly colored Navajo blankets at ten dollars each and one small saddle blanket of good make and fine colors for these articles. These small rugs or saddle blankets I took each at five dollars a piece; thus, two large blankets and one small one representing twenty-five dollars were given to me for each one of the Springfield muskets or Sharps carbines. The same price was settled upon for the cap-and-ball pistols with holster and belt. Then followed our trade of silver work along similar lines of value. Next came our trade for colored cotton goods in piece or by the bolt, cotton shirts, Indian beads, paints, knives, needles, scissors, spectacles or looking glasses, and Jews' harps or mouth organs.

On the evening of the second day we had disposed of the entire stock of guns and pistols, ammunition, knives, and other lines of goods that I had from my original stock and also all that I had obtained at Fort Verde. In exchange, I had 151 Navajo blankets and small rugs, fifty-five pounds of silver Navajo jewelry of all sorts, thirty-one spurs, and some fifty other articles of Navajo manufacture.

Knowing we would be expected to feed our customers, I purchased from Mr. Hawley ten head of sheep at two dollars per head, ten bushels of potatoes at one dollar per bushel, three bushels of wheat, a quantity of salt, and four gallons of sorghum molasses. I rented from him two large oblong metal copper-bottomed tanks or molasses pans in which to boil sorghum when making molasses, then purchased from him a wagonload of cedar wood. He and my Chinese cook, Quong Hing, slaughtered the sheep and put in three of the sheeps' carcasses at a time into one of the large molasses tanks. A fire was started in the furnace under the tank, and another fire in the furnace under the other tank. Into the second tank were put three bushels of potatoes and carrots. In a large boiler we had with us we prepared a plentiful supply of coffee. I purchased forty pounds of brown sugar from Mr. Hawley at forty cents per pound and gave fifteen dollars to Mrs. Hawley for one hundred loaves of bread that she had been two days baking in a large outdoor Mexican oven.

On the afternoon of the second day's trading, the big dinner was ready, and about one hundred and twenty men, women, and children were given such a feast as they seldom enjoyed in their own hogans. There was enough left to give them another respectable meal at noon the following day. By that time all of our trading was over. Both the Indians and I were satisfied, and I paid Mr. Hawley for mule stabling and grain, lucerne hay, bread, potatoes, sugar, salt, carrots, the mutton of ten sheep, and store rent the sum of ninety-three dollars.

For two evenings and for part of the last day at Moencopi I very industriously interrogated their chief Manuelito relative to their history, their ways of living, their government, courtship and marriage customs, their religious beliefs, and all that appertained to them as a people. In numbers at that time the Navajos consisted of between eighteen and twenty thousand souls, men, women, and children. They were more civilized than the Utes, Paiutes, Apaches, Commanches, Mojaves, or other wild tribes of Arizona, but not so much so as the Hopi groups of Pueblo Indians to the east. They occupy a large area of rather poor country in northeastern Arizona, southeastern Utah, and northwestern New Mexico. Most of their territory is in Arizona.

As to appearance in face and form, these Navajo Indians run about average in size, weight, and stature with most other men, white or colored. There is greater diversity in their facial features than is usual amongst Indian tribes. Many of them have Roman noses, with other bold commanding features. Usually the eyes and mouth wear a pleasing expression. With the women, the eyes have a very kind and pleasing look. As to morals in chastity and honesty, the Navajos do not seem to average up to the Pueblo people. The Navajos in many cases live to great ages, although most die before the age of sixty.

They own considerable numbers of small Mexican horses, burros, and mules, and large flocks of sheep and goats. From the wool of their sheep they make the famous Navajo blankets, saddle cloths, and small rug-like blankets, and headbands and belts for women, as previously stated. They are exceedingly clever workers in silver, brass, copper, iron, and steel but do not know anything about mining or smelting of any kind. They are also successful in dyeing wool and cotton fabrics, thread, and woolen or cotton twine. Some of their colors they obtain from plants and barks growing in their country, and others are obtained from the post traders at Wingate, Fort Defiance, or Santa Fe, Taos, and Albuquerque.

The Navajos are what we might call a pastoral people, living largely from the proceeds of their flocks of sheep and goats, their few head of cattle, their bands of rather inferior horses. Their limited areas of land produce corn, melons, squash, beets, cabbage, and turnips, and they own scattered peach orchards in the Canyon de Chelly, Canyon del Muerto, and elsewhere.

A unique feature amongst the Navajos is that men and women are on terms of perfect equality. Men and women or husband and wife discuss all business and domestic matters before entering into any business relations with a stranger. For good and sufficient reasons titles, names, and family inheritance descend from the mother's side of the house, and interest in family possessions is held during the life of father and mother or wife and husband as fifty-fifty, or equal in ownership; but at the death of either husband or wife all of the joint property goes to the remaining wife or husband.

They have a queer custom of matrimony. Usually, when a man's wife dies, she (as will be shown why) is often much older than her husband. When she dies, the family wealth passes to her husband, who is now from thirty-five to fifty years of age. At the end of from three to six months he tries to find another wife among Navajo girls from fifteen to twenty years of age. When they are married, the property he has becomes joint in ownership.

As a rule, the Navajo husband, if he is not killed by Apaches or by some other savage Indians, lives until he is about sixty-five or seventy years of age. He then dies and leaves all to his wife, who by this time is maybe thirty-five to fifty years of age. After three to six months, or at the most one year, she suffers much from loneliness. At that time she begins to weave a blanket, or, if she is not an expert weaver, she employs someone who is. Directly the word goes out that the rich widow is weaving a blanket, which means that she is contemplating matrimony. About the same time, quite a number of young bucks in age from about seventeen to twenty-five years begin making her visits dressed in their very best shirts and blankets and riding their best horses. Each of these young fellows she treats with respect and much courtesy. Perhaps six weeks after her fine blanket is completed she has a number of her lady friends assist her in preparing a grand feast. For this she produces boiled or roasted mutton of sheep or goats, boiled beans with boiled jerked meat, parched corn, stewed peaches, and Navajo baked loaves, or, if the season is right for it, ripe peaches or other fruit.

When this great feast is given, from ten to twenty of her admirers are invited, each coming dressed in his very best, riding one horse and leading another packed with his extra belongings. When all the candidates have arrived, they are seated, if the weather is favorable, in a circle outdoors and given each a liberal share of food. After the feast, the beautiful widow comes out of the nearby hogan, carrying the beautiful blanket which is to proclaim the future happiness of one of the young bucks seated in that circle. After making several turns around the circle, the widow throws the blanket around the neck and shoulders of the one she loves best. On that same day the happy couple take two riding horses and from two to four pack horses and depart on their honeymoon. This takes place in some deep but interesting canyon or a wooded mountain glen, where for three to six weeks they live retired from the world.[26]

Like all Indian tribes, the Navajos are extremely superstitious. For example, when a man, woman, or child dies in the hogan, never again will that family occupy the old residence. The corpse is brought forth and laid to rest by night and the hogan is destroyed by fire if built of wood or grass and left to fall into ruin if built of stone. It frequently occurs, however, that if the hogan is of more than usual value, being well constructed of stone and otherwise attractive, when they find that the sick person is certain to die, he is taken out on a stretcher and allowed to breathe his last a few hundred feet outside the residence, thus saving their hogan from destruction. They have a holy fear of going near or touching the clothing or any article on the corpse.

Under no condition will a Navajo touch or eat fish. They tell that this is because very long ago the now dead towns and cliff dwellings north of the San Juan River were occupied by a race of men who were numerous, very warlike, and great enemies of the Navajos. For a long time the Navajos were little better than slaves to these people, being compelled to carry wood or corn or other produce on their backs for long distances to the homes of the Cliff Dwellers and also to do other difficult and menial acts of service.

At length, after many generations of this sort of slavery, a very large and handsome man came from the east. He appeared to rise out of where the sky and earth join together. He carried with him a long rod or staff, and when he came amongst the Navajos, he saw how they were being treated by their masters and he was much displeased. He then told the Cliff Dwellers that their ill treatment of the Navajos must cease or they themselves would get into serious trouble, whereupon the Cliff Dwellers told him that he could go to the devil. Who was he that he should dictate to them, the greatest people in the world? They said further that the Navajos were their slaves and they would continue to do with them and for them as they pleased, and it was not for him or anyone else to tell them what they must do.

When he heard these things, the man told the Navajos to wait and keep quiet until the next new moon, at which time they were to procure things for a great feast. They must obtain wild turkeys, stewed rabbits, green corn, paper bread, and other delicacies and prepare this feast along the south bank of the San Juan River and at places along the banks of the Little Colorado. Three days before the feast, they were to invite the Cliff Dwellers, their enemies, to come, make peace, and eat.

So the Cliff Dwellers, who were great gluttons, started forth on the day of the great feast. As they rushed forth to cross the San Juan River, the great wise man stood on the south bank, and when they were about in the middle of the river he waved his long rod and they were instantly turned into fish. The Navajos themselves ate the great feast prepared for their enemies and became a free people; but they never to this day eat fish, for they are the descendants of the Cliff Dwellers. In proof of this wonderful event, the cliff dwellings of that entire region stand accursed and lonely and uninhabited save by the ghosts of the cliff dwellers.

I found the Navajos to have scores of astounding traditions similar to this great fish story. They tell of their wars with the Hopi or Moquis or Zunis and with the Utes and Apaches, in all of which troubles the Navajos come out best. They also tell of how they once fought with the Spaniards and Mexicans, and their wars with the Americans, of their wars with Kit Carson and his soldiers, and of how they made peace with the United States and their present agreeable standing with the Great Father at Washington.

Family pride and family traditions and social standing go along in the lives of Navajos as amongst the white race. Love and hate, good family government, domestic broils and scandals take place in the great Navajo reservation just as in Boston, St. Louis, or San Francisco. There are hundreds of ways of making trouble in a Navajo household, just as in the home of a Methodist minister.

Amongst the Navajos the number of sheep, goats, jackasses, pinto ponies, family silver ornaments, and many-colored family blankets go very far to give a family standing in Navajo society. When midwinter comes, it is frequently the case that quite a number of Navajo families, through gambling, high living, or other bad management, are compelled to take their family silver ornaments to the traders and pawn them for food, tobacco, and other necessities. In the summer, when wool and blankets are sold to the traders, the family silver is taken out of hock and each member takes particular pride and care to wear again his or her share of the family jewels. But should they fail to redeem their jewels, they at once and forever lose their high standing until by some turn of good fortune they again become rich.

Certain places amongst the Navajos possess peculiar virtues and powers of good and evil. One very prominent old Navajo named Juan Blanco told me that Navajo Mountain, Canyon de Chelly, and Canyon del Muerto are amongst the places where spirits of the dead are very active at certain seasons, and such places are frequented by living Navajos only during the times when the ghosts are either absent or in deep sleep. It may be stated that the above localities are quite rich in old ruins, so it is quite natural that a people like the Navajos would attach mystic powers to such localities. I very much regretted that the above regions were much too far away to allow our visiting them on that occasion. At Moencopi I learned that from that point I could have gone to the Hopi villages over a much shorter and no doubt better route than the one I took from the Mormon fort at Sunset. I was, however, much pleased that even though I could have made a much shorter route I yet saw that strange but interesting little nation.

Beyond Moencopi the same deep red and pink expression of the Painted Desert region was yet upon the country. From time to time we saw more of the ancient ruins. It was early in the morning when we left Moencopi, but so rough and rocky was the road that we did not make more than twenty miles that day. About four o'clock in the afternoon, Isadore Mooncraft shot a very young and fat buck deer, which Quong Hing and Con Dawson dressed. We had venison for supper, breakfast, and noon the next day. Our camp that first night out from Moencopi was near some water tanks in the red sandstone, and some scattering juniper or cedars furnished very good fuel for our fires. Although we saw fires on far-off buttes, it may have been Navajo shepherd boys watching their flocks of sheep or goats. The weather had been exceedingly fine, blue skies with fairly pleasant clear nights, since the days when we passed such wild winds and deep snows in crossing the Mogollon Range of central Arizona. Owing to the sheep, goats, cattle, and ponies of the Navajo feeding over the region through which we passed, grass was rather poor; but, as we had taken from Mr. Hawley's place a plentiful supply of barley, our mules fared very well on the first day out.

Our second day's drive was but twenty-five miles. There was a small pond of water in a shallow sandstone basin where we camped for the night; and, having learned that wood was scarce at this place, through the day we gathered a quantity of dead cedar and cottonwood along the way sufficient for our fire that night.

We met one small party of Navajos on their way to Canyon de Chelly and Fort Wingate, and we overtook a fighting family of Danes who were going back into Utah from a small Mormon settlement on the headwater of the Gila River in Arizona. There was the father, mother, a son of about nineteen years, a daughter of sixteen years, and a small boy and girl. They were either Danes, Swedes, or Norwegians. Their name was Jensen, and of all the quarrelsome people I ever saw on any road in any country they were the most pronounced fighting family.

This family first overtook us at the Mormon fort at Sunset Crossing. They were camped near that river, and as we came up there was a family fight between father and son, backed by mother and daughter on opposite sides. As we drove up, there were cries of "Murder! Help! Help! Murder!" Dawson, Quong Hing, and I left the wagon, ran forward and found that the young man had his father, a man of about sixty-five years of age, down and was pummeling him unmercifully with his fists, while the girl was crying and trying to pull the boy away from beating their father. The mother was crying to the girl to let her brother alone, as he was giving his father what he richly deserved. The other two children, boy and girl, were up on the family wagon crying lustily for help.

Our party quickly drew the young man off from beating his father, and then asked what all this trouble was about. The father, who had been crying "Help!" and "Murder!" began his story; but soon father, mother, and daughter each began to talk at the same time. The father, whose face and hands were bleeding, said that four or five years earlier his trouble with the boy began. The mother began her story at an even earlier date, before they left Scandinavia. The young boy, Erastus, started his story the morning they left Cottonwood, below Salt Lake City, Utah, on their journey to Arizona the previous year. He said the fighting started that morning and continued ever since. The young woman, Olga, began her story when they started from the upper Gila River on their present journey back to Cottonwood in Utah. The family told us they were going to take their troubles into the Bishop's Court at Sunset for an amicable settlement.

During my journey to the Hopi pueblo, this turbulent family did have their troubles aired in the Bishop's Court, seemingly in a very satisfactory manner. But, upon resuming their journey, it was a fresh fight every ten miles. My own party passed and repassed them five times between the Mormon fort and Lee's Ferry, and on each occasion there was a family fight, either as we came up or before we passed their camp.

On the second day after leaving Moencopi, this Mr. Jensen and his warlike household passed us at noon. They had with them two dogs that were on no good terms with each other, and one of their horses was extremely vicious, whilst another was balky. As they passed us, I rather hoped that they would proceed so rapidly that we could never more overtake them, but the sequel will prove to the contrary.

Almost half an hour after this combative aggregation of domesticity passed us for the fourth time and while we were preparing dinner a party of four Navajo men, five women, and eight children came to our campfire. They had with them a quantity of fresh venison and desired to share our fire for preparing their own dinner of fresh meat and boiled corn. We gladly allowed them to do so, and besides furnished them each with a large tin cup full of well-sweetened coffee from our large coffee boiler.

Some of this party of Navajos were from Fort Wingate and the others were from near Navajo Mountain in southeastern Utah. They had with them a quantity of very beautiful garnets of varied colors of red and pink, in size from one to ten karats, to the amount of about six quarts, and about two quarts of peridots, or green garnets, of fine color, as well as a quantity of evanturine quartz, or sunstones, and two small bags of turquoise of clear, rich, blue color. These they had collected between where we were then and within a few miles of Fort Wingate. They were free to tell me where they gathered the garnets and peridots but would give me no information as to where they obtained the turquoise, as they value it highly and are jealous lest white men should run into the locality where they mine it.

I well knew that we were now within the precious-stone region of northeastern Arizona and would very much like to have camped for a week and range over the hills there to search for gems; but, as we were in the Navajo country, it would not do, as they would not knowingly let us pick up any sort of ore or mineral the size of a pin from their country. But with this party of Indians I traded a quantity of tobacco, coffee, vermillion or red paint, glass beads, of which we yet had a small lot, and a half-dozen skinning or hunting knives for two hundred ounces of fine garnets, fifty ounces of peridots or Arizona emeralds, fifty ounces of sunstones, and ten ounces of very choice turquoise, things that I had been very anxious to secure.

When we camped the next night, we found nearby our fighting Scandinavian family, Mr. Olaf Jensen and children, with his red-eyed, red-haired, warlike wife, Christiana. Meeting with them thus time and again proved to be a rather disagreeable incident in our passage across the Painted Desert, and their exhibit of life was a most pitiable example of domestic misfit and family warfare. The grass at this water tank was somewhat better than what we had already found since leaving Moencopi. After our mules had each eaten a good measure of water-soaked barley, we hobbled them on this grama grass, which was abundant. We set out our guards for the night and there spent our last night on the long, lonely, but interesting region south of the Colorado River, the Painted Desert.

The next day at a very early hour we left the sandstone water tanks, passed above the camp of our fellow travelers, the fighting Scandinavians, and went over a very rough road. From two barrels attached to the sides of our wagon we drew sufficient water for ourselves and mules at the noon hour, as we had done on previous days. After a rest of an hour and a half we continued over the road that was becoming worse and more difficult, until at length after a terrible uphill pull over a tract of wagon road where stones of all sizes made traveling difficult, we reached the high elevation above the Colorado River, just about three-quarters of an hour before sundown. We were in sight of Lee's Ferry and the residence of the now deceased but famous John D. Lee.

After calling loudly for a time, and three or four rifle discharges to attract the attention of the people of the ferry on the north side of the river, we at last heard voices saying, "All right! We will soon be over there." Within three-quarters of an hour and in the rosy twilight, we found ourselves across the river and making ready to camp for the night.

Lee's Ferry was built by the famous John D. Lee, who was credited with having been the leader of the Mountain Meadows Massacre of 137 persons in September, 1857, emigrants on their way to California. For that awful crime he had been executed in 1877 on the same field where the massacre had taken place. Lee had been a polygamist with ten wives, one of which, Mary, was now there with her children conducting this ferry. She had a hired man of all work named Samson.[27]

I told her that I wanted to purchase a liberal supply of lucerne or alfalfa hay for my four mules, as well as barley and oats. For my men and myself, I wanted milk, vegetables, eggs, and possibly a few chickens to be converted into pot pies or fried in a long-handled spider frying pan or dutch oven. She said that she would be most happy to furnish us with anything around the place that we might want, and at the most reasonable prices possible. Upon learning that she had a shop with a forge, blacksmith- and woodworking tools, and material for horseshoeing, I told her that our long march from Sunset Crossing was so difficult that our mules were needing rest and shoe repairing and that our wagon also required a once-over because of the frightful condition of the country over which we had traveled for the past forty-eight hours.

In the morning, we all felt exceedingly well rested and refreshed, as the night previous was the first night for almost five months, save at Prescott or at Colonel Joe Melvin's ranch at Fort Verde, in which we did not have to stand guard watching our wagons, mules, and camp. I was really glad to reach the north bank of the Colorado River, for that part of my journey after leaving Prescott, while it held many features of deep interest, was a wild, dangerous, and difficult region. The passage of the Mogollon was one of the most difficult weather experiences I had ever known. In passing through that wilderness of more than six hundred miles, I carried a large sum of money, mostly in United States currency. Had my little command of four men and myself been killed and my outfit taken, no doubt the hiding place of that money in one of the sideboards of the wagon bed might never have been discovered. Possibly the large roll of United States currency enclosed in tough brown paper and buried in a keg of axle grease might have been found, perhaps not. I had taken chances, as has been seen, when I left my outfit at the Mormon fort and visited the Hopi villages for several days and when I went on the hunting expedition at Chaves Pass in the Mogollon. But now that I was at Lee's Ferry, even yet in a wild country but across the Colorado, my nerves felt easier.

After breakfast, I ordered Quong Hing to begin his laundry work, which meant to wash sheets, table linen, towels, and the personal underwear of five men, as soap, water, and wood were abundant. Our last laundry work had been done at the Mormon fort on Sunset Crossing. The other three men reshod the mules, repaired the wagon, washed and oiled the harness, and cleaned guns, thus putting our outfit in good condition for continuing our journey, which was yet over a difficult road.

I left the work to my men and started to make a study of our surroundings. Mrs. Mary Lee was the youngest of John D. Lee's ten wives.[28] She was then, I would judge, between thirty-five and forty years of age. By birth she was English, in height about five feet six or seven inches, about 183 to 187 pounds in weight. In complexion she was a cross between a blonde and a brunette, her hair of a light cast, neither red nor auburn. She had fine teeth, well-shaped nose and mouth, small hands and feet, pleasing manners, and was rather inclined to smile than to be solemn in expression. In speech, she plainly indicated her nationality of the working classes of England. Her family then consisted of one boy of perhaps fourteen years of age, twin girls of twelve, quite handsome, and two small boys of eight and ten. The twin girls were of light complexion and of pleasing manners.[29]

The Lee home was a one-story log structure of six rooms, including kitchen, the southwest of which was the sitting or living room. In one corner stood a half-dozen shotguns and an old smoothbore United States musket, and one brass-mounted jaeger or Fremont rifle. On the walls hung three Colt's pistols. Other wall decorations included a picture of Joseph and Hyrum Smith, the Mormon prophets, standing in a side view and each leaning on a walking stick. There was also a picture of Brigham Young, another of Heber C. Kimball, and in an oval frame a photograph of John D. Lee. The walls of this sitting room were papered over with copies of the *New York Sun*, *Deseret News*, and *New York Tribune*. The furniture of this and other rooms of the house was homemade of native timber. Withal, the house bore a comfortable expression.

Mrs. Lee had an enclosure of about sixteen acres connecting with the house and outer structures, eight acres of which were under cultivation with vegetables, corn, and lucerne or alfalfa hay, four crops of which were produced annually. The ferryboat was strongly built, but of small dimensions. Two wagons and eight horses were all that it could carry at a single crossing.

The setting was a bowl-like depression on the great Colorado River. In the southeast, north, and northwest, cliffs of red sandstone shut out all view of the outer world. Blue sky above and a wagon road, with an open space quite narrow, shot out from this celebrated spot into the southwest, and a short distance from the place, going out by this road, the country opened out into considerable width and the surface showed a dry desert.

Mrs. Lee told of coming as a Mormon immigrant to Utah, of having married into the Lee family, and her general experience as a polygamous wife. She told of how Lee had taken her, his latest matrimonial acquisition, because of constant dread of the wrath to come, into that far place, made their home, built the ferry, cultivated that small area, and for a time felt that his seclusion was so complete that the federal officers could never secure his arrest. But in the early days of November, 1874, he was arrested at the town of Panguitch, where two of his wives and families resided. His arrest was made by William Stokes, a deputy United States marshal.

She related how he was taken to Beaver, Utah, tried and found innocent by a most peculiar jury, but later retried and found guilty in the federal court at Beaver. On March 23, 1877, at Mountain Meadows in Washington County where he and his men had committed the atrocious murders, he was shot to death by a detail of United States infantrymen from Fort Cameron near Beaver. As she related this to me, Mary Lee said that she would have been contented in mind if bishops Haight, Higbee, Dame, and Klingonsmith and their assistants Stewart, Adair, Jones, and George A. Smith, who had instigated the massacre, had all been apprehended and executed at the same time and place with her husband. Bishop Klingonsmith, who had gone out of Utah and was living with an Indian wife far down on the western banks of the Colorado River in San Bernardino County, California, came forward and turned state's evidence and thus escaped punishment. Of the others named, not one of them was apprehended, and in time they died in hiding.

I had yet with me one bale of merchandise. She desired to make some purchases, but claimed that she had but little real money. She had, however, a wonderful Navajo blanket that John D. Lee had with him when executed, and which had been spread over his coffin when it was taken from that field to Panguitch, where he was buried. This blanket was given to her later. She also had many other fine articles of Navajo manufacture, as well as a quantity of most beautiful garnets. She exchanged those articles, together with a wonderful Navajo willow water jar and a beautiful Hopi woman's belt, peculiarly woven, for a quantity of my goods.

About the blanket, she related a strange, gruesome history. She said that it was an accursed object that had come into John D. Lee's possession in exchange for a horse, and that from that time to the day of his death he had bad luck and trouble. Because of its history, I was glad to get it; but let me digress here to state that the same blanket did not bring any good luck to me. Whilst in eastern Montana down on the Yellowstone, I either lost it out of a spring wagon I was driving, or it was stolen, and I later learned that because of it, three men were killed in a gunfight. But it was the most beautiful and valuable Navajo blanket I had ever seen. Because of all the troubles and misfortunes associated with this blanket, I named it Helen of Troy. There were other articles that once belonged to Lee that I could have obtained, but I did not want them, and as events went later I regretted having taken the blanket.

During our rest at Lee's Ferry, a slightly built man named Darrel, a son-in-law of John D. Lee, came in. He was one of the men at the Lee home in Panguitch when Lee was arrested. He was a peppery but agreeable sort of fellow. He crossed the Colorado on the ferry for some business in the Navajo country about an hour after we saw him and just about the time we were about to pull away from Lee's Ferry.

After three days, we settled all accounts and took our departure, coming out of the ramparted cove at Lee's Ferry to the wide open Paria Plateau. Our road ran somewhat to the southwest and soon reached a point near the abrupt walls of the Grand Canyon of the Colorado. Halting our mule team on the highway, we all went down to the steep rim of the canyon to gaze into the depths below. Words cannot describe the awfulness of that tremendous depth at the bottom of which flows the Colorado River. The depth at that point is about four thousand feet, and looking down it seemed not more than twenty feet across the waters of the Colorado River. In order to look down with safety, we were compelled to crawl near to the rim, then, each lying down his full length and gazing into the depths below, we beheld one of the most wonderful and awe-inspiring sights in the world.

We reached House Rock Springs in House Rock Valley that evening, where we camped at a cattle ranch the first night out from Lee's Ferry. The next day was over a rough road. Late in the afternoon we crossed once more the northern boundary of Arizona, and night brought us into the

Mormon town of Kanab, later the county seat of Kane County, Utah. Kanab is situated in the vicinity of numerous prehistoric remains. In the year 1873 while employed a short time with Major Powell's command in government exploration, I had seen this region to the north and investigated many of these ruins, so that now the face of the country was quite familiar to me.

From Kanab our road went over the wild, fantastic red, white, and green sandstone formations that continue down to Rockville and Virgin City in the upper regions of the Virgin River. In those towns we again met some of the men who hauled my loads of freight down to Cerbat and Mineral Park. After two more days we passed through Toquerville and Leeds, and landed in Silver Reef, where I had employed Con Dawson. As he had interests in the silver mines of that camp, Dawson left our command. He was a most faithful man and served me well for almost five months of that expedition. I never saw him again. He died at Los Angeles and lies buried there.

I remained two days at Silver Reef, one of the most interesting and unique silver-mining regions of the world, as its silver ores lie wholly in sandstone and the cause of that occurrence remains a mystery to science. The stratified measures of sandstone cover an area of about four square miles, showing conditions of mineral enrichment found nowhere else. There are two principal measures resting one against the other on an incline on which we find the silver values. In one of these the silver lies in an oxidized state with sulphurets and native silver, and the silver as taken from the ores of this reef is almost one thousand fine. The silver ore in the other reef contains a considerable percentage of copper. A curious feature of the silver ores of this locality is that some of the richest ore is found in fossilized or petrified wood and other vegetable matter lying between the laminations of these sandstone measures, some examples of which would run up to five thousand ounces of silver per ton.

At Silver Reef I again met my friends Colonel John Wall; James Linch; John Diamond, deputy sheriff of the camp killed in a gun battle some days later; my friend Jacob Sultan, a merchant; friends Kate Duggery and Margaret Carr of the local hotel; and a few others. It was late winter; but in that locality below the rim of the Great Basin the weather was springlike and the trees were putting forth their leaves.

We continued to Milford, where my friend Eusebius Sieboldt left my command to return to Duck Creek, White Pine County, Nevada, where his sister Katherine was yet teaching school and where he had joined us the previous autumn. He was a good and most faithful man. Later, both he and his sister went to California, where each of them married and made their homes.

At this point in my narrative, the interested reader may ask what became of the fighting family, the Jensens, who traveled the same road as my party. I learned in reaching Kanab that they were anchored in that town. Some three years later I met a party from Kanab who said that the elders of the church in Kanab felt that the father and mother of this Jensen family were uncongenial to each other, so they were given a divorce. The father Jensen some two weeks later married an old-maid Danish girl, and mother Jensen married a man whose two wives had died of pneumonia some three months before. Olga, the daughter, was taken as a fourth wife by the bishop's counselor of Panguitch. The minor children, boy and girl, were divided, the mother taking the little girl, and the father the boy. The older boy, Erastus, who used to take so much pleasure in beating his father, went back to Arizona, where he drove a freight team of mules and was killed during an Apache outbreak near Globe. So doubtless peace and contentment were the portions meted out to the remainder of that Jensen family ever after.

My remaining two men and I eventually reached Salt Lake City and Ogden, where I paid them off. I retained Mooncraft a few days, however, to assist with my mules and in packing my load of Navajo blankets, silverwork, and other Indian goods for shipment to New York City.

Between the United States currency hidden in the outside brace board of my wagon, and a large roll of bills hidden in the gallon keg of axle grease, and other cash within that wagon, when I arrived at Ogden I had $17,477. A little over half of this was profit, although $1,650 of this profit was commission on mining transactions I helped to carry out in Mojave and Yavapai counties, Arizona. I put my currency, gold, and silver into a knapsack and took train at Ogden for Salt Lake City. At Wells, Fargo & Co. bank in that city I purchased bank exchange on New York City for seventeen thousand dollars. I returned to Ogden and sold my four remaining mules and harness to Charlie Reed and Thomas Maguire, Montana freighters at Corinne, Utah, for $750—a few dollars less than the lot cost me at Corinne and Ogden the year before. The remaining wagon, tents, and camping outfit I sold to a man in Ogden. My carbine, short shotgun, and pistols, and a considerable lot of trophies including gold and silver specimens, Apache Indian bows, knives, the famous John D. Lee Navajo blanket, and other Indian work I put into storage at Ogden, reserving some articles for friends in New York City.

After I paid Isadore Mooncraft for his services the last few days in Ogden, we parted at the old Union depot in Ogden, he taking train for Sacramento, California, and I starting for New York. We never saw each other after that morning.

My pup Moses I took east and gave to my father and mother. He lived many years, and after they passed away he came to my home and lived until he was about fifteen years of age. The fossils, Indian weapons, petrified wood, human bones, ancient stone axes, knives, and other articles of antiquity collected in Arizona I sent away to my eastern home to take their place with my collection of similar articles from other parts of the world.

I reached New York City on May 5, 1879, to meet my principals and friends in that city. After resting a few days, I met my brokers and completed my business with them. The Navajo rugs and blankets, silverwork, and other Arizona Indian varieties I collected I sold at excellent prices to some Indian curio dealers up near Union Square adjacent to Fifth Avenue.

I visited Gilmore's Gardens, which at the time of this visit were being used for international walking and racing matches. I went directly to the management and discussed with them the proposition of having from ten to twenty Moqui Indians brought to New York City to walk in matches against any man from any part of the world, knowing how long-winded and prodigiously capable those Indians were in walking or footracing. The management agreed that if I could succeed in bringing them to New York City I would receive fifty percent of the profits arising from their work in the arena. I immediately ran down to Washington City in order to obtain a government permit to bring the Indians to New York City; but, after laying my proposition before the United States Indian Department and making all kinds of good promises of good care and great profit to those Indians, I was informed that such would not be permitted, so I was compelled to drop the scheme, much to my sorrow.

So ended my third and last trading and mining expedition into Arizona. These expeditions between 1877 and 1879 comprised one of the most interesting, important, and graphic periods of my life. I was the only man ever to undertake such work over the routes I had taken. My operations in Arizona and Mexico took place when those regions stood between barbarism and civilization, where there was not a railroad into northern Mexico and none in Arizona, and a single military telegraph line reached some one or two parts of Arizona, like Prescott, the capital.

In looking back over those days, I marvel at what I dared to do in my youth, and wonder that I escaped robbery or death in a country where life was held cheaply and where civilized and savage brigands watched every opportunity of exercising their motto, "Seize who may and hold who can." For three years I had been quite fortunate both in my commercial ventures and mine investigations, exploration work, and in the study of the Indian tribes. I studied the social and political conditions of northwestern Mexico and the prehistoric remains of the extinct occupants of ancient Arizona, both by investigating the standing ruins at many places and by excavating the buried habitations and mounds. My opportunities enabled me to collect valuable ethnological data, both from ancient ruins and living tribes, and to gather a great many valuable mineral specimens and crystalizations. I made the most of my opportunities, thereby securing much that was to be of great value in the future.

I deemed myself extremely fortunate in having escaped robbery or death or both. It was during the latter part of my third expedition that I began to realize fully that should I continue to risk life and property in those fields, disaster would inevitably overtake me, either from those in my employ, banditti or highwaymen, or from Indian attacks. My presence in that region became well known, and although I always found the officers of the law ready to perform their official duties, I well knew at the same time the country was too vast for any officials to cover. Therefore I wisely concluded to cease my profitable, interesting, but dangerous undertakings in that country.

I was fortunate or lucky in the men whom I employed. When it is called to mind that on each expedition I had in employ different men, although they all proved faithful to me, it is not unlikely that disaster might eventually have come from those I so implicitly trusted, or from other sources. The reader can fully realize the chances I took when burying treasures at points to which I might not again return, and the risks I ran when I hid away $10,500 in the channeled outside brace of a wagon bed and at the same time buried in a keg of axle grease a large lot of currency. But, of course, none of my men realized that such an amount of treasure was in any such way hidden there. I simply took chances and won.

Adieu, dear, dangerous, romantic Arizona of the old days. I acquired knowledge and fortune within your borders. I was happy under your sunlight and your starlight, and loved to listen to the pattering of the friendly rains upon my tent in April. If my men, myself, and my suffering mules underwent unspeakable pains, trials, and tribulations in our crossing of the Mogollon against the winds and snowstorms of February, we had ample compensation when we sat around the pleasant campfires in mountain glen or open plains, or even in the silent, solitary desert where we halted for the noonday meal or camped after days of weary travel. I well remember the murmur of the pines in the Santa Cruz, the Bradshaws, or the far-off Mogollon.

Of course, I am free to admit that I cursed your red-eyed rattlesnakes, your hated tarantulas, your villainous blowflies, your forty-seven kinds of lizards, and your repulsive, death-dealing Gila monsters. But the Big Sandy, the Santa Maria, the glades of Salt River, the valley of the Verde, the broad miles of the Hassayampa, and the plains of the Gila were friendly regions, and your men and women—Americans, Mexicans, and

Hopi Indians—became near and dear to me. At times I would that I could live that life again. But it cannot be, and so, peering through the mists of years from the days and nights that I spent amid your fields, your valleys, your deserts, and your timbered hills, I utter the poet's cry of "Hail and farewell!"

Notes

Notes to Introduction

1. The entry under Maguire's name in J. Cecil Alter, ed., *Utah: The Storied Domain* (Washington, D.C., 1932), II, 32–36, bears indications of Maguire's writing style, and Charles Kelly, "Don Maguire—Pioneer," *Utah Motorist* (April 1933): 8–9, came from Alter's book and interviews with Maguire.
2. The Maguires were stalwarts of the embryonic Catholic community in Ogden when regular masses began to be said there in 1873 by Father Patrick Walsh. The Very Reverend Denis Kiely, "A Brief History of the Catholic Church in Utah," MS at the Utah State Historical Society, lists four brothers—Michael, John, Charles, and Dominick Maguire—their sister, Mrs. Brown, and "their aged and respected parents" as members of the congregation. Bernice Maher Mooney, *Salt of the Earth: The History of the Catholic Diocese of Salt Lake City, 1776–1987* (2nd ed., Salt Lake City, 1992), 73, reports that the first regular mass in Ogden was celebrated in the home of Michael Maguire on 5 January 1873.
3. Charles Nettleton Strevell, *As I Recall Them* (Salt Lake City, 1943[?]),133–35, describes some of Maguire's archaeological work and claims that some of the Anasazi mummies and artifacts he took from Grand Gulch became a part of the Temple Square museum exhibits in Salt Lake City. Neil M. Judd, *Archaeological Observations North of the Rio Colorado* (Washington, D.C., 1926), 54–55, describes Maguire's excavations at Paragonah, as does Maguire himself in "The Paragoonah Fortress," *Salt Lake Tribune*, 30 January 1893, 2. Kelly, "Don Maguire—Pioneer," 8, identifies the site of Maguire's San Juan County excavations as "Grand Wash," but it is clear that he means Grand Gulch.
4. Maguire's letters to Kelly are in the Charles Kelly Papers at the Utah State Historical Society, as are some brief notes on Maguire's career gleaned through interviews.

5. *Ogden Standard Examiner*, 8 January 1933, 1, and 9 January 1933, 10.
6. Maguire to Charles Kelly, 15 and 23 April and 2 August 1931, Charles Kelly Papers, Utah State Historical Society.
7. See, for example, *San Francisco Chronicle*, 11 February, 12 March, and 29 April 1877 for descriptions of Maguire's journey from Benton, California, to Hackberry, Arizona.
8. The economic and social circumstances of Arizona's mining districts at this time are concisely sketched in Rodman Wilson Paul, *Mining Frontiers of the Far West, 1848–1880* (Albuquerque, 1963), 155–60.
9. Howard R. Lamar, *The Trader on the American Frontier: Myth's Victim* (College Station, Texas, 1977).

Notes to Chapter One

1. The name is given as Gardner in the biographical sketch in J. Cecil Alter, *Utah: The Storied Domain* (Washington, D.C., 1932), 34.
2. The first railroad to reach Arizona was the Southern Pacific, which reached Yuma in 1877 and continued across southern Arizona and New Mexico to link up with the Texas Pacific near El Paso in 1881. Maguire could have used this line even on his first expedition, but it would have put him far to the south of the mining districts west and northwest of Prescott and even farther from the Nevada mining districts, his two most profitable arenas. Henry P. Walker and Don Bufkin, *Historical Atlas of Arizona* (Norman, OK, 1979), 46.
3. Christopher Layton (1821–1898) was Mormon bishop of Kaysville for seventeen years and a prosperous resident credited with introducing dry farming to Davis County, Utah. Maguire also bought most of his animals for his other two expeditions from Layton. Andrew Jenson, *Latter-day Saints Biographical Encyclopedia* (Salt Lake City, 1901), I: 363–64.
4. Patrick Edward Connor opened the first mine at Stockton, which became the Honorine, in 1865. During the 1870s there were several smelters at Stockton, and it is impossible to tell which one Maguire is describing. He may be describing three at once, for Stockton seems to have had none the size he indicates. Ore in the area was much less rich in gold than Maguire reports; it was primarily lead and silver, with small proportions of gold and zinc. Mary Helen Parsons, "Stockton," in Tooele County Daughters of Utah Pioneers, *History of Tooele County* (Salt Lake City, 1961), 343–44.
5. Maguire's geography is in error here. Given the direction he was traveling, he would have passed through Tooele before reaching Stockton.
6. This is Orrin Porter Rockwell (1813–1878), who developed his ranch in Skull Valley during the years after 1873.
7. Maguire's biography of this controversial Mormon frontiersman reflects standard anti-Mormon views. For a much less violent interpretation of Rock-

well see Harold Schindler, *Orrin Porter Rockwell: Man of God, Son of Thunder* (Salt Lake City, 1966).

8. These are Gosiutes, not Paiutes, though the culture is similar. Jesse D. Jennings, "Prehistoric and Historic Peoples of Utah," in Jennings, et al., *Indians of Utah: Past and Present* (Salt Lake City, 1959), 16–19.

9. After some Gosiutes massacred twenty-three California immigrants at Gravelly Ford on the Humboldt River in 1862, Connor retaliated in a bloody campaign that resulted in pacification of the Indians. Brigham D. Madsen, *Glory Hunter: A Biography of Patrick Edward Connor* (Salt Lake City, 1990), 61–63.

10. Alphaeus Cutler Worthington's father, James Worthington, was one of the original settlers of Deep Creek Valley in 1858. James and Rachel Worthington lived there until 1883; "Cut" and his wife Priscilla lived there only temporarily. Ronald R. Bateman, *Deep Creek Reflections* (Salt Lake City, 1984), 52–53.

11. Maguire has just crossed the Snake Mountains and reached Spring Valley, Nevada.

12. This is present-day Wheeler Peak, renamed in 1869 for Lt. George M. Wheeler, who explored the area that year. Harlan D. Unrau, *Basin and Range: A History of Great Basin National Park, Nevada* (Denver, 1990), 57.

13. A. C. Cleveland (1803–1903) was a Maine native who mined in California from 1858 to 1868, then moved to White Pine County, Nevada, and created the livestock and farming empire Maguire describes. Effie O. Read, *White Pine Lang Syne* (Denver, 1965), 180–81.

14. William Burke had come to Schellbourne during its mining boom in the early 1870s and stayed on into its ghost-town phase, as Maguire indicates. The Burke family was still there in 1925; Read, *White Pine Lang Syne*, 122. See also Stanley W. Paher, *Nevada Ghost Towns & Mining Camps* (Berkeley, 1970), 240.

15. The 1870 census gives his name as Nathaniel Kinsley and identifies him as a single rancher, born in Illinois, and thirty-eight years of age.

16. At the time of Maguire's visit, Cherry Creek was between two mining booms, 1873–75 and 1880–83. The town burned in February 1901, but photographs in Paher, *Nevada Ghost Towns*, 243–45, corroborate Maguire's description of rational town planning.

17. Maguire's description is too vague to allow precise location of this ranch, which was somewhere near present-day Ely, nor can Mrs. Killfor be located.

18. This unusual name, which I have been unable to locate in either the censuses or local historical literature, suggests a spelling error introduced in dictation, but the only real names I have located that Maguire might have intended are Guilford and Killgore, both single male ranchers, and Henry Gilbert, a farmer aged forty-eight in 1880, with a wife, Susan, age thirty-three, and a seventeen-year-old daughter. None of these appear to fit the bi-

ography Maguire gives. The colorful nature of Maguire's story here also supports the suspicion that he invented the whole thing.

19. Robinson, also known as Mineral City and Lane City, reached its peak as a mining center in 1872, when it had a population of six hundred. In 1876, evidently not long before Maguire's arrival on this occasion, the mines played out, and later in the year it was almost completely abandoned. Later attempts to mine the area also failed, and shortly after 1908 the town was deserted. Paher, *Nevada Ghost Towns*, 232.

20. The Hamilton gold rush began in 1868 and declined during the 1870s, as Maguire indicates. Paher, *Nevada Ghost Towns*, 247–50.

21. Treasure City grew at the same time and rate as Hamilton, and although the mines were rich (Paher, *Nevada Ghost Towns*, 252, estimates some $20 million in silver was taken out in less than ten years), it was, as Maguire indicates, subject to overspeculation and declined quickly after 1870. A fire in 1874 destroyed most of the town, and it was not rebuilt.

22. All three of these men appear in either the 1870 or 1880 census. Richard Barnes was a farmer, born in Kentucky, age forty-nine in 1870, living with his Irish wife, Sarah, forty-five. J. B. Saborn in 1880 was a forty-five-year-old farmer living with a twenty-one-year-old black female, Lizzie Saborn. Alexander McCulloch, born in Virginia, was thirty-eight and single in 1870; by 1880 he had a wife, S. A., age forty-four, a three-year-old daughter, and a black servant boy, age thirteen.

23. This is Warm Springs, south of Tybo, where a small settlement existed after 1868. Paher, *Nevada Ghost Towns*, 176.

24. The Tybo boom began in 1874 and lasted until 1879, though mining continued there until World War II. As Maguire indicates, he was there during its greatest production. Paher, *Nevada Ghost Towns*, 348–53.

25. This is Maguire's phonetic spelling of "Two G." See Paher, *Nevada Ghost Towns*, 348.

26. Charles Garrett appears in the Tybo census in both 1870 and 1880. In the first he is listed as a thirty-five-year-old merchant born in Ohio. In 1880 he is listed as a publisher.

27. Belmont's decline came after the discovery of the deposits at Tonopah in 1885, which drained Belmont's population to the richer lode. Nell Murbarger, *Ghosts of the Glory Trail* (Palm Desert, CA, 1956), 41–49.

28. Maguire slights Jefferson, which was at its height as a mining community, with a population of eight hundred in 1876. Murbarger, *Ghosts of the Glory Trail*, 261.

29. Austin is one of Nevada's most famous mining towns. Founded in 1874, it became an important supply point for prospectors operating throughout southern Nevada. The Manhattan Silver Mining Co. had purchased most of the important mines by 1871 and was enjoying great prosperity at the time of Maguire's visit. Paher, *Nevada Ghost Towns*, 166–71.

30. Eureka was a vitally important transportation center for southern Nevada

because of the Eureka & Palisade Railroad, which linked the community to the rest of the country via the Central Pacific Railroad in October, 1875. Paher, *Nevada Ghost Towns*, 181.

31. Mining had begun at Ione in the early 1860s and enjoyed considerable prosperity in the early 1870s, but, as Maguire indicates, it was in a state of decline at the time of his visit; by 1880 it was pretty much abandoned. Paher, *Nevada Ghost Towns*, 379–80.

32. Patsy M. Boler, a stock raiser thirty years of age, born in Ireland, appears in the 1880 census with his wife Ellen, thirty years of age, and three daughters and one son.

33. The ruins of the old stamp mill would have been visible to Maguire, but it is curious that he fails to mention the ruins of the old San Antone Stage Station, which Stanley Paher calls "Nevada's most famous stage station, a twenty-room two-story structure of adobe and brick," which was built in 1865. Though later abandoned, it was undoubtedly still standing when Maguire passed through. Paher, *Nevada Ghost Towns*, 362.

34. Maguire arrived in Belleville at the beginning of its prosperity, though his estimate of only about 240 inhabitants seems far too low. Paher, *Nevada Ghost Towns*, 452, estimates the population in 1876 at about 400 people. This would grow to 500 or 600 by 1877; then decline set in after 1882.

35. Maguire's count is not far off: Paher, *Nevada Ghost Towns*, 444, says there were eleven saloons. The town was only founded in 1876, so it was brand new at the time of Maguire's visit. His impression of the wild living there was correct; it was, Paher says, "one of Nevada's toughest camps."

36. On Francis M. "Borax" Smith and the borax industry in this part of Nevada and eastern California see Paher, *Nevada Ghost Towns*, 426–31.

37. Maguire's directions are inaccurate here. Bodie is almost due west of Columbus, though enough to the north to justify "northwest." Benton, however, is southeast of Bodie, not farther to the northwest. An explanation perhaps lies in the fact that Maguire did not visit Bodie and was thus unsure of its exact location.

38. If this relationship is true, these would have been pretty elderly men. Emma Smith was born in 1804, the youngest of seven children, and had four older brothers. The family religion was Methodist Episcopal. Linda King Newell and Valeen Tippetts Avery, *Mormon Enigma: Emma Hale Smith, Prophet's Wife, "Elect Lady," Polygamy's Foe* (Garden City, NY, 1984), 3.

39. Owens Valley was known as Round Valley in Maguire's time. See frontispiece map in Willie Arthur Chalfant, *The Story of Inyo* (Bishop, CA, 1922).

40. Thomas Williams is listed in the 1880 Inyo County census as a forty-year-old farmer born in Wales and living with his twenty-five-year-old wife, Susan, born in Michigan, and their two-year-old daughter, Winiford. I have been unable to locate any of their neighbors whom Maguire names, perhaps, as he hints, because of the transitory nature of their tenure in the area.

41. The only person of this name I have been able to locate is probably one of

Hessian's sons, a twenty-five-year-old laborer named Dick Hessian who appears with his twenty-year-old wife, Mary, in the 1880 census.

42. This is the area of ancient bristlecone pines, the oldest living things, some of which are as much as 4,600 years old. Maguire seems to have confused the name of Big Pine with that of nearby Lone Pine, which was built near a huge solitary pine tree that blew down in a storm in 1876. Mildred Brooke Hoover et al., *Historic Spots in California* (Stanford, CA, 1966), 118.

43. Camp Independence was established on 4 July 1862 to protect the few white residents of the area from Indians and to defend against secessionists in Nevada and Arizona. It was abandoned in July 1877. Hoover et al., *Historic Spots*, 116. It is best known today as the home of writer Mary Austin, who lived there during the 1890s. See Mary Austin, *Earth Horizons* (Boston, 1932), 284–89.

44. Perhaps not surprisingly, no one with this famous name appears in the census or in any other records I have consulted. It is almost certainly a nickname or an invention of Maguire's to fill in his faulty memory or notes.

45. Discovered in 1865 by a Mexican named Pablo Flores and two partners, the Cerro Gordo mines were the richest in Inyo County, producing an estimated total of $28 million. Although Maguire reports finding few people there, several thousand lived in the region. See Hoover et al., *Historic Spots*, 118–19; Philip Varney, *Southern California's Best Ghost Towns: A Practical Guide* (Norman, OK, 1990), 11–16; Remi Nadeau, *City-Makers: The Story of Southern California's First Boom, 1868–76* (Los Angeles, 1965), 73–80.

46. Although I can find no record of Tommy Passmore, the site of this station is almost certainly Swansea, where a smelter once existed to reduce Cerro Gordo ores. In 1874 the smelter was flooded in a cloudburst, but there is evidence that the site continued to be used afterwards, probably as the travelers' station Maguire found. Varney, *Southern California's Best Ghost Towns*, 9–10.

47. Remi Nadeau made a fortune freighting ore from Cerro Gordo to Los Angeles and returning with agricultural produce from the San Fernando Valley. It was this commerce that gave the valley its first great economic encouragement. A descendant, also named Remi Nadeau, tells the story in *City-Makers*, 63–72. See also Varney, *Southern California's Best Ghost Towns*, 13; and Chalfant, *The Story of Inyo*, 277–83.

48. Truman Raymond, a stationkeeper born in Illinois and age forty-five, appears in the 1880 census with his fifty-two-year-old wife, Hanah.

49. C. Saunders, born in England, ran the Point of Rocks Station with his wife, Elizabeth. Saunders was sixty years of age at the time of the 1880 census, his wife sixty-three. Neither appears in the 1870 census, but an anonymous traveler in 1871 reported that Mrs. Saunders pointed with pride to her nearby five-acre cornfield, raised in refutation of older settlers who deemed the soil too alkaline for agriculture. Clifford Walker, *Back Door to California: The Story of the Mojave River Trail* (Barstow, CA, c. 1986), 283. A photograph of the site in 1863 is on page 288. Contrary to what Maguire says, Point of

Rocks was not at the forks of the road at present-day Barstow which gave westbound travelers an alternative of going to either Los Angeles or San Bernardino, but rather at modern Helendale. Nor is this to be confused with another station called Forks of the Road, farther east at the point where eastbound travelers could turn off toward Salt Lake City or continue on to Arizona. A map between pp. 22 and 23 in Erma Peirson, *The Mojave River and Its Valley* (Glendale, CA, 1970), shows the early geography of this area.

50. On his return trip, Maguire recorded a rather unflattering description of Saunders's Station in his diary (left here unedited):

> If the emagination can contemplate a little house of 4 rooms having a voranda around it built of adobe roofed with cottonwood poles a fence near the house on the south side and a large pasture on the north side with my horse [illegible] in it then he will have a pretty good picture of Mr Sanders ranch. . . .
>
> [A little dog and a derelict sheepherder occupied the living room.] On the wall hung a variety of newspaper ads some very pretty and all neatly arranged in the north east corner of the sitting room there were a few shelves and thereon were placed a few groceries for sale to the poor weary traveler at Six Hundred per cent. A fire place in the west end of the room a fire board upon it. . . . in the window sill forner there was a small sea [?] box on it a Russian slave box along side of it a little piece of board on that a pair of specks next a hole next a dirty tin plate next a flask of Kentucky rifle powder next an old oyster can with a stick in it. Over the south door which was shut there hung a picture of Napoleon's Grand Opera House in Paris.

51. This is the Mojave Road, also known as the "Old Government Road" or the 35th Parallel Route, which linked Los Angeles with Arizona via the Mojave Desert. It was as arduous, desolate, and dangerous as Maguire indicates. Father Francisco Garces, the tireless Spanish missionary, was the first white man to traverse the desert, during his journey of January–May 1776 in an attempt to develop a route from Santa Fe to Monterey. It was opened as a wagon road in 1859 and was superseded by a railroad in 1883. John Galvin, ed., *A Record of Travels in Arizona and California, 1775-1776, Fr. Francisco Garces* (San Francosco, 1967), 26–60. See also Dennis G. Casebier, *The Mojave Road* (Norco, CA, 1975); and Herbert M. Hart, *Old Forts of the Far West* (New York, 1965).

52. This is apparently Hawley's Station, run by Isaac Hawley and his wife, Emily Bartholomew Blackburn Hawley. The "Miss Blackburn" would be either Alice Miranda Blackburn or Emily Lucetta Blackburn, daughters of Thomas and Emily Blackburn. See Will Bagley, ed., *Frontiersman: Abner Blackburn's Narrative* (Salt Lake City, 1992), 214; and Patricia Jernigan Keeling, ed., *Once Upon a Desert* (Barstow, CA, 1994), 188.

53. Although I have been unable to identify McConnell, Maguire's diary on

his return trip says this was the Fish Pond Station, which appears on the map in Casebier, *The Mojave Road*. Peirson, *The Mojave River and Its Valley*, 156, says this station was run by Lafayette Meacham at about this time.

54. This rawhide furniture fashioned from readily available materials was common in pioneer homes in the desert Southwest. Its major objectionable quality is its squeakiness when sat upon; otherwise, its flexibility makes it surprisingly comfortable.

55. Camp Cady was sporadically occupied by United States troops from 1859 to 1871. The structures Maguire saw were erected in 1868. See Leonard Waitman, "The History of Camp Cady," *Historical Society of Southern California Quarterly* 36 (March 1954): 49–91; Casebier, *The Mojave Road*, 110; and Hart, *Old Forts*, 124–26.

56. Maguire's diary places these dying sheep between Soda Lake and Rock Springs.

57. The Caves is a natural rock shelter used as a stopping point on the Mojave Road. Casebier, *The Mojave Road*, 111, includes a photograph of the site.

58. Soda Lake is a large sink at which the Mojave River terminates. Although it contains a significant quantity of water during the wet part of the year, during the summer it dwindles to little or nothing. Drinking water is available at nearby Zzyzx Springs, as Maguire indicates in the next paragraph. Fort (or Camp) Soda, like Camp Cady to the southwest, was a sporadically occupied military outpost at this point during the 1860s.

59. Maguire's diary makes no mention of this man on either the outward or homeward legs of the expedition, and his fanciful name, like that of the Countess Du Barry, suggests that this story is entirely a fabrication.

60. Maguire's diary mentions only two Indians, naming only Black Jim.

61. This is probably Rocky Ridge, on the northern slope of the Kelso Mountains.

62. This is Marl Springs, a waterhole at which, like Camp Cady and Camp Soda, the army established an occasionally occupied outpost in the 1860s. Its good water made it a natural stopping place for travelers. Hart, *Old Forts*, 120–21.

63. Camp Rock Springs was another sporadically occupied military installation during the 1860s. It was less used than Marl Springs because, as Maguire indicates, the water supply was uncertain. Hart, *Old Forts*, 119, reports a tradition that Rock Springs was used by the army as a morgue where casualties of the conflicts with the Paiutes could be kept until the arrival of burial wagons, and the remains of this usage may have been the "graves" Maguire saw.

64. Maguire's diary adds, "in the North side is a tunnel in the rock to serve as a fort against the attack of Indians," and notes that "There was a tough old crowd" there.

65. Fort Paiute was located at the summit of Paiute Hill because of the plentiful water of Paiute Creek, which Dennis Casebier estimates flows at a rate of

250,000 gallons per day. Although the creek quickly disappears into the dry desert, it was a delightful anomaly for thirsty travelers like Maguire.

66. Students of the Mojave Road will note that Maguire bypassed with no mention several stations on the western part of the road, such as Cottonwoods, Grapevine, and Forks of the Road. This may be because he was using pack animals that proceeded faster than wheeled vehicles and thus had no need of the extra stops. In addition to the 1871 traveler's report given in Walker, *Back Door to California*, and the sites mapped in Casebier, *The Mojave Road*, see Henry P. Walker, "Soldier in the California Column: The Diary of John W. Teal," *Arizona and the West* 13 (Spring 1971): 33–82; and the narrative of December 1876–January 1877 by Alphonse Pinart, *Journey To Arizona in 1876* (Los Angeles, 1962). Pinart followed most of Maguire's route into central Arizona later the same year.

67. William Harrison Hardy (1823–1906), a native of New York, earned the title "Captain" when he was elected head of an immigrant wagon train to California in 1849. He purchased the ferry at what became known as Hardyville in 1864 and ran it until the second of two devastating fires largely destroyed the community in 1873. The ferry passed out of use when the railroad was built across the river at Needles in 1883. Maguire's favorable assessment of Hardy's character is corroborated by other records. See James E. and Barbara H. Sherman, *Ghost Towns of Arizona* (Norman, OK, 1969), 74.

68. Built in 1859, then abandoned during the Civil War, Camp Mojave after the war became both a prominent army installation and a village that was designated the seat of Mojave County in 1866. The town's heyday occurred during the 1880s, but decline set in when the army abandoned the post permanently in 1890. In 1941 all remaining buildings were destroyed. Sherman and Sherman, *Ghost Towns of Arizona*, 102. See also Hart, *Old Forts*, 112–15.

69. Maguire's descriptions of the Mojave and other Arizona Indians apparently represent both his own observations and information gotten from local agents. Richard J. Hinton, *The Hand-book of Arizona* (New York, 1878), an early reference book, was in Maguire's possession, for a copy with his bookplate is now at the Utah State Historical Society library. However, Maguire's account goes beyond Hinton and sometimes contradicts him.

70. Mineral Park's star was rising at the time of Maguire's visit. Established in 1871, it grew rapidly because of the prosperity of its silver mines, and it became the seat of Mojave County in 1877. Its population in the 1880s was 700 people. Sherman and Sherman, *Ghost Towns of Arizona*, 100–101. Maguire visited Mineral Park on all three expeditions and traded profitably there.

71. Hinton, *Hand-book of Arizona*, 355, sketches Hualapai Charlie's character.

72. Note that Maguire revisited Hackberry on his second and third trips and found business better than on this first visit, though trading with the cattle-

men seems to have been almost as profitable as trade with the miners. Gold was discovered at Hackberry in 1870 by Sam Crozier and three others. Will C. Barnes, *Arizona Place Names* (Tucson, 1960), 211–12.

73. William Franklin Grounds (1851–1930) was an Arkansan who perhaps reached Arizona through Texas, for his wife was a Texan. He was the first man to bring cattle into Mojave County. Grounds and his wife left Arizona for Fresno, California, in 1901. His son, W. F. Grounds, Jr., married a daughter of Samuel Crozier and turned the WF Cattle Company in the region of Hackberry and Kingman into one of Arizona's largest livestock companies. See Edward H. Peplow, Jr., *History of Arizona* (New York, 1958), III: 440.

74. This can only be one of Maguire's youthful romantic flights of fancy. Franciscan Father Francisco Garces (1738–1781), who explored northern Arizona in 1775 and 1776, was one of the most memorable adventurous missionaries of Spanish Catholicism. He ranged, usually with only an Indian guide, for hundreds of miles from San Xavier del Bac under the most dangerous and arduous conditions to take Christianity to the Indians of Arizona and California. Although his detailed journals contain a wealth of geographical information, even to the extent of allowing modern scholars to retrace his routes, Garces's missionary purpose generally crowds out of his journals the kinds of description Maguire would need to identify such a campsite definitively. See Garces's journals in Elliott Coues, ed., *On the Trail of a Spanish Pioneer*, 2 vols. (New York, 1900).

75. The 1880 census lists George Russell, fifty-three years of age, born in Oregon, and farming on the Big Sandy thirty miles north of Signal. By this time he was divorced, but his son, Frank L., seventeen years of age and born in Oregon, lived with him.

76. Greenwood grew up around the stamp mill erected to process ore from the McCracken silver mine, discovered in 1874. It was in its heyday at the time of Maguire's visit, and attained a population of some four hundred. But its prosperity was short lived, for a bigger stamp mill erected at nearby Virginia City in 1878 took the McCracken business away from Greenwood. Sherman and Sherman, *Ghost Towns of Arizona*, 72. Note that while Maguire visited Greenwood again on his second trip and found it still booming, he declined to return on his last expedition, "as we learned that the mills down in that region were shut down, and the mines employing but very few men."

77. This may have been the Davis House, which was famous for its comfortable rooms and sumptuous meals. Sherman and Sherman, *Ghost Towns of Arizona*, 72.

78. Maguire's diary characterizes Greenwood as "a poor miserable spot made of Cottonwood Palisades," all the houses having dirt floors and cane roofs. "I found Seven women and about 200 men," he adds, "dogs on top of dogs and no two alike. . . . Whiskey is plenty and food is dear."

79. The identity of Poker Smith is uncertain, but a man named Fatty Smith

did run a famous saloon in Greenwood. Sherman and Sherman, *Ghost Towns of Arizona*, 72.

80. Either Marooney or McRooney is probably Fred Mulroney, whom the 1870 census lists as a thirty-five-year-old farmer born in Ireland. The name is spelled "Morony" in the 1880 census. Maguire applies the given name Malachi to Marooney, but none to McRooney; however, neither person appears in either census exactly as Maguire names him.

81. Daniel Hatz (b. 1831) was a Swiss emigrant who came to Prescott during its early mining boom in 1864 and stayed to become a prominent hotelier as well as a noted botanist. The Pioneer Hotel was the name of Dan Hatz's establishment, and the correct name of the Hotel Prescott was the Prescott House. Sue Abbey, Sharlot Hall Museum, to the editor, 2 September 1993; and clipping files, Sharlot Hall Museum.

82. All of these people, as Maguire indicates, were prominent Prescott citizens. Levi Bashford (c. 1836–1899) was born in New York and became prominent in the railroad business in Illinois. President Abraham Lincoln appointed him Surveyor General for Arizona Territory in 1863, and he founded the Bashford-Burmister mercantile establishment in Prescott. Cotesworth Pinckney Head (d. 1887) was another New Yorker who entered the mercantile, stock-raising, and mining businesses in Prescott in 1869. John Goulder Campbell (1827–1903) was a Scottish emigrant who ran a cattle ranch near Prescott; after 1895 he ran the Depot House hotel. Morris Goldwater, uncle of Senator Barry Goldwater, ran a department store and later served as mayor of Prescott. Thomas Matthew Alexander (1822–1910) was a farmer, rancher, and miner; and Edmund George Peck (1835–1910) was a prosperous miner and army guide. I am indebted to Sue Abbey, archivist at the Sharlot Hall Museum, who provided this information from the museum's clipping files.

83. An otherwise undated newspaper clipping at the Sharlot Hall Museum dates this felling of the pines on the Prescott plaza in 1876 but does not identify the perpetrator. C. A. Luke and Lucius Jewell were both early mayors who had businesses located on the plaza, but not on the east side. Morris Goldwater had a business on the east side, but was not mayor until later. Sue Abbey to the editor, 2 September 1993.

84. Yaki Wilson's early years are obscure, but he came to Arizona shortly before this time with a price on his head for having led a revolt of Yaqui Indians against the government of Sonora. He worked as a cook at Smith's Mill, then opened this stage stop at Antelope Creek. A defrocked priest named Charles Stanton coveted Wilson's business and tricked a neighbor, an Englishman named Partridge, into murdering Wilson. After Wilson's death, however, a man named Timmerman proved he had loaned Wilson money and was thus a partner, and he took over the stage stop. Dan B. Genung, *Death In His Saddlebags: Charles Baldwin Genung, Arizona Pioneer* (Manhattan, KS, 1992), 138–40.

85. Although Maguire dates its founding a little early, his history of Wickenburg's mining days is essentially accurate. Founded near the Vulture Mine, which Austrian immigrant Henry Wickenburg discovered in 1863, the town was one of Arizona's largest communities, and missed becoming the state capital in 1866 by only two votes. Although the mining boom days were almost over at the time of Maguire's visit, the community of Wickenburg continued as the center of a ranching district. See Works Progress Administration (WPA), *Arizona: A State Guide* (New York, 1940), 356–57; and Sherman and Sherman, *Ghost Towns of Arizona*, 164–65.

86. Abraham Harlow Peeples (1822–1892) left Yuma with the famous Arizona scout Pauline Weaver in 1863 on a prospecting expedition. Although they found some gold, and Peeples started a ranch in what came to be known as Peeples Valley in 1865, he had sold out by 1870 and become a saloon keeper in Wickenberg. Barnes, *Arizona Place Names*, 353. It is possible that Maguire confused Peeples with Johnny Peebles, the proprietor of the Palace Saloon in Tybo, Nevada, whom he had met earlier on this trip.

87. Mary Elizabeth Sanger (1846–1902) was known, among other nicknames, as Mollie Monroe. Although she was probably not a member of a gang, and was born in New Hampshire instead of Massachusetts, Maguire's other facts are generally correct. See "Times and Trials of Mollie Monroe," *Sharlot Hall Gazette* (Prescott, AZ) 9 (December 1982): 1–2.

88. This is a pseudonym, as Maguire reveals during his dealings with the man on his second expedition.

89. Smith's Mill was built in 1874 by W. C. Smith. By 1 May 1877 the post office there was discontinued. Barnes, *Arizona Place Names*, 193. Maguire did not visit the site on subsequent trips.

90. Alphonse Pinart, a French traveler who followed essentially the same route as Maguire into central Arizona later in the year, recorded the name of this rancher as Bowers, and the editor of Pinart's narrative identifies Bowers as a founder of a flour mill in Agua Fria Valley in 1869. Pinart, *Journey to Arizona in 1876*, 32.

91. Phoenix, which has become Arizona's largest city and one of the West's major metropolitan centers, was still young in Maguire's day. As the WPA guide puts it, "The present city was founded and has developed within the span of one human life." *Arizona: A State Guide*, 219. First established as a hay-cutting camp for the animals at Fort McDowell in the late 1860s, the community began to grow as an agricultural center during the early 1870s when a prospector named Jack Swilling and some partners began enlarging some prehistoric Indian canals and diverting the Salt River into them for irrigation. As the city began to develop in the 1870s, it became a popular recreational center for the Fort McDowell soldiers. Its 1880 population was 1,708. Rufus Kay Wyllys, *Arizona: The History of A Frontier State* (Phoenix, 1950), 231–36.

92. Maguire's diary adds, "The men look as though they had been drawn on

a rack in the time of the inquisition and the women look as though they could enjoy a bit of divorce twice a [year?]"

93. An unfulfilled promise. Maguire did not visit Phoenix on his third expedition, and makes no mention of prehistoric sites in the area in the narrative of the second.

94. Charles Trumbull Hayden, father of long-time Arizona Congressman Carl Hayden, had built a ferry and mill on the Salt River. In 1882 he sold out to the Mormons from nearby Mesa, who built a town on the site and called it Tempe. James H. McClintock, *Mormon Settlement in Arizona: A Record of Peaceful Conquest of the Desert* (Phoenix, 1921), 219.

95. Generally spelled Sacaton, this is, as Maguire later notes, the headquarters of the Pima Reservation.

96. The following description of the Pimas is evidently based on Maguire's own observations and on-site research, for it contradicts Hinton, *Hand-book of Arizona*, 357, the 1878 reference book which we know Maguire owned, perhaps at the time he wrote these narratives, and almost certainly by the time he prepared the final typescript. Hinton considered the Pimas morally degraded.

97. Except for his acerbic assessment of some of the citizens of Florence, Maguire's description is generally fair and accurate. Founded in 1866 by Levi Ruggles, Florence was one of Arizona's first white communities. It became a supply center for mines in the area and a stage station. Its 1880 population was 902—probably not much different from the population Maguire found—and it was impressive enough to have been considered for the territorial capital. WPA, *Arizona: A State Guide*, 292–94.

98. Father Kino discovered Casa Grande in 1694. See Robert H. and Florence C. Lister, *Those Who Came Before: Southwestern Archeology in the National Park Service* (Tucson, 1983), 101.

99. By far the oldest of Arizona's major cities, Tucson began to grow as Spanish settlers followed Father Eusebio Kino into the area after 1700, when he founded Mission San Xavier del Bac and they settled near springs along the Santa Cruz River. It became a Spanish, then Mexican, and later American military outpost against the Indians. It began to expand after the Civil War, and especially after the territorial legislature awarded it the university, not long after Maguire's visit, in compensation for having given Phoenix the capital. WPA, *Arizona: A State Guide*, 256–58.

100. San Xavier del Bac was abandoned when the missions were secularized after Mexican independence in 1821. Between then and 1906, when it was reoccupied and restored, the church fell into the disrepair Maguire describes. See WPA, *Arizona: A State Guide*, 265.

101. Maguire visited Mesa on all three expeditions and, evidently because of his liking for Daniel W. Jones, overcame his dislike for Mormons and Mormonism enough to appreciate their heroic efforts in colonizing the Arizona desert. See his fuller accounts of Mesa in those narratives, and see also the note on its history in the second expedition.

102. Fort McDowell was built in 1865 by General George Crook as a base from which to attempt to control the Apaches. It was abandoned in 1890. Hart, *Old Forts*, 157–58.
103. Maguire's diary says, "That night we put up with the dirtiest woman in the United States a widow lady named Scroggin from among the poor white trash of S. Carolina."
104. At this point, Maguire seems to be rushing to finish his narrative, and shortchanges a rather interesting homeward leg of the expedition. His diary appears to indicate that he picked up another shipment of goods at Mojave: "found my goods all right," he says upon arriving there on 22 April; he then spent the following day preparing for the rest of the journey, which must mean loading his animals. Despite what he says in the narrative, he traded extensively on the way home, indicating in his diary that he "done pretty well" at Tybo, Nevada, and "done well" on Kern Creek. A sore throat forced him to lay over for four days, and a can of meat "which had entered into a state of decomposition" made him ill in the eastern Utah desert.
105. Alexander Toponce (1839–1923) was a French emigrant who came to Utah in 1857 as assistant wagon boss with the federal troops under Albert Sidney Johnston. He spent most of the rest of his life in Utah, particularly the Gentile (non-Mormon) center of Corinne, where he was a freighter and supplier. Though he was not a Mormon, the Mormons respected him for his honest dealings. See Dan L. Thrapp, *Encyclopedia of Frontier Biography*, III: 1435–36; and Alexander Toponce, *Reminiscences of Alexander Toponce: Written By Himself* (Norman, OK, 1971).

Notes to Chapter Two

1. By "condemned," Maguire must mean "surplus." His term implies that the guns were defective, which does not seem to have been the case. At the beginning of the Civil War, the army replaced the old smoothbore musket with the muzzle-loading rifle, a much more accurate and longer-range weapon, and the older guns thus became available to civilians like Maguire. Bruce Catton, *America Goes to War* (Middletown, CT, 1958), 15–18, discusses the relative merits of the two weapons.
2. For a fuller account of this expedition see Gary Topping, "A Trader in the Rocky Mountains: Don Maguire's 1877 Diary," *Idaho Yesterdays* 27 (Summer 1983): 2–12.
3. Brigham Young died 23 August 1877, and the funeral was on 2 September and corresponded closely to Maguire's description. Leonard Arrington, *Brigham Young: American Moses* (New York, 1985), 398–401.
4. He also secured the third teamster, Bernard Foley, whom he neglected to mention until Foley left him at Provo and was replaced by Sam Roberts.
5. His diary gives the departure date as 14 January.

6. Maguire's memory is faulty at this point. The Walker House guest registers at the Utah State Historical Society archives contain no entries for Maguire or any of the other parties he mentions during the entire month of January 1878.

7. Benjamin Morgan Roberts (1827–1891) was a private in Company D of the Mormon Battalion. Carl V. Larson, *A Data Base of the Mormon Battalion* (Providence, UT, 1987), 145.

8. Maguire's diary indicates that Roberts's wages were fifteen dollars per month and board.

9. Edward Wheelock Tullidge (1829–1894) had no official position as church historian and as a matter of fact apostasized, being one of the instigators of the Godbeite schism. As Maguire indicates, Tullidge was a prolific writer and an important cultural figure. In addition to his biographies of Smith and Young, his major works include a massive history of Salt Lake City, a history of Mormonism in northern Utah and southern Idaho, and *The Women of Mormondom*. He was publisher of *Tullidge's Quarterly Magazine* and of the *Mormon Tribune,* which became the *Salt Lake Tribune*. See William Frank Lye, "Edward Wheelock Tullidge, The Mormons' Rebel Historian," *Utah Historical Quarterly* 28 (January 1960): 56–75.

10. While few modern readers of Eliza R. Snow (1804–1887) would seriously dispute Maguire's assessment of "Zion's Poetess," her importance as a cultural figure was very great. See Maureen Ursenbach Beecher, "The Eliza Enigma: The Life and Legend of Eliza R. Snow," in Thomas G. Alexander, ed., *Essays on the American West* (Provo, UT, 1976), 29–46.

11. Sarah Elizabeth Carmichael (1838–1901). See Miriam B. Murphy, "Sarah Elizabeth Carmichael: Poetic Genius of Pioneer Utah," *Utah Historical Quarterly* 43 (Winter 1975): 52–66.

12. In spite of his elaborate descriptions of Provo and of Mormon society there, Mormonism tended to bore Maguire, and extended stays in Mormon communities gave him itchy feet. As he left Provo at the beginning of his third expedition, he recorded in his diary that "The Mormon people have treated me well and it is but charity in me to state that I owe them nothing and they owe me the same amount."

13. Abel Butterfield was one of the early settlers of Santaquin, Utah, settling there in 1852. His physical appearance was much as Maguire describes it, and he was known as a fearless Indian fighter. See Emma N. Huff, comp., *Memories That Live: Utah County Centennial History* (Springville, UT, 1947), 474–77; and Peter Gottfredson, *Indian Depredations in Utah* (Salt Lake City, 1969), 80.

14. Founded in 1851 as a way station on the so-called "Mormon corridor" from Salt Lake City to San Bernardino, California, Fillmore was named for President Millard Fillmore (as was Millard County, of which Fillmore is now county seat) in gratitude for Utah's territorial status, which was granted during his administration as part of the Compromise of 1850. Although

Brigham Young designated Fillmore the territorial capital in anticipation of its central location in his colonization plan, Utah's population has in fact remained concentrated along the Wasatch Front from Ogden to Provo, and only the 1855 legislative session met there before the capital was transferred to Salt Lake City. Milton R. Hunter, *Brigham Young the Colonizer* (Salt Lake City, 1940), 263–70.

15. Maguire's description is about the only record of the Bourne family, and it is at odds in two respects with the 1870 census: it lists five daughters and one son, ranging in age from twenty-seven to ten, and he has their names wrong.

16. Cove Fort was built in 1867 during the Black Hawk Indian War to protect travelers between the Mormon settlements in northern and southern Utah. Ward J. Roylance, *Utah: A Guide to the State* (Salt Lake City, 1982), 529.

17. Maguire is wrong in this, of course. Prairie dogs are common at various places in the Great Basin.

18. Ira Nathaniel Hinckley (1828–1904). If there was a relationship to Brigham Young, either by blood or marriage, it does not appear in his biography, Parnell Hinckley, "Events in the Life of Ira Nathaniel Hinckley, 1828–1904: Pioneer, Churchman, Rancher," manuscript at Utah State Historical Society library.

19. Maguire's fascination with these famous ruins led to his excavating them in 1893. See Neil M. Judd, *Archaeological Observations North of the Rio Colorado* (Washington, D.C., 1926), 54; and Don Maguire, "The Paragoonah Fortress," *Salt Lake Tribune*, 30 January 1893, 2.

20. Daniel Page is listed in both the 1870 and 1880 censuses as a farmer, though he could have functioned also in the roles Maguire indicates. In 1878 he was forty-nine years of age and had a wife twenty years younger. They had five daughters and one son in 1880, though one daughter was not yet born in 1878, and Page's father, Daniel, Sr., age seventy-eight, lived with them.

21. Henry Lunt (1824–1902), born in Cheshire, England, was bishop of the LDS Cedar City Ward, 1859–1878. Andrew Jenson, *Latter-day Saint Biographical Encyclopedia* (Salt Lake City, 1920), 3: 446–47.

22. This is probably Peter Shirts, "a Daniel Boone type of pioneer who shunned the proximity of his brethren and usually located on the outermost fringe of Mormon exploration." After 1866, church authorities required him to live with his co-religionists, which is why Maguire encountered him in Kanarrah. P. T. Reilly, "Historic Utilization of Paria River," *Utah Historical Quarterly* 45 (Spring 1977): 189. Eventually Shirts's desire for isolation got the best of him, for Mormon scouts for the San Juan Mission of 1879—the famous Hole-in-the-Rock expedition—found him living alone at the mouth of Montezuma Creek in southeastern Utah. David E. Miller, *Hole-in-the-Rock: An Epic in the Colonization of the Great American West* (Salt Lake City, 1959), 25.

23. Few other visitors agreed with Maguire's anti-Mormon contrast, for Silver Reef, then at the height of its mining boom, was a typical western mining town, "a treeless, grassless, red-sand location," as one historian characterizes it, "a shack town, its main street lined with saloons, gambling places, and other conveniences for sinners." Most Mormon towns, even on the southern Utah frontier in the 1870s, were neat and orderly. Nels Anderson, *Desert Saints: The Mormon Frontier in Utah* (Chicago, 1942), 428–29.

24. At this period, Joseph Smith's "Word of Wisdom" against consumption of alcohol by Mormons was only a recommendation, and both production and consumption of local wine in southern Utah were common, even among church authorities. Maguire's characterization of its potency is not, as one might expect, another anti-Mormon thrust. One former resident of Silver Reef recalled that although other liquors were locally made or doctored to add potency, "it was Dixie's red wine that had a kick worse than a government mule, as many newcomers learned to their sorrow." Anderson, *Desert Saints*, 434.

25. I have not been able to identify any Pulsipher who meets Maguire's description fully. The only "downeast Yankee" among them was Zera, the head of the family, who settled in Hebron, Utah, not Santa Clara, and died in 1872. His son John, born in Spafford, New York, in 1827, could be the one Maguire met, though he too was living in nearby Hebron. This information comes from Mormon family group sheets in the Church of Jesus Christ of Latter-day Saints Family History Library, Salt Lake City, Utah.

26. Edward Bunker (1822–1901) founded Bunkerville, Nevada, in 1877 and served as bishop in the Mormon church there until his death. Bunker's three wives bore him twenty-eight children. His second counselor was Myron Abbott (1837–1907). See the autobiography of Edward Bunker, Utah State Historical Society, 12–14; and Frank Esshom, *Pioneers and Prominent Men of Utah* (Salt Lake City, 1966), 707.

27. Maguire's diary says he found Hendricks working for "a man from California with sheep," and that Hendricks had "once been surgeon in the Irish Legion of Chicago during the American Civil War." He says Hendricks had a young wife and child in Kansas City.

28. This is Isaac, not William, Jennings, who arrived at St. Thomas in 1870, became Indian agent, and bought up considerable property from Mormons who were abandoning the impoverished Muddy Mission in 1871. Arabell Lee Hafner, *100 Years on the Muddy* (Springville, UT, 1967), 129–30.

29. The reservation is now in Clark County, which was created from the southern part of Lincoln County in 1908. Hafner, *100 Years on the Muddy*, endpaper map.

30. Fanny was Mrs. Jennings's daughter by a previous marriage, while Lydia was born to the Jennings at St. Thomas and could hardly have been much more than half the age Maguire estimates. Hafner, *100 Years on the Muddy*, 130.

31. Stone's Ferry was established by the fall of 1871 by James Thompson and a partner named Stone. They sold out to Daniel Bonelli evidently just after Maguire's visit. See Melvin T. Smith, "The Colorado River: Its History in the Lower Canyon Area" (Ph.D. dissertation, Brigham Young University, 1972), 420–21. Maguire's diary adds that "The ferry is small and each team that crosses it pays 8 dollars." The diary calls Thompson "Tony" and characterizes him as "a very nice little fellow."

32. Maguire's diary identifies a "Mrs. Thomas" teaching at St. Thomas.

33. Mining began in Cerbat in the late 1860s and flourished during the 1870s, but by the time of Maguire's second expedition it had begun to decline; the seat of Mojave County, for example, passed to Mineral Park in 1877. James E. Sherman and Barbara H. Sherman, *Ghost Towns of Arizona* (Norman, OK, 1969), 21–22.

34. Mineral Park was in the ascendant during Maguire's second expedition. It had just lured the county seat from Cerbat (1877) and boasted a newspaper, the *Mojave County Miner,* and a population of nearly seven hundred. Sherman and Sherman, *Ghost Towns of Arizona*, 100–101.

35. Richard E. Lingenfelter, *Steamboats on the Colorado River* (Tucson, 1978), 66, identifies this Indian as Iretaba.

36. The diary gives the date as 27 February.

37. On the settlement of Mesa see James H. McClintock, *Mormon Settlement in Arizona: A Record of Peaceful Conquest of the Desert* (Phoenix, 1921), 211–24.

38. Daniel W. Jones, *Forty Years Among the Indians* (Salt Lake City, 1890), 309ff.

39. In the first narrative, Maguire says he met Reverado at Wickenburg, and in the third narrative regrets, when passing through Wickenburg, that he had no time to call on the Reverados.

40. Maguire's description suggests that this may have been Colossal Cave east of Tucson, an immense cavern extending many miles into the earth and reputed to have been a rendezvous point for shady or nefarious activities such as Maguire reports and in which he was engaged. The smoke stains are still visible on the walls, but the bat guano on the floor is not. However, the commercial value of the guano could have led to its removal subsequent to Maguire's visit. Colossal Cave is located in the Rincon Mountains, not the Santa Cruz, which I have not been able to identify. The Santa Cruz River flows nearby and may have confused Maguire's nomenclature. A more serious problem is that Colossal Cave is not reachable from Florence in one day on horseback; but Maguire's reported departure time of three a.m. indicates his vague memory of a hard journey that could have extended to more than one day. On the other hand, there are other caves in that part of Arizona that could have served as the rendezvous point. Stan Jones of Page, Arizona, author of a tourist brochure on the cave, contributed to the above speculations. See also WPA, *Arizona: A State Guide*, 383.

Notes to Chapter Three

1. York, Utah, fifteen miles north of Nephi, was the southern terminus of the Utah Southern Railroad in 1878. The line had been built south from Provo in 1877 to serve the Tintic mining district, and was welcomed by the farmers of Juab County as well. As the line continued to be extended to the south in 1879, York was abandoned in favor of Juab, about thirteen miles south of Nephi. Stephen L. Carr, *The Historical Guide to Utah Ghost Towns* (Salt Lake City, 1972), 99.
2. Daniel Bonelli (1836–1903) came to Utah in 1859, went to Santa Clara in 1861, and bought Stone's Ferry in the late 1870s. He moved the ferry upriver to the east side of the mouth of the Virgin River, where he established a settlement called Rioville. Melvin T. Smith, "The Colorado River: Its History in the Lower Canyon Area" (Ph.D. dissertation, Brigham Young University, 1972), 423–25.
3. Charles B. Genung was a New Yorker who joined the gold rush to California, but arrived in northern Arizona in July 1863 still in search of gold but also of relief from a mysterious lung ailment. He discovered the Montgomery Lode in the Yavapai Hills, and in July 1864 he helped Henry Wickenberg build the first arastra (an ore-crushing apparatus) at the Vulture Mine. He remained in Peeples Valley as a miner, farmer, and Indian fighter until his death in 1916. See Edward H. Peplow, *History of Arizona* (New York, 1958), II: 179, 186; John Alexander Carroll, ed., *Pioneering in Arizona: The Reminiscences of Emerson Oliver Stratton & Edith Stratton Kitt* (Tucson, 1964), 28–29; and Dan B. Genung, *Death In His Saddlebags: Charles Baldwin Genung, Arizona Pioneer* (Manhattan, KS, 1992).
4. Ed Schieffelin and his brother Al came to Arizona in 1877. Ed made the first strike of silver ore at what became Tombstone in February 1878. See Sherman and Sherman, *Ghost Towns of Arizona*, 153; and Rodman Wilson Paul, *Mining Frontiers of the Far West, 1848–1880* (Albuquerque, 1963), 159.
5. This is an anachronism, for the famous town of Tombstone was not founded until later in 1879. What Maguire visited was a small boomtown known as Watervale, near Ed Schieffelin's Lucky Cuss Mine. As Maguire indicates, it was a new strike, and the town was probably as wild as he indicates, though he is probably reading back into his memories some of what he knew Tombstone became during the 1880s.
6. Albert Sieber (1844–1907) emigrated from Germany as a small boy, served in the Civil War, and moved to Arizona about 1868. He became General George Crook's chief scout in 1871 and served in that capacity until 1890. Although, as his biographer points out, "his education was rudimentary[,] he was highly intelligent, honest, intrepid, loyal and worthy of the many encomiums from army officers for whom he served." He died under a falling rock during construction of the Roosevelt Dam, perhaps dislodged by a grudge-bearing Apache. See Dan L. Thrapp, *Encyclopedia of Frontier Biogra-*

phy (Glendale, CA, 1988), III: 1305–7; and Thrapp, *Al Sieber, Chief of Scouts* (Norman, OK, 1964).

7. This is almost certainly W. W. Snyder, who ran a stage stop called Snyder's Station at Bumblebee. Although there was a temporary army post at Bumblebee in about 1860, and there was a certain amount of gold mining in the area, the travelers' accommodations Maguire describes were the settlement's most lucrative source of income. Sherman and Sherman, *Ghost Towns of Arizona*, 16.

8. Anson Peacely-Killen Safford enjoyed the longest tenure of any of Arizona's territorial governors (1869–1877) and earned a reputation as one of the best governors in Arizona history. Safford brought order out of chaos during perhaps Arizona's most lawless period. In addition to suppressing Mexican and Apache raiders, Safford supported his governmental authority by creating the territorial prison at Yuma. Perhaps his greatest achievement, however, was his creation of the Arizona public school system. Jay J. Wagoner, *Arizona Territory, 1863–1912* (Tucson, 1970), 101–23. Safford had been governor during Maguire's first visit, and Maguire had good reason to be grateful to Safford, for it was his suppression of raiders and highwaymen that in large part had made Maguire's expeditions possible.

9. Although the reputation of John Charles Fremont (1813–1890) has been a matter of controversy among historians, to Americans of Maguire's generation he was a charismatic, popular hero whose exciting reports on his Western explorations of 1842 and 1843 provided their first knowledge of the American West. Even after his colorful role in California's Bear Flag Revolt ended in court-martial, and his two last exploratory ventures ended in tragedy, Fremont remained a larger-than-life figure to many. Nevertheless, his star had definitely descended when Maguire met him. He had been appointed territorial governor only the previous summer, and his brief term of office (1878–1881) was not a happy experience. He took the role very seriously, but his frequent and prolonged absences from Arizona to raise money for various development plans were resented by the people of the territory, and the Arizona climate did not agree with his wife. Ferol Egan, *Fremont: Explorer For A Restless Nation* (Reno, 1985), 520–22.

10. Maguire's reckoning of longitude is confusing but accurate enough when properly understood. Camp Verde, Arizona, is at roughly 112 degrees west longitude, reckoned from the Greenwich Meridian. Washington, D.C., is about seventy-three degrees west longitude. This places Camp Verde, as he says, about thirty-five degrees west of Washington.

11. Fort Verde was established under the name Camp Lincoln in 1865 and used by General George Crook as a base from which to subdue the Apaches. Its name was changed to Camp Verde in 1868, then Fort Verde in 1879. It was abandoned in 1890. Herbert M. Hart, *Old Forts of the Far West* (Seattle, 1965), 159–61.

12. This was an eastward extension, in other words, of the road over which

Maguire had crossed southern California to Hardyville, Arizona, and returned on during his first Arizona expedition.

13. The name was the Prescott-Santa Fe Stage Line. Henry P. Walker and Don Bufkin, *Historical Atlas of Arizona* (Norman, OK, 1979), 41.

14. An earlier version of the following pages appeared as "Don Maguire's Trading Expedition in Northern Arizona, 1879," *Utah Historical Quarterly* 53 (Fall 1985): 380–95.

15. Lot Smith (1830–1892) was a hot-tempered Mormon warrior who had made a name as leader of the Saints' resistance to federal troops on the Wyoming plains in 1857. In 1876 he was sent to Arizona to become, with James S. Brown and Daniel W. Jones, one of the competitors in the curiously divided leadership of the Mormon colonies there. The identity of the counselor is uncertain. The only possibility I can suggest is Ralph Ramsey (1824–1905), an English convert to Mormonism who arrived in St. John's, Arizona, from Richfield, Utah, in September 1879. Maguire may have encountered him at Sunset, which was on the way from Richfield to St. John's, earlier in the year. See Charles S. Peterson, " 'A Mighty Man Was Brother Lot': A Portrait of Lot Smith—Mormon Frontiersman," *Western Historical Quarterly* I (October 1970): 393–414; and *Deseret Evening News*, 3 February 1905. I am indebted to Harry F. Campbell for calling my attention to the latter reference, Ramsey's obituary.

16. On the United Order of Enoch see Leonard J. Arrington, *Great Basin Kingdom: Economic History of the Latter-Day Saints* (Cambridge, 1958), chapter 11; and Charles S. Peterson, *Take Up Your Mission: Mormon Colonizing Along the Little Colorado River, 1870-1900* (Tucson, 1973).

17. John Taylor (1808–1887) was not formally "sustained" (installed) as president of the Mormon church until 1880; but, as president of the Quorum of the Twelve Apostles at Brigham Young's death in 1877, he was de facto leader of the church. Howard R. Lamar, ed., *The Reader's Encyclopedia of the American West* (New York, 1977), 1161.

18. These of course are the Hopi villages due north of the Mormon colonies. "Moqui" is an archaic term for the Hopi.

19. This is probably mistaken, since the Snake Dance traditionally occurs in August, and Maguire later says it was early February 1879 when he left the Mormon colonies.

20. I have corrected Maguire's spelling of the names of all the Hopi villages.

21. I have been unable to find examples of either of these phenomena among the Hopi.

22. This account of Smith's death is erroneous. He was shot by a Navajo named Chachos on 21 June 1892 after Smith tried to drive some of the Indian's livestock off his land at Moencopi. Peterson, " 'A Mighty Man Was Brother Lot,' " 412–13.

23. Maguire is almost certainly pulling the reader's leg here. The Petrified Forest is *east* of the Mormon colonies, and thus significantly out of his way to

Moencopi and Lee's Ferry; so Maguire obviously made a deliberate detour to see it. Although he may have been, as he says, unaware of its distance or extent, he must have known his party was approaching it, and at any rate it is unlikely, even at a late hour, that his men would have mistaken petrified logs for real ones.

24. Cyrus Benjamin Hawley was born in Canada in 1824 to a westering New Yorker named William J. "Cap" Hawley, who converted to Mormonism and came to Utah in 1852. The Hawleys were among the pioneers of what came to be known as Pleasant Grove, and the Ben Hawley house is one of that community's architectural treasures. Maguire's mention of Hawley's presence at Moencopi and his role there is the only record I have found of that phase of his life. I am indebted to Roger Roper for calling my attention to Hawley's meager biographical data. See *Pioneers and Prominent Men of Utah* (Salt Lake City, 1913), 925; and Utah County Daughters of Utah Pioneers, *Timpanogos Town* (Salt Lake City, 1947), 49, 53. The map following page 58 shows the location of Hawley's house.

25. Clifford E. Trafzer, *The Kit Carson Campaign: The Last Great Navajo War* (Norman, OK, 1982), 212–23, characterizes the great headman Manuelito as the Navajo Geronimo, a great warrior who spent his life fighting Mexicans, Utes, Pueblos, and Americans. Manuelito led the last desperate Navajo resistance against American troops under Kit Carson, and his surrender in the fall of 1866 ended the war.

26. This account of Navajo marriage ceremonies is completely inaccurate. The actual ceremony is described in Raymond Friday Locke, *The Book of the Navajo* 4th ed. (Los Angeles, 1989), 20–23.

27. "Samson" must have been Warren Marshall Johnson, who worked for Emma Lee at the ferry, then succeeded her when she left in May 1879. He stayed until 1896. See P. T. Reilly, "Warren Marshall Johnson, Forgotten Saint," *Utah Historical Quarterly* 39 (Summer 1971): 3–22, and W. L. Rusho and C. Gregory Crampton, *Desert River Crossing* (Salt Lake City, 1975), 25–46.

28. This is Emma (not Mary) Batchelor Lee, later French (1836–1897), who first arrived at Lee's Ferry in 1871 with her husband, another of his wives, Rachel, and their families. Emma was Lee's seventeenth wife; he had a total of nineteen, not ten, as Maguire says. Juanita Brooks, *John Doyle Lee, Zealot—Pioneer Builder—Scapegoat* (Glendale, CA, 1961), 379–84; and Brooks, *Emma Lee* (Logan, UT, 1975).

29. The twin girls were Ann Eliza and Rachel Emma; the "fourteen-year-old" boy was probably Ike (Isaac), who was actually sixteen. Emma Lee had two daughters younger than Ike—Frances Dell (seven) and Victoria Elizabeth (five)—but no younger sons. The two younger boys Maguire mentions are inexplicable, unless he mistook the daughters for boys. Warren Johnson had no boys that old who might have been mistaken for Emma's. See Brooks, *John Doyle Lee*, 383–84; and Reilly, "Warren Marshall Johnson," 6–14.

Bibliography

Articles

Kelly, Charles. "Don Maguire—Pioneer." *Utah Motorist* (April 1933): 8–9.

Lye, William Frank. "Edward Wheelock Tullidge, The Mormons' Rebel Historian." *Utah Historical Quarterly* 28 (January 1960): 56–75.

Murphy, Miriam B. "Sarah Elizabeth Carmichael: Poetic Genius of Pioneer Utah." *Utah Historical Quarterly* 43 (Winter 1975): 52–66.

Peterson, Charles S. " 'A Mighty Man Was Brother Lot': A Portrait of Lot Smith—Mormon Frontiersman." *Western Historical Quarterly* 1 (October 1970): 393–414.

Reilly, P. T. "Historic Utilization of Paria River." *Utah Historical Quarterly* 45 (Spring 1977): 188–201.

——. "Warren Marshall Johnson, Forgotten Saint." *Utah Historical Quarterly* 39 (Summer 1971): 3–22.

"Times and Trials of Mollie Monroe." *Sharlot Hall Gazette* 9 (December 1982): 1–2.

Topping, Gary. "A Trader in the Rocky Mountains: Don Maguire's 1877 Diary." *Idaho Yesterdays* 27 (Summer 1983): 2–12.

——. "Don Maguire's Trading Expedition in Northern Arizona, 1879." *Utah Historical Quarterly* 53 (Fall 1985): 380–95.

Waitman, Leonard. "The History of Camp Cady." *Historical Society of Southern California Quarterly* 36 (March 1954): 49–91.

Walker, Henry P. "Soldier in the California Column: The Diary of John W. Teal." *Arizona and the West* 13 (Spring 1971): 33–82.

Books

Alexander, Thomas G., ed. *Essays on the American West*. Provo, Utah: Brigham Young University Press, 1976.

Alter, J. Cecil, ed. *Utah The Storied Domain*. Chicago and New York: The American Historical Society, 1932.

Anderson, Nels. *Desert Saints: The Mormon Frontier in Utah*. Chicago: University of Chicago Press, 1942.

Arrington, Leonard. *Brigham Young: American Moses*. New York: Alfred A. Knopf, 1985.

——. *Great Basin Kingdom: Economic History of the Latter-Day Saints.* Cambridge, MA: Harvard University Press, 1958.

Austin, Mary. *Earth Horizons*. Boston: Houghton Mifflin, 1932.

Bagley, Will, ed. *Frontiersman: Abner Blackburn's Narrative*. Salt Lake City: University of Utah Press, 1992.

Barnes, Will C. *Arizona Place Names*. Tucson: University of Arizona Press, 1960.

Bateman, Ronald R. *Deep Creek Reflections*. Salt Lake City: s.p., 1984.

Brooks, Juanita. *Emma Lee*. Logan: Utah State University Press, 1975.

——. *John Doyle Lee, Zealot—Pioneer Builder—Scapegoat*. Glendale, CA: Arthur H. Clark, 1961.

Carr, Stephen L. *The Historical Guide to Utah Ghost Towns*. Salt Lake City: Western Epics, 1972.

Carroll, John Alexander, ed. *Pioneering in Arizona: The Reminiscences of Emerson Oliver Stratton & Edith Stratton Kitt*. Tucson: Arizona Pioneers Historical Society, 1964.

Casebier, Dennis G. *The Mojave Road*. Norco, CA: Tales of the Mojave Road Publishing Co., 1975.

——. *The Mojave Road Guide*. Norco, CA: Tales of the Mojave Road Publishing Co., 1986.

Catton, Bruce. *America Goes to War*. Middletown, CT: Wesleyan University Press, 1958.

Chalfant, Willie Arthur. *The Story of Inyo*. Bishop, CA: Chalfant Press, 1922.

Coues, Elliott, ed. *On the Trail of a Spanish Pioneer*. New York: F. P. Harper, 1900.

Driggs, Howard R. *Timpanogos Town*. Manchester, NH: Clarke Press, 1948.

Egan, Ferol. *Fremont: Explorer For a Restless Nation*. 2nd ed., Reno: University of Nevada Press, 1985.

Esshom, Frank. *Pioneers and Prominent Men of Utah*. Salt Lake City: Pioneers Book Publishing Co., 1913.

Galvin, John, ed. *A Record of Travels in Arizona and California, 1775–1776, Fr. Francisco Garces*. San Francisco: J. Howell Books, 1967.

Genung, Dan B. *Death In His Saddlebags: Charles Baldwin Genung, Arizona Pioneer*. Manhattan, KS: Sunflower University Press, 1992.

Gottfredson, Peter. *Indian Depredations in Utah*. Salt Lake City: s.p., 1969.

Hafner, Arabell Lee. *100 Years on the Muddy*. Springville, UT: Art City Publishing Co., 1967.

Hart, Herbert M. *Old Forts of the Far West*. Seattle: Superior Publishing Co., 1965.

Hinton, Richard J. *The Hand-book of Arizona*. San Francisco: Payot, Upham & Co., 1878.

History of Tooele County. Salt Lake City: Tooele County Daughters of Utah Pioneers, 1961.

Hoover, Mildred Brooke, et al. *Historic Spots of California*. Stanford: Stanford University Press, 1966.

Huff, Emma N., comp. *Memories That Live: Utah County Centennial History*. Springville, UT: Art City Publishing Co., 1947.

Hunter, Milton R. *Brigham Young the Colonizer*. Salt Lake City: Deseret News Press, 1940.

Jennings, Jesse D., et al. *Indians of Utah: Past and Present*. Salt Lake City: University of Utah Press, 1959.

Jenson, Andrew. *Latter-day Saints Biographical Encyclopedia*. Salt Lake City: Deseret News, 1901.

Jones, Daniel W. *Forty Years Among the Indians*. Salt Lake City: Juvenile Instructor Office, 1890.

Judd, Neil M. *Archaeological Observations North of the Rio Colorado*. Washington, D.C.: Government Printing Office, 1926.

Keeling, Patricia Jernigan, ed. *Once Upon a Desert*. Barstow, CA: Mojave River Museum Association, 1994.

Lamar, Howard R. *The Reader's Encyclopedia of the American West*. New York: Thomas Y. Crowell Co., 1977.

———. *The Trader on the American Frontier: Myth's Victim*. College Station, TX: Texas A&M University Press, 1977.

Larson, Carl. *A Data Base of the Mormon Battalion*. Providence, UT: K.W. Watkins, 1987.

Lingenfelter, Richard E. *Steamboats on the Colorado River*. Tucson: University of Arizona Press, 1978.

Lister, Robert H. and Florence C. *Those Who Came Before: Southwestern Archeology in the National Park Service*. Tucson: Southwest Parks and Monuments Association, 1983.

Locke, Raymond Friday. *The Book of the Navajo*. 4th ed., Los Angeles: Mankind Publishing Co., 1989.

Madsen, Brigham D. *Glory Hunter: A Biography of Patrick Edward Connor*. Salt Lake City: University of Utah Press, 1990.

McClintock, James H. *Mormon Settlement in Arizona: A Record of Peaceful Conquest of the Desert*. Phoenix: n.p., 1921.

Miller, David E. *Hole-in-the-Rock: An Epic in the Colonization of the Great American West*. Salt Lake City: University of Utah Press, 1959.

Mooney, Bernice Maher. *Salt of the Earth: The History of the Catholic Diocese of Salt Lake City, 1776–1987*. 2nd ed., Salt Lake City: Catholic Diocese of Salt Lake City, 1992.

Murbarger, Nell. *Ghosts of the Glory Trail*. Palm Desert, CA: Desert Magazine Press, 1956.

Nadeau, Remi. *City-Makers: The Story of Southern California's First Boom, 1868–76*. Los Angeles: Trans-Anglo Books, 1965.

Newell, Linda, and Valeen Tippetts Avery. *Mormon Enigma: Emma Hale Smith, Prophet's Wife, "Elect lady," Polygamy's Foe*. Garden City, NY: Doubleday & Co., 1984.

Paher, Stanley W. *Nevada Ghost Towns & Mining Camps*. Berkeley: Howell-North Books, 1970.

Paul, Rodman Wilson. *Mining Frontiers of the Far West, 1848–1880*. Albuquerque: University of New Mexico Press, 1963.

Peirson, Erma. *The Mojave River and Its Valley*. Glendale, CA: Arthur H. Clark Co., 1970.

Peplow, Edward H., Jr. *History of Arizona*. New York: Lewis Publishing Co., 1958.

Peterson, Charles S. *Take Up Your Mission: Mormon Colonizing Along the Little Colorado River, 1870–1900*. Tucson: University of Arizona Press, 1973.

Pinart, Alphonse. *Journey to Arizona in 1876*. Los Angeles: The Zamorano Club, 1962.

Read, Effie O. *White Pine Lang Syne*. Denver: Big Mountain Press, 1965.

Roylance, Ward J. *Utah: A Guide to the State*. Salt Lake City: Utah Arts Council, 1982.

Rusho, W. L., and C. Gregory Crampton. *Desert River Crossing*. Salt Lake City: Peregrine Smith, 1975.

Schindler, Harold. *Orrin Porter Rockwell: Man of God, Son of Thunder*. Salt Lake City: University of Utah Press, 1966.

Sherman, James E., and Barbara H. Sherman. *Ghost Towns of Arizona*. Norman: University of Oklahoma Press, 1969.

Strevell, Charles Nettleton. *As I Recall Them*. Salt Lake City: Stevens & Wallis, 1943[?].

Thrapp, Dan L. *Al Sieber, Chief of Scouts*. Norman: University of Oklahoma Press, 1964.

———. *Encyclopedia of Frontier Biography*. Glendale, CA: Arthur H. Clark, 1988.

Toponce, Alexander. *Reminiscences of Alexander Toponce: Written By Himself*. Norman: University of Oklahoma Press, 1971.

Trafzer, Clifford E. *The Kit Carson Campaign: The Last Great Navajo War*. Norman: University of Oklahoma Press, 1982.

Unrau, Harlan D. *Basin and Range: A History of Great Basin National Park, Nevada*. Denver: National Park Service, 1990.

Varney, Philip. *Southern California's Best Ghost Towns: A Practical Guide*. Norman: University of Oklahoma Press, 1990.

Wagoner, Jay J. *Arizona Territory, 1863–1912*. Tucson: University of Arizona Press, 1970.

Walker, Clifford. *Back Door to California: The Story of the Mojave River Trail*. Barstow, CA: Mojave River Valley Museum Association, c. 1986.

Walker, Henry P., and Don Bufkin. *Historical Atlas of Arizona*. Norman: University of Oklahoma Press, 1979.

Works Progress Administration. *Arizona: A State Guide*. New York: Hastings House, 1940.

Wyllys, Rufus Kay. *Arizona: The History of a Frontier State*. Phoenix: Hobson & Herr, 1950.

Unpublished Manuscripts

Family group sheets. Family History Library, Salt Lake City, Utah.

Clipping files. Sharlot Hall Museum, Prescott, Arizona.

Hinckley, Parnell. "Events in the Life of Ira Nathaniel Hinckley, 1828–1904: Pioneer, Churchman, Rancher." Utah State Historical Society, Salt Lake City, Utah.

Kelly, Charles. Papers. Utah State Historical Society, Salt Lake City, Utah.

Kiely, The Very Reverend Denis. "A Brief History of the Catholic Church in Utah." Utah State Historical Society, Salt Lake City, Utah.

Maguire, Don. Papers. Utah State Historical Society, Salt Lake City, Utah.

Walker House Guest Registers. Utah State Historical Society, Salt Lake City, Utah.

Dissertation

Smith, Melvin T. "The Colorado River: Its History in the Lower Canyon Area." Ph.D. dissertation, Brigham Young University, 1972.

Newspapers

Ogden (Utah) *Standard Examiner*
Salt Lake Tribune
San Francisco Chronicle

Index